To my old
Eric Newman
with best wishes

B Wilson
Mg 2005

THE SEARCH FOR ERNEST BRAMAH

THE SEARCH FOR

ERNEST BRAMAH

Aubrey Wilson

CREIGHTON & READ

British Library Cataloguing in Publication Data
A catalogue record for this book is available from the British Library.

ISBN 978-0-9553753-0-9

Typeset by Amolibros, Milverton, Somerset
This book production has been managed by Amolibros
Printed and bound by T J International Ltd, Padstow, Cornwall, UK

CONTENTS

Illustrations facing page xvi and page 1:

Ernest Bramah in the Royal Army Defence Corps, 1916.
'An aged Mandarin of ancient lineage and ripe culture'. John Connell.
(Provided with kind permission by the National Portrait Gallery.)

ACKNOWLEDGEMENTS

Inevitably, many years of researching for this book brought me into contact with numerous individuals and organisations. Almost without exception they were extremely helpful and co-operative. If I have omitted to mention anyone in my chaotic filing system I hope they will forgive me.

My overwhelming thanks must go to two people without whom it could be truly said that the book could not have been completed.

First, I have three substantial reasons for being grateful to William Charlton. He has acquired the few remaining years of Bramah copyright and has been successful in arranging reprints of previously unpublished material. In this respect, all Bramah devotees also owe a debt of gratitude to him. He has freely given me permission to use all of his Bramah material as will be obvious from the copious quotations I have used. This book could not have been written without his agreement to allow me to plunder his property. I have been able to take advantage of his considerable knowledge of Bramah's works many of which, with incredible skill and perseverance, he has managed to transcribe from execrable handwriting, unreadable to almost everyone else, into immaculate typescripts. Finally, he read my manuscript and saved me from many errors of fact and interpretation.

Second, Professor Gertrude White who gave me access to her late husband, Professor William White's, archives and research and permission to use them in anyway of my choosing. He attempted a biography many years ago but was defeated by the distance between himself in America and the many sources of information on Ernest Bramah in Britain. He had to begin with a blank sheet of paper and did not have the huge advantages I have enjoyed; the enormous coverage the Internet provides and rapid communication through e-mail. Nevertheless he laboriously assembled a cornucopia of material which gave my own research its starting torque. It is obvious from William White's letters that he was generous in sharing his considerable knowledge of Bramah with others, even with those would-be authors who were also attempting to write Bramah's biography and would have competed with, but doubtfully rivalled, his own.

Two other benefactors must also be singled out. Professor Peter Gaspar a long-time Bramah enthusiast and like Bramah himself, a committed coin collector. His guiding hand, most particularly for Chapter Fourteen, has provided an insurance policy against numismatists who would have unquestionably exposed my total ignorance of the subject. Taking advantage of the Chair of Chemistry which he occupies with distinction at the Washington University, St. Louis, I also benefited from his advice on the reality or otherwise of the chemicals which Bramah introduces into some of his stories thus separating Bramah's vivid imagination from authentic science.

Tara Wenger, Research Librarian at the Harry Ransom Humanities Research Center at the University of Texas, Austin, never failed to respond to my bombardment of requests and interpreted my needs with the accuracy that only a highly skilled librarian could possibly achieve. Her co-operation removed the 3,500 miles that separated me from the seminal collection of Bramah material held at the Center.

Very late in the writing of this book the now elderly nephew and niece of Bramah's widow, Rosemary Smith (it is coincidental that she married a 'Smith' and was not part of the Bramah/Smith family) and John Barker were located. Although they were both young when Ernest was alive, their memories, letters and photographs proved of enormous value. They solved a number of mysteries that enabled me to correct several errors of fact and to adjust a number of what were speculative statements.

There are of course others who must be acknowledged and thanked for their help and for their permission to use their copyrighted material; Mike Berro whose Internet Bramah newsletter was a mine of information both from Mike, an avid collector, and from contributors. The newsletter unites Bramah lovers' world-wide. He also compiled the most complete bibliography in existence and I am indebted to him for allowing me the use of copies of book jackets he laboriously collected.

I am grateful to the B.B.C. for their permission to quote extensively from John Connell material in *The Listener*; *The Book Collector* for Mark Valentine's insightful comments on collecting Bramah books; *The Birmingham Post* for allowing me to reproduce, some almost fully, Bramah's earliest journalistic efforts

Acknowledgement is also made to; Dover Publications for the E. F. Bleiler excerpt from his Introduction to *The Best of Max Carrados*; Sean Haugh and Robert Fransen for the use of their reviews of *What Might Have Been*; Cosmos Books permitted me to quote extensively from David Langford's essay on Ernest Bramah; The Folio Society agreed to my use of part of Rosalind Vallance's Introduction to their edition of *Citizen of the World*; Penguin Books and the Penguin Collectors' Society for searching their archives to establish the size of the various editions of Bramah's books and also for allowing me to quote from Grant Richards' autobiography *Author Hunting* and from Pêh Der Chen's *Honourable and Peculiar Ways*; Peters, Fraser and the Dunlop Group on behalf of the estates of J. B. Priestley and Hilaire Belloc to use extracts from *The Edwardians* and the Introduction to *Kai Lung's Golden Hours*; Anthony Rota permitted important correspondence between his father and William White to be included; The Royal Archives for the several letters I have reproduced; the Society of Authors on behalf of the Bernard Shaw estate for their agreement to reproduce one of his inimitable post cards. A. P. Watt, Bramah's agent, for releasing the Bramah-Jerome K. Jerome letters to me; The High Master of the Manchester Grammar for information on Bramah's schooldays and for quotation from the school magazine; *Tribune* for the permission to use the Orwell extract; *Punch* was able to trace previously unknown articles which were thought to be unattributed but which had appeared in their index as the work of E. B. Smith.

Among others whose help I sought and which was gladly given were; Mr. Jeremy Bramah, Mrs Elizabeth Lazerno both of whom allowed me to search their archives; Mr. Michael Sharp of A. H. Baldwin the Numismatists and Mr. Tom Eden of Sotheby's for valuable information on Bramah's coin collection; Professor Pierre Coustillas and Madame Jane Gissing who gave me access to George Gissing's letters; Ms Viriginia Murray who delved deeply into the John Murray archive and located a small treasure trove of Bramah material; Mr. Aaron Saltzman who doggedly pursued my requests for material only to be found in the U.S.A; Christine Thomas for her outstanding genealogical skills that led to many important discoveries; my long-suffering amanuensis, Dorothy Storr, who was always available when needed; my old friends and colleagues; Joan Nicholson and Christopher West, who witnessed both conception and parturition of the book and who volunteered to read a not particularly well presented draft which they did with meticulous care. Their suggestions for changes and omissions were invaluable to one who has been too close to his subject for too long. I accepted all their proposals for changes with gratitude; Bernard Wilson was my man on-the-spot in Manchester and saved me numerous journeys to Manchester where he found evidence relating to Bramah's early years.

It has been a pleasure to deal with a number of archivists and librarians. Their assistance has been invaluable. They are invariably efficient, helpful and courteous. I would like to thank all the Libraries and Local Studies and Archives Centres whose services I used extensively. These include: The Bibliographical Society of America, City of Birmingham, The Bodleian Library, The Charles Deering Mcormick Library, Cheshire Diocesan Record Office, Northerwestern Univesity, The Boroughs of Bexley, Hastings, Barnet, Haringey, Hammersmith, Richmond, Islington, The British Library, British Numismatic Society, Bristol University Library and their Department of Drama, Rare Books and Special Collections Library, Jerwood Library of Performing Arts, *Journalism Quarterly*, Royal Boroughs of Kensington and Chelsea and of Kingston, Lambeth Palace Library, Lancashire Record Office, University of London George Orwell archive, University of Illinois, Manchester City Council, National Portrait Gallery, New York Public Library's Berg Collection, North Somerset Council, Northwestern University Special Collections, The National Archive, The Royal Archives, University of Virginia's Alderman Library. Warwickshire County Council. The Wellcome Institute.

Jane Tatam of Amolibros, the finest of hand-holders, helped me negotiate the numerous pitfalls between manuscript and the finished book and whose gentle but firm criticism has eliminated what would have been unforgivable errors.

I must pay tribute to my wife, Gina. It was only her enthusiasm and encouragement which, never wavered over a whole decade, that kept the project alive through those black periods when the research appeared to be leading nowhere. Without her unswerving support it can be truly said the book would never have been written.

At the end of every acknowledgement the author invariably offers the courtesy of exonerating from any errors or omissions all those who helped and takes on him or herself full responsibility. Never was such a caveat more justified than for this book.

WHAT OTHER WRITERS THOUGHT
ABOUT ERNEST BRAMAH

'There are volumes of Kai Lung waiting for you…I can assure you that you will have joined some of the wisest and choicest spirits of this age – a kind of Kai Lung conspiracy.' *J. B. Priestley*

'It is not extravagant praise. It is merely a judgement: a putting into as carefully exact words as I can find the appreciation I make of this style and its triumph.' *Hilaire Belloc*

'Ernest Bramah showed a stroke of distinct originality in creating his blind detective Max Carrados.' *Julian Symonds*

'Ernest Bramah achieves a delicate balance of humane and intellectual elements.' *Dorothy L. Sayers*

'It [The Wallet of Kai Lung] is quite certainly one of the great books of the language.' *G. K. Chesterton*

'My proselytising fervour [for Kai Lung} has led me, over the years, to thrust volumes into the hands of potential converts…. . If the proselytising worked let the converts be easy in their consciences, for if they are now in the company of the blessed, I bear them no grudge for their depredations.' *Bernard Levin*

'Bramah's place is in the more elevated, refined and sequestered reaches of the large and multifarious bazaar in which literary wares are offered for sale.' *Times Literary Supplement*

'But what is remarkable about Mr. Bramah's work is the undeviating fidelity and sureness with which he adheres to his idiom. Never for one moment does Mr. Bramah allow himself to be seen or felt behind the bland mask of Kai Lung. The impersonation is complete.' *Edward Shanks*

'I do not know if Ernest Bramah ever dreamed of the keenness of joy that has been created by him.' *E. C. Bentley*

'...in these [stories] Bramah's genius – a big word which, I do not use loosely - for identifying himself with what he conceived to be a Chinese mental and spiritual mode came unfalteringly to fruition.' *John Connell*

Ernest Bramah in the Royal Army Defence Corps, 1916.

'An aged Mandarin of ancient lineage and ripe culture'. John Connell

INTRODUCTION

Enthusiastic readers of Ernest Bramah's works, and world-wide there are many of them, have long wanted to know something about the author they so much admired. These are not only the now-ancient survivors from the years when Bramah was at the height of his popularity. They include a growing band of younger readers who, after a gap of some years when the books were out of print and often not available in libraries, can now purchase from an increasing number of new editions or they can download complete books off the Internet. More and more of Bramah's works are being reprinted so a new generation is discovering, and older generations re-discovering, the delights of his wit, prescience, imagination and erudition. They can meet or renew their acquaintance with the ingenious and loveable Kai Lung, the comic naivety of Kong Ho and the gifted blind detective, Max Carrados with his uncanny powers of observation.

They are asking, "Who was Ernest Bramah?" – a contemporary of, and in his time as popular as, Conan Doyle, Arnold Bennett, H. G. Wells and W. W. Jacobs. His work never really attained best-seller status and is perhaps better classified as 'long selling' rather than 'best selling'. Nevertheless, he never ceased to have devoted and distinguished admirers. What was lacking in numbers was certainly compensated for in the quality of a small and prominent group that included Hilaire Belloc, G. K. Chesterton, Sir John Squire, E. C. Bentley, Arthur Quiller-Couch, J. B. Priestley and Dorothy L. Sayers, all of whom had a deep and lasting admiration for the author. Today, the addictive quality of the stories would classify them as 'cult' books.

His humorous works were ranked with Jerome K. Jerome's and W. W. Jacobs'; his detective stories with those of Conan Doyle; his science

1

fiction with H. G. Wells and his supernatural stories with Algernon Blackwood. George Orwell acknowledged that a Bramah book [*What Might Have Been*] influenced his seminal *Nineteen Eighty-Four*.

If the man, rather than his writings, is unknown, it is because he chose not to reveal himself to his public or indeed to the literati of contemporary London. His defence of his privacy was almost paranoiac. Very few successful writers have so completely avoided personal publicity as Ernest Bramah, aided by the fact that his real name was Smith. According to Peterborough writing in the *Daily Telegraph* at the time of Bramah's death:[1]

> No one has ever known anything about him except the fact, which leaked out somehow that his full name was Ernest Bramah Smith. His age was never disclosed while he lived. His publishers and literary agents were sworn to secrecy about everything connected with his personal life. He never appeared in public.

Indeed, Grant Richards, his publisher, felt the need to write in an Introduction to the 1923 reprint to *The Wallet of Kai Lung*:[2]

> Finally, I do assure his readers that such a person as Ernest Bramah does really and truly exist. I have seen and touched him. His portrait has been published although I am not sure that even this statement carries conviction.

Bernard Levin in an article *The Times* in 1977[3] commented on the Professor William White's microscopic study of the cornucopia of documents relating to Ernest Bramah held at the Harry Ransom Humanities Research Center at the University of Texas and White's assiduous research in England. Levin wrote that [White] 'was able to piece together about as much biographical material as would cover a match box label or two'. Levin, one of the small, influential band of enthusiasts, gave absolution to those who failed to return copies of his Kai Lung books because 'they are now in the company of the blessed'.

But the statement about the lack of personal information is only partly true. In 1926 Bramah sent the Editor of an American newspaper *The Ashville Times* some autobiographical material he had prepared in

1923 for *The Bookman* and which he asked them to 'knock it into shape and out of the first person'. He also wrote that 'it told all about myself that I considered required telling'. This invaluable document provides insight into his early years making it possible to assemble facts about both his childhood and early adult life. After that Andrew Motion's criterion for good biography is not easily met. 'I regret the absence of personal detail which even the most vigorous of biography needs to bring to life. I want to know when people had their hair cut as well as when they wrote their great works.'

After about 1900 the trail becomes more difficult to follow although Bramah's work is well documented. Personal information relating to the years of his success is fragmentary. Memories of Bramah and his wife of their now elderly nephew and niece who knew them in the last years of their lives, although fragmentary, did fill a number of gaps and enabled some speculative statements to be confirmed or refuted. Thus it is possible to piece together aspects of his life, character, interests and attitudes; certainly from his books, published and unpublished, through comments by critics and others, and partly through the relatively few extant letters from and to Bramah and about him.

In the search for Bramah the passage of time is indeed regrettable. William Charlton in an article bemoans[4] 'In Bramah's case someone working fifty years ago would have had a chance. His wife Maisie died only in July 1957. He and she had a living nephew and niece to whom they were close and whose addresses are given in their Wills, the Bramah archive was not sold and dispersed until 1959. The 'living nephew and niece' were not to be found, alas, for another fifty years.

William White, among others believed there was a manuscript of an autobiography. Neither Bramah's agents nor the widow of Watt's son, who had inherited the copyrights, claimed to have any knowledge of such a document – but it did exist. A letter to A. P. Watt from Bramah's Solicitors and Executors stated:[5]

There are certain sealed parcels at the Hammersmith Branch of Midland Bank Ltd. One of these parcels contains [a] manuscript which Mrs. Smith informs us consists of the late Mr. Smith's own personal autobiography. Mrs. Smith informs us that she does not desire this manuscript to be opened and read. It would appear necessary for Probate purposes for the manuscript to be valued and we shall be glad if you would kindly arrange with Mrs. Smith [to] take the necessary steps in this connection.

HSBC Bank, which acquired Midland Bank, state they do not hold the material, probably because all papers are normally destroyed five years after a relationship has ceased and twenty-five years for documents such as deeds and leases. However in the Sotheby's February 24th 1959 sale item 465 reads.

Bramah (Ernest) THE AUTOGRAPH MANUSCRIPT OF HIS AUTOBIOGRAPHY WITH REVISIONS AND DELETIONS, *written in seventeen notebooks, original wrappers 8v; together with a Typescript of the work, 750 ll. 4to. unbound*
This very full and interesting account of the author's career up to the time of his marriage is UNPUBLISHED.

Item 466 appears to be a barely disguised autobiography of Bramah's school days.

Bramah (Ernest) THE SCHOOL DAYS OF PHILIP JENKINS The autograph Manuscripts of his story, with revisions and deletions c. 85pp., written in a dummy copy "of The London Handbook" for 1897, original pictorial wrappers 8vo together with two Typescripts of the story, wrappers 4to. This autobiographical story, which Bramah utilised in his Autobiography (see Lot 465) is apparently unpublished. Included in the lot is a series of 31 A. Ls.s written by Bramah as a small schoolboy to his family, covering the period of 1877-79, a collection of his school reports for the same period, a few letters from his schoolmaster to his father, and few other related pieces.

Both items offered for sale two years after Maisie's death were described as, 'The property of a gentleman' and both were withdrawn before the sale. Who 'the gentleman' was is not known although an inspired guess might be his agent W. P. Watt. It would seem unlikely that these were the documents Maisie ordered to be destroyed and it is more than possible a full autobiography covering his whole life was the document deposited at the Bank. These two early autobiographical efforts probably still exist somewhere but there has been no sighting of a full autobiography and, if it did exist, alas, must now be presumed destroyed.

The literary detective is set an extremely difficult task; only fragmentary and distant family memories, no autobiography or biographies, no diaries, no contextual anecdotes or contemporaries to interview, few letters, many indecipherable and mostly only referring to publishing matters and which contain little personal content. Nevertheless, the scattered pieces have been collected and assembled into what is hoped is a coherent picture of a learned but secretive man. Never have truer words been written than those of Justin Kaplan when he declared that the biographer needs 'an ox-like endurance, resignation to the rapid passing of time without much to show for it and the capacity to feed on your own blood when other sources run dry'.[6]

Many of Bramah's extant drafts are almost impossible to decipher most particularly those found in dummy copies of *The London Handbook*. Pages are not numbered and following the sequences is an arduous task. It is not made any easier by his idiosyncratic omission of titles, writing in the margins and using both sides of what was thin paper with the ink showing through. Thus valuable textual analysis which could show the development of the story or article is always very difficult and often impossible. Such analysis might reveal whether the final published text varied from earlier versions and shows the development of the book. It is some consolation that, knowing Bramah was such a perfectionist, it is unlikely the final document was not immaculate, and in total accord with his high standards.

Bramah has never been a forgotten author but has been given up for lost as a biographical subject. In 1964 Professor William White signed an agreement with a publisher for a book which was to be partly biographical and partly a critique of Bramah's works and style. It was to be another thirteen years before White considered he had enough material to proceed. The publishers gave a deadline of January 1978 but this was not met and the contract was cancelled. There were however still references to the putative book in White's correspondence as late as 1986.

If an author struggled hard and continuously to maintain his privacy during his lifetime is there any justification for seeking to reveal the person behind the creative artist? I believe there is. Understanding the man enables the reader better to appreciate his art, his skill, his imagination and his erudition and to appreciate what influenced the writing and formed his character – in Bramah's case a remarkable and impressive one. It provides in the words of the biographer Martin Stannard[7], 'a mental landscape to historicise critical interpretation' but more importantly and in less academic terms, better to enjoy what Bramah produced solely for our amusement.

My own acquaintance with the author began very many years ago. The school library always pinned to its door the jackets of new acquisitions. A picture of a Chinaman, although of the most benign appearance, led me to believe this might be a new Fu Manchu or Charlie Chan-type novel. The evil Dr. Fu Manchu's nefarious activities were followed tenaciously every Sunday afternoon on crackling Radio Luxembourg and no Charlie Chan film was ever missed.

If my expectations of thrilling action packed adventures were not fulfilled I did find instead, to use a Bramah term 'gravity removing' tales of immense attraction, even if at that immature age, I was not able to appreciate the elegance of the language nor the subtlety of the satire. I was hooked. From then on everything Bramah wrote was devoured rather than just read – the 'serious' books as well as the humorous ones.

I could find out nothing about the author other than the brief biographical notes that appeared on the Penguin Books editions, and later fuller, but still scant, information in the various biographical dictionaries. *Who's Who* listed his books and nothing else. It was many years before there was time to undertake the investigation that started in 1995 and has continued ever since and which, in the end, revealed more information than at the outset had been dreamed possible.

There are two widely disparate views of literary biographers. They have been criticised as flesh-eating bacilli or more wittily in Oscar Wilde's terms: 'Every man has his disciples and it is always Judas who writes the biography.' Lytton Strachey's totally contrary view was that it was the most delicate and the most humane of all branches of the art of writing.

Biographers are accused of craving acquaintance through the act of writing. This is probably true but who would not gladly substitute a few hours with the author for years spent locating and perusing secondary sources. Chronologically, for me, such a meeting would have been just feasible but highly unlikely to have been granted.

Both Dr. Johnson and Bertrand Russell provide more than adequate criteria to judge the success of a writer. The former wrote that the only end of writing is to enable the readers better to enjoy life or endure it and the latter that 'Each of them [stories] was written for its own sake, simply as a story, and if it is found either interesting or amusing, it has served its purpose.' Bramah succeeded on both counts.

Why a writer of such immense talent fell into partial obscurity is as difficult to understand as why, in more recent years, a new interest has emerged. This led, and is leading to more and more reprints and the emergence of previously unpublished material.

What the research has revealed is an erudite, witty, extremely hard working, shy man – a man who was kind, courteous and generous. But this book is not a hagiography. Bramah could be illiberal, prejudiced and could not resist embellishing some of his narratives with sadistic incidents and descriptions.

Nevertheless the book is written with affection for a man who gave so much pleasure to so many people – but it is affection that I am sure Ernest would have rejected.

Sources & Notes

1   *Daily Telegraph*. June 30th 1942.

2   Ernest Bramah. *The Wallet of Kai Lung*. Grant Richards. London. 1923. Grant Richards. *Introduction*.

3   Bernard Levin. 'Wanted some impeccable tales of Kai Lung. *The Times*. London. December 30th 1977.

4   William Charlton. 'Challenge to the Biographer' *Wormwood* No.1. Tartarus Press. Leyburn. Yorkshire. 2003.

5   Correspondence between A. P. Watt and Bramah's solicitors provided by Mike Berro.

6   Justin Kaplan. Chapter One 'A culture of biography' *The Literary Biography*. Dale Salwak (Ed.) Macmillan Press. Basingstoke. 1966. p.8.

7   Martin Stannard. *The Literary Biography*. op. cit. Chapter Four. 'The Necrophilic Art?'

MONEY EQUIVALENTS

There is no accurate way of comparing monetary values of previous ages with today's values. The patterns of purchasing were very different. At the time of Ernest Bramah's birth, 1868, the pound would have been worth the equivalent of £45.78 in today's terms and a gentlemen with a wife and family could have comfortably supported himself on £400 a year.

Except where a parallel contemporary value is significant all monies quoted in this book are given at their values current at the time. As an aid to obtaining even a rough idea of the purchasing strength of a pound the following table is offered. It is compiled from various recognised sources and is available from the Bank of England.

Taken by decades up to the date of Ernest's death in 1942, the values given (where not converted in the text) can be compared to the twenty-first century equivalent by applying the following multipliers.

Multipliers to convert the value of the pound for any quoted year to 2005 values

£1 in	1870 =	£47.62
£1 in	1880 =	£50.36
£1 in	1890 =	£62.40
£1 in	1900 =	£59.45
£1 in	1910 =	£59.54
£1 in	1920 =	£22.10
£1 in	1930 =	£34.83
£1 in	1942 =	£37.50 (The year of Bramah's death)

It can be seen over his lifetime there were wide fluctuations – 1920 values were a third of those of 1890. Thus care is needed to ensure the multiplier for the right decade is applied.

THE PARADOX

Ernest Bramah was an enigma – a man of contradictions and contrasts. A paranoia to maintain his privacy and seclusion battled with his skill in self-promotion and marketing; strong right wing political views held alongside his essential kindness and concern for the underdog; the macabre and sadistic elements in his writing that belie his courteous, urbane and cultured life; a strong personal moral code clashed with his obvious delight in outrageous advocacy of issues that offended contemporary mores; a fascination with the supernatural and occult but a love of all that was sanctified by age and custom.

Together these paradoxes produced a writer of great erudition and knowledge and whose skills spread over many styles; a great short story writer but not a great novelist; a deadly serious man but also a humorist who invented a whole new style of 'Mandarin English' that has never been copied; a blind detective with incredible powers and a host of well drawn, fascinating characters who people his stories and articles and which continue to attract readers more than half a century after he completed his last book.

CHAPTER ONE

A VICTORIAN CHILDHOOD

Ernest Brammah Smith's antecedents were most certainly working class and not likely, except for the very few, to provide a milieu which gave opportunities for personal development, financial success, social acceptance and esteem. To be born into a working class family in the mid-Victorian period was to enter a world of pestilential rookeries, with thousands of people herded together and horrors more akin to a slave ship than a city. Crowded houses reeked of poisonous malodorous gases generated by sewage and refuse in the courts and streets into which the sun, clouded by factory smoke, rarely reached. Rooms were small, walls black with the accumulation of years of dirt that penetrated through cracked walls and broken windows. The workers and their families, most particularly the children, were chronically unhealthy, stunted in growth and ill-formed.

The conditions in the windowless factories were appalling. The hours were long, not infrequently fourteen, fifteen and sometimes sixteen each working day. Both the conditions and the work were unpleasant, unhealthy, dirty, dangerous and noisy. Employers were dictatorial, unpredictable and ruthless. Truly 'dark satanic mills'.

Life without money was wretched. Pauperism and fear of the workhouse dominated everyday existence. Keeping heads above water was paramount and being able to pay your way the limit of working class ambition.

Ernest Brammah Smith's family were skilled or semi-skilled workers or tradesmen. His maternal grandfather was a double-matcher (a process in textile dyeing that was both unpleasant and sometimes toxic) but he was not without means. His Will shows he owned four cottages with an estate not exceeding £200. This, on the death of his wife, was left to his five children, one of whom was Ernest's mother. Ernest's paternal grandfather traded as a butcher.

His father, Charles Clement Smith, was a textile worker who had experienced the horrors of the textile mills with the incessant roar of the machinery and the clattering of the driving belts, the air heavy with lint which clogged the lungs. Charles however was not the average mill worker. He was self-taught, clever and ambitious and probably a little unscrupulous. Over the years he rose to the positions of 'buyer' and 'mill manager'. His wife, Susannah, whose maiden name was Brammah, was illiterate, was probably a mill girl and was described by the family as 'one of the people'– the marriage certificate gives an X as her mark. It has been suggested by the living descendants of Joseph Bramah, the famous engineer, that it is feasible that the Brammahs were a branch of their family.

At the time of the birth of their first child, Emily Jane in 1854, the Smiths were living in North Street, Audenshaw. In 1858 there was a second child, Charles Percy. Sometime between the birth of Charles Percy and the next child the family moved to Hulme. A second daughter, Rose, was born in 1865. It is suspected by the family that she was mentally retarded. There were almost certainly infant deaths, which accounts for the long gaps, by Victorian standards, between the children.

Hulme was a small town with well-landscaped areas and large houses with gardens occupied by those with business interests in the centre of Manchester. But there was another Hulme, the Hulme described by Frederik Engels. This consisted of poor quality, crowded, back-to-back houses constructed for the influx of workers from the countryside who came to work in the rapidly growing textile industry. Apart from the cotton mills, chemical and dyeing works there was also a large barracks with housing around which was described as 'dingy' and 'tumble down', 'public houses of the lowest class' and marine stores and rag and bone shops.

It was this environment, not the affluent Hulme, into which Ernest Brammah Smith was born at 10 Rushton Street on April 5th 1868. Ernest was christened with his mother's maiden name, Brammah, as his own second name.

According to Citizens Role, Medlock Street Ward, the family left Rushton Street in 1869. They next appear in Census of 1881 although Rose was not living with the family but with her aunt, a publican. The Role shows them now living at Birch Field, Worsley, a much more prosperous area. Although it too comprised textile mills there were a number of small estates including the house the Smiths occupied. It was next to Ryland's Dacca Mill. Charles was employed at the mill and his senior position justified the provision of the house as a 'tied cottage'. Just when the Smiths arrived in Worsley is not known but one of the many mysteries surrounding the Smith family was the rapid improvement in Charles's finances. In thirteen years the family appears to have gone from the slums to a large house surrounded by a two-acre garden with tennis courts and a lake. Apart from the home there is ample evidence that by the 1880s Charles was a man of some wealth.

◆

There are references to Charles's occupation as 'warehouseman', 'buyer coloured' and also 'mill manager'. While 'warehouseman' might summon up the vision of a brown-overalled minion in fact it could refer to the ownership of a warehouse. It is conceivable that at some time he was the 'Smith' of Smith & Crofton, in Blackfriars Street, Manchester who were textile warehousemen and shippers selling to India, China and the Levant. John Barker, Bramah's nephew by marriage, heard frequent references to 'a warehouse in Manchester', which would fit the location since Worsley where Charles is known to have worked was then some way outside Manchester.

In the Census of 1901 Charles described himself as a 'Retired buyer of textile goods'. Charles's prosperity could not be explained by Susannah having received her share of her father's estate as this, divided equally between her siblings would have been less than £50. A less flattering, but likely, possibility is that as a buyer and mill manager he was able to amass his wealth through bribery and other inducements to purchase from a supplier.

Settled comfortably in their Worsley home Charles had given his eldest child, Emily Jane, a good education and was supporting her at an art school. The second child, Charles Percy was by all accounts an excellent scholar and won a place to read Theology at Oxford leaving with a BA and First Class Honours and was eventually ordained.

Ernest Brammah Smith while not born into a wealthy family arrived at the time of their rapidly improving prosperity. A large part of his boyhood was spent in his own spacious and well-equipped home with its large garden. He also mentions having the illicit run of the neighbouring cotton mill with its forge, carpenter's shop and the 'fascinating society of boilermen, blacksmiths, stokers and other delightful people'.[1] There is little doubt from his meagre notes he had a happy and fulfilled childhood in a warm, loving family.

The years of Ernest's childhood were ones of great political turmoil and change; The Married Women's Property Act, Employers' Liability Act, The Irish Land Act, The Factories and Workshop Act, the legalisation of the Trade Unions and the secret ballot were all innovations which occurred within ten years of his birth. These changes were to impact later on his unsuccessful farming career and on his writing. They were also the years that saw the births of his great contemporaries H. G. Wells, Marcel Proust, Stephen Crane, Somerset Maugham, G. K. Chesterton and André Gide.

◆

Ernest's education began at a dame school[2] and a private boarding school. From here in 1880 he was sent to the Manchester Grammar School (where he seems to have dropped the second 'm' in his name) which then, as now, had a reputation for outstanding teaching and results. Many years later he wrote that in Dr. Samuel Dill's day 'it was a good public day-school where De Quincey was educated though he was not very grateful to it'.[3]

However Ernest was a poor scholar. William White writing in the summer edition 1966 of the school magazine[4] about Bramah's time there begins his article: 'If there had been a poll at the Manchester Grammar School in 1884 on the Student Least Likely to Succeed, one of those in the front running would have been Ernest Bramah or, as he was then known. Ernest Brammah Smith'. The missing autobiographical story manuscript, *The School-days of Philip Jenkins* would doubtless have given a much more detailed description of life at the Manchester Grammar School in the last quarter of the nineteenth century.

His reports must have left his parents, so ambitious for their children, distraught. In the Middle 1st form he was thirty-first out of thirty-one; in the Upper 1st Classics sixteenth out of twenty-six. His usual position in most subjects was in the lower half of the class. With neither School Certificate nor Matriculation he could not enrol at any University and certainly not Oxford to follow in the steps of his elder brother Charles.

At a time when compulsory education was only up to the age of 10, all that could be said was that he had at least completed most of his secondary education. He may only have been able to reach a middle of the class position in Classics but the successful writer he became was able to introduce, effortlessly, references to and comparisons with classical figures and situations. Similarly his unremarkable performance in science did not damp his interest in the subject and many of his successful books and stories were to have scientific contents central to the plot.

He did however acquire one important interest while at school and which he carried into his adult life and became an acknowledged leading world expert – coin collecting or, as he preferred to call it, numismatics. It is not always easy to trace any autobiographical material in Bramah's stories but there is one article that can be verified as a true account of the origin of a lifetime hobby. In 'Through the eyes of a child'[5] he relates the genesis of his interest in numismatics. He writes of a small shop in a passageway called Half Street alongside the cathedral that sold (among other things), coins. The proprietor was a D. T. Batty. Bramah wrote:

> When he learned I wanted to inspect the contents of the penny bowl I regret to say he groaned audibly. Conversation as to the relative merits of the various penny coins that I coveted, he did not encourage..... . I graduated from the penny to the twopenny bowl and ultimately to trays. I was even permitted on some few special occasions to glance at the more expensive stock in the room above.

David Batty did indeed exist, his shop is listed in an 1850 Directory. He authored *Descriptive Catalogue of the Copper Coinage of Great Britain*,[6] which preceded Bramah's own *A Guide to the Varieties and Rarity of English Regal Copper Coins. Charles ll – Victoria 1671-1860* some sixty years later.

At the end of the autumn term of 1884 his parents removed him from the Manchester Grammar School. What happened to his education in the next year is not known. Possibly he had a private tutor – his father could certainly afford it – or he went to another school.

At the age of seventeen Ernest's parents were doubtless greatly concerned when they had to decide, with him, just what career he could follow. University was not an option given his poor academic record. His 'fixed intention to have just such another shop [as Batty's] if I failed to induce Mr. Batty to take me into partnership meanwhile when in the progress of growing up I should be called upon to choose a career'[7] was firmly rejected by his parents.

That his parents consented to him giving up his education suggests that they were both wise and indulgent or both, or maybe just desperate. Ernest had expressed an interest in a career in farming because in his own facetious words 'of a pleasure I derived from keeping ducks'. They acceded to his choice and they generously arranged to fund his pupillage and provide an income to support himself during his apprenticeship. Circumstances proved that this was not to be the least of their expenditure. As events turned out their agreement to this career choice may have been a mistake. Circumstances were to prove that this was not to be either the last or the least of their expenditure.

Sources and Notes

1   Ernest Bramah. Autobiographical note. Typescript held in the Ernest Bramah Collection at the Harry Ransom Humanities Research Center. [H.R.H.R.C.] University of Texas at Austin. Undated. No published version found.

2   Dame schools were the equivalent of infant or nursery schools today, usually run by women in their own homes. The children were taught the alphabet and some reading and given household chores to do.

3   H.R.H.R.C. op. cit. Autobiographical note.

4   William White. 'Ernest Bramah at MGS.' *ULULA The magazine of the Manchester Grammar School*. Manchester. Summer 1965.

5   Ernest Bramah. 'Through the eyes of a child'. Typescript. op. cit. H.R.H.R.C. n.d.

6   David Batty. *Descriptive Catalogue of Copper Coinage of the British Empire*. Forsyth. Manchester. 1868.

7   H.R.H.R.C. op. cit. Autobiographical note.

CHAPTER TWO

TO BE A FARMER'S BOY

Even Ernest realised that fondness for ducks and an urban childhood did not equip him to go straight from school to being a farmer. He understood that he had to have a basic knowledge of farming methods, animal husbandry, crops, finance and at least some ideas of the problems he would face and the opportunities open to him.

Bramah's farming career can be traced from his first book *English Farming and Why I Turned It Up*.[1] The title was the invention of his somewhat unconventional publisher, Andrew Tuer, founder of the Leadenhall Press, who had a partiality for quaint titles and eccentric format, but it also reflects Bramah's own drollery. Bramah explained the book was 'an autobiographical account of my farming days treated from a light and anecdotal standpoint.' This tongue in the cheek narrative of his venture into agriculture is probably a reasonably accurate description of his experiences even though there has been a considerable embellishment of the characters in the book – neighbours, labourers, landowners and agents and his fictional wife with the exotic name of 'Altera'.

Having decided to farm the first thing was to get some practical knowledge. No doubt influenced by his unimpressive record at the Manchester Grammar School, he turned down the opportunity to go to an agricultural college on the grounds 'that horses might be studied more economically than by keeping a stud of horses and that billiards was not an essential item except perhaps for elephant farming.'[2]

Thus at seventeen years of age Ernest set out on his farming career. He had absolutely no knowledge whatsoever relevant to his chosen vocation. The only alternative to attending agricultural college to learn the basics that had to be mastered was to obtain a pupillage since his father did not want his son to be a farm hand. There was a world of difference between a farm hand and a farm pupil. The farm hands were servants who did what they were ordered to do. A pupil lived as a member of the family and was instructed in the skills of running a farm.

Sometime in 1885 an introduction from one of his father's contacts found him a place on a farm Ernest called 'Erith'. This is the first instance of the wish to conceal facts about himself to avoid publicity. Like many things associated with Bramah the actual locations of this and his subsequent pupillage are disguised in his account of his farming career. It was not the fear of libel that caused to him to do this, since on his own admission later, he knew nothing about the law of libel. The desire for privacy ensured every geographical location, every town, every village, every topographical reference and every person mentioned in the book were changed to prevent identification. Thus it is pointless to speculate whether this was the name of the farm or the district it was located in. Kent County records show no farm or farmer in Erith with any of the names in the book.

Ernest stayed at 'Erith' for fifteen months where he applied himself to learning farming far more assiduously than to his schoolwork. Having completed what might be called a 'foundation course' he was ready to apply for a pupillage.

♦

He returned to Manchester and began a systematic search to find the most suitable Pupil Master farmer. The first step was a search through the classified advertising columns in the appropriate farming periodicals. There was no shortage of opportunities. Over fifty 'possibilities' were identified and Ernest wrote an initial letter to all of them requesting full particulars.

With his father's help, the replies received were subjected to a selection process using criteria that appear to be as arbitrary as his choice of farming as a career. First, anyone seeking more than 100 guineas per year (over £6,000 today) was eliminated as '…we regarded such a sum as uncompetitive'. That was true since the agricultural press contained advertisements from farmers requiring as little as thirty guineas per year. 'A gentleman who mentioned a steam yacht was excluded, as was one who offered an exceptional chef. A farmer who always took first prize at county shows and an offer which assured the would-be pupil that the farmer only took the sons of gentleman were eliminated, as was one which included 'an introduction to all the county families'.

Similarly, a rejection factor was the inducement of plentiful hunting, yet another because of a requirement to buy the farm at the end of the apprenticeship. One respondent 'anticipated that I would object to taking my hunters so far, an easily surmounted difficulty as he knew of one of two very suitable horses for sale in the neighbourhood'.[3]

However frivolous the primary selection process was, within a few weeks he was settled in a farm he called Tudorlands and, as events turned out, it was a good choice. The location of this mixed farm of some 300 acres remains a mystery. However a fragmentary statement among Bramah's papers, apparently written about 1940 and now held at the Harry Ransom Humanities Research Center, University of Texas at Austin, referred to his being a 'mud student' in Cheshire and Devonshire. In his book he records that his second pupillage was 150 miles away from the first and 20 miles from the sea. If 'Erith' was in Kent, this would place 'Tudorlands' crudely in the Okehampton area of Devon which is the only place in the England that fits the co-ordinates.

◆

According to Ernest's own account, after about two years he felt himself sufficiently competent to rent a farm of his own. The search for a suitable holding took twelve months during which time he 'looked across the greater part of England'. He was 'almost tired of the whole business and was in a ripe mood to take any place that had no glaring setbacks'. Finally, almost as an act of desperation, he settled on a farm, and this time it is one that can be identified – Packwood Hall Farm – located between Packwood and Knowle in Warwickshire. In his book he called it 'Redeaves'.

The house still exists and can be positively identified since Bramah mentions a moat around the house and describes the main living area as it exists today. There is only one house in and around Knowle that fits the description of Packwood Hall, a largely unspoilt sixteenth century building. Substantial additions were made in 1910 long after Bramah had left the farm. As it stands now it would appear to have been very large for occupation by a bachelor with few, if any, staff but in Bramah's time it was much smaller.

At the time Bramah leased the farm it was part of the Wykeham-Martin estate, and was 180 acres which he rented for £200 per annum (approximately £11,500) – no mean sum to find from the yield from 180 acres. He, or his father, negotiated a rent of £1.1s. per acre (£66.00) against an asking price of £1.5s.which was probably about twelve per cent below the average going rate.

The farm was not a success and although it was on a yearly tenancy he persevered for three years before he finally gave up any hope of making a living as a farmer and abandoned the attempt in September 1892. He did so with regret as his encomium of the farming life shows:

> For it is a grand life itself. There is a straight simple dignity in its daily round, an exquisite beauty in its gradually unfolding life and a direct honesty in its inviolable laws that raise it above all common considerations. It opens the portals of a world of new emotions that dwellers in cities never feel; emotions that live and die in the fibre of the communicant and are untranslatable beyond.[4]

He took part in the country sports such as hunting and shooting and kept his shotgun for many years after he had no further use for it eventually giving it to his nephew John. Despite Ernest's obvious love of the countryside he was to spend all but the last year of his life in London.

If the entry into farming was unfortunate the exit was timely. Immediately after he gave up farming there was a devastating drought followed in 1894 by an exceptionally bad harvest. Ernest attributed his own failure to a toxic mixture of under-capitalisation inherent in the economic conditions and the bloody-minded conservatism of agricultural labourers. Their views were somewhat different to those of their employers as their wages and hours had changed little from those prevailing fifteen year earlier.

In the Preface to his book[5] he makes a cryptic reference to 'a person may be sure a would-be farmer would be £500 (£29,500) a year better off' not to farm. If this figure is anything like correct it can be safely assumed that his farming career cost his father a great deal of money, probably over £100,000 in today's terms, taking into account the cost of the pupillage, his twelve months' search for a rented farm and buying stock and equipment for the farm. Oddly enough, at exactly the same time, a near contemporary author, Algernon Blackwood, managed to lose his father £130,000 at current values in an unsuccessful farming venture in Canada.

An interesting insight into farm economics is given from a statement that one landowner would not accept any tenant without his having the capital equivalent of £10 per acre. If this was typical of the times it implies that with 180 acres Ernest had to have had capital of £1,800 (over £108,000) – a very large sum by any standards and one which was quite outside any possibility of Ernest possessing. Unless the Wykeham-Martin estate from which Bramah rented 'Redeaves' did not apply this financial requirement, the capital backing must have come from his father – one more proof he was a wealthy man.

◆

The chronology of Bramah's farming career is hard to re-constitute but from fragmentary comments and some, perhaps dubious, calculations it would appear to be:

> Erith – fifteen months 1885-1886
> Tudorlands – two years 1886-1888
> Search for a rented farm – one year 1888-9
> Tenancy of Redeaves – three years 1889-1892

The fact that his book *English Farming and Why I Turned It Up* was published two years after leaving Redeaves (or Packwood Hall Farm) gives credence to this chronology.

At some stage the family, always a close one, decided that they would move from Lancashire to be near Ernest. The 1891 population census shows Charles, who was now retired, Susannah and daughter Rose living in the nearby village called Knowle, just a few miles from the farm.

Emily Jane was not with the family at Knowle but was living with Ernest and keeping house at Packwood Hall Farm and was probably the model for the fictional wife, Altera.

If nothing else, Charles was able to witness just how the money he had provided for Ernest was lost. It is reasonable to deduce that he did not blame Ernest for the failure or if he did, he forgave him, because he continued to provide him with financial support for some years more.

Retrospectively it can be seen that Ernest had not chosen the most propitious time to enter agriculture. The 'Great Depression' as it was called lasted for some twenty-five years and hit agriculture particularly hard. In addition, almost every calamity known to farmers took their toll – blight, mould and mildew in crops, foot-and-mouth disease, pleuro-pneumonia, and liver rot in animals. Prices were falling, the average yield of wheat per acre fell, foreign imports increased. Ernest concluded that 'no other trade or profession, yields so small a return in proportion to the risk on the invested capital'.[6]

Ernest complains in his book that political agitators periodically brought his employees to a rebellious point. It was pure coincidence that Redeaves, or to give it its real name, Packwood Hall Farm, was less than twenty miles away from the Barford Farm of Joseph Arch – a Primitive Methodist preacher, a successful agitator for unionisation of agricultural labourers and who was elected to Parliament in 1885. The deep resentment among the agricultural workers was well enunciated by Joseph Arch in 1898 a few years after Ernest had given up his disastrous farming career. In his book *Joseph Arch – the Story of his Life told by himself*, he wrote:

'Their [the employers] policy has been to do with as little labour as possible, and the labour they did employ was never paid sufficiently to enable the men to do a good day's work. They have half-paid labour, and the result is half-fed labour.'

Perhaps Ernest's unsuccessful foray was as much a matter of timing as lack of experience or even incompetence. It was fortunate for all those who were later to enjoy Bramah's skill, humour and inventiveness that his farming career was not a success. The loss to literature would have been great had the enterprise proved a profitable venture.

♦

It was while Bramah was struggling to make a living from the farm that he, accidentally, took the first steps that were to lead him to his subsequent successful career (and, in parenthesis, enabled the geographical location of the farm to be identified). Acting as secretary to his village agricultural show he sent a paragraph about it to the *Birmingham News, South Edition*. This was inserted and the Editor wrote asking him if he would become a regular correspondent for the district. Since the outcome had such a profound affect on his future it is worth quoting at length Ernest's own description of the circumstances. He wrote:[7]

> The district included about a quarter of an English county and would have required three horses to cover properly. One could deal with anything from a dog fight or a very large mushroom to an earthquake (which never actually occurred) or a good murder (which was even rarer). The rate of payment was five shillings (25p) a column, the column being about 2,000 words. Two columns a week would be expected. I accepted this offer in the same lavish spirit and did my best, but I am afraid that it generated in me a fondness for the more lucrative branches of literature that pursued me ever since.
>
> In addition to hard and fast reporting we were much encouraged to comment in a light and persiflagellatory spirit on passing events. I understand that my paragraphs in this department afforded frequent amusement and on Saturday evenings at the village green, aged rustics might be heard asking one another with senile chuckles whether they had "seen master's latest". It is a living wonder to me now that I didn't land the paper in for a libel action over something or another, and I hadn't the faintest notion of what "sub judice" implied. These risks accepted light-heartedly but not so the numerous misprints which (I considered) covered me with shame, and the occasional excision necessary, no doubt, from the sub-editorial point of view, of some paragraph over which I had perhaps taken considerable trouble.
>
> Periodically smarting under some humiliation I threw in the job, but on each occasion the resignation was declined and I was

lightly implored not to take life and letters quite so seriously. Finally the Editor solemnly undertook (entirely his own idea) to pay for everything that I sent in, whether it was used or not. Alas! I have never since found another Editor who even approached that fine standard.

It would seem that his territory was both Packwood and Lapworth, just about half way between Birmingham and Stratford upon Avon. The contributions are what might be expected in a local newspaper, highly parochial and factual. Hiding behind the not very inspired pseudonym of 'Packwoodsman' he gathered confidence and, doubtless with the Editor's approval, his humour begins to be displayed.

Commenting on warnings printed on the reverse of dog licences concerning rabies he advises his readers not to interpret them too literally. Among the symptoms, dog owners are warned of:

…a change of habit, restlessness, hiding in dark corners, altered voice, uttering the peculiar noise in which the howl predominates, surly but not vicious, on the contrary often affectionate…. Dogs showing *any* of these symptoms should be at once isolated… . I only know one man who implicitly followed this advice…returning home after a long absence his dog greeted him with unusual affection, and was immediately isolated in the coal cellar, where it rapidly developed another symptom – an utterance of a peculiar noise in which the howl predominated – and on seeing his master approaching armed with a poker, it confirmed his worse fears by retiring into a dark corner.[8]

Reporting on a County Councillor's speeches:[9]

On Monday the address read uncommonly like the painstaking effort of an advanced schoolboy whereas on Wednesday, Mr. Ramsden spoke with the easy flow and conviction carrying arguments of a finished orator. By what ill-advised chance he happened to read his Tuesday's address I cannot pretend to say but I sincerely hope that in justice to himself he will not repeat the experiment. By this Mr. Ramsden will learn that he made a slight mistake on the latter occasion as I was present, but unfortunately, reporters are not yet compelled to wear brass plates, with numbers, like cabmen. Should the County Council require more funds, they may remedy this omission by taxing and licensing us, and then even the above happy consummation may be effected, although it is quite unnecessary as the eagle eye of experience can mark us, as easily as the proficient thief can spot the indifferent-looking man, gazing abstractedly at the pavement to be a detective. Besides a brazenly shabby appearance, and a bulging breast pocket, caused, not by a roll of bank-notes, but by an over-fed note book, most of us have a hunted look, as though dreading a meeting with the gentleman whose name was mis-spelt, or the lady whose coiffure we tried to describe, in the previous weeks issue. Mr. Ramsden is not yet proficient in all this, so I will consider his remarks to be delivered sub rosa, and they must be forever lost.

Headed 'Of Two s' in the March 7th 1891 issue he was writing about the noxious smell of a local gas works and the then prevalent view that inhaling the aroma would cure whooping cough. He writes: '…were I offered the alternative of a perfect cure or malignant whooping cough I would unhesitatingly choose the latter'.

His last contribution to the paper was in September 1892. This coincides with his abandoning farming, although he was able to extract something from his experience in writing his first book a few years later. Another career had now to be sought.

Sources & Notes

1 Ernest Bramah. *English Farming and Why I Turned it Up*. Leadenhall Press. London 1894.

2 op. cit. p.17.

3 op. cit. pp.38-39.

4 op. cit. p.180.

5 op. cit. Preface.

6 op. cit. p 141.

7 H.R.H.R.C. op. cit. Autobiographical note.

8 *Birmingham News. South Edition*. January 17th 1891.

9 op. cit. 12th February 1891.

CHAPTER THREE

THE JOURNEYMAN

There is little doubt that Charles Smith was an indulgent father. He was also uncritical and still optimistic about his son's future. Despite the heavy losses Ernest incurred in his disastrous farming career his father now agreed to him trying his hand at journalism in London. He gave him an allowance as well as, to quote from Ernest's autobiographical note, 'a small assortment of works all explaining how large incomes might be made in various branches of literature, none of which, I regret to say, I have yet found time to read, much less profit by.' The allowance, as Ernest later remarked, had guaranteed to save him from the romance of actually starving as George Gissing and Jerome K. Jerome had done. He arrived in London probably some time in 1893.

Heading for Grub Street, inhabited by indigent writers and journalists and from which they all aspired to escape, must have been an unnerving experience for a young man whose previous existence had either been with his family in the suburbs of Manchester or in the country. He was not rich so could not share the paradise that London offered to the wealthy nor, fortunately, was he poor so forced to experience the hell that London was for the impoverished. The migration from the country to the town was still in full flow. Crowded, the population of London had grown to six and half million by 1900, it was as filthy, foggy and squalid as the Gustave Doré's drawings depicted it. A gloomy sink of soot and screeching iron, huddled tenements, tiny back yards with a privy and washing lines and everywhere stench and smoke. The destitute, who Jack London called 'people of the abyss', crammed into any space, most particularly churches, to fester and die.

This was the London to which Ernest now journeyed and hoped to make both his fortune and his reputation. He described himself as 'timorous' so that the move was an act of considerable bravery. Unlike Arthur Waugh whose father had also given him an allowance to try his luck in London as a free-lance journalist he did not have Waugh's advantage of being a relation of Edmund Gosse who introduced him into the glittering literary scene of London. Bramah knew few, if any, people in London and he had to face the problems of finding suitable accommodation within his limited means, employment and making friends and contacts. Journalism was his new chosen career but his achievements to date as a free-lance correspondent for a local paper would not impress any would-be employer.

He wisely spent his first months in London acquiring skills that were necessary accomplishments for journalists and learned shorthand, like Dickens before him, and typing. The growth in literacy had led to an explosion in the numbers and types of newspapers and journals which were started to meet a huge public demand for features and fiction. This provided the opportunity for free-lance work, something that he showed considerable knowledge of in his later writings. Nothing with a Bramah by-line has been located and it might be inferred his freelancing was not very successful.

Clearly his network in the literary world had not yet developed to the extent of providing him with the personal contacts and introductions he needed. But for once fate was on Ernest's side. The college where he was acquiring his secretarial skills also had an employment agency that sent him to see Jerome K. Jerome, the author of the highly successful *Three Men in a Boat* and publisher of the very popular magazine, *The Idler*. Jerome was about to launch *To-day* magazine and 'wanted someone to do his correspondence'. Ernest would suit. He was now on the first step of the literary ladder.

His lowly position did not at first give him an entry into the company of the successful authors who were both contributors to *The Idler* and personal friends of Jerome K. Jerome. Extant letters from Jerome to Ernest Bramah all appear perfunctory, indeed brusque, and show no warmth or amicability.[1]

Dear Smith,

Send the Geo.Moore M.S. to "Station Hotel" Newcastle on Tyne "To await arrival" & register it. Also send proofs of magazine page re Bert [Sic] Harte. Publish Chapters 4 & 5 or Part II the same week.

Yours truly

JKJ
I have not corrected for technical errors.

Dear Smith,

I enclose a cheque for Moore. But don't give it up unless he delivers the whole of the M.S. to the end. Find out what we owe Vivien for M.S. of his in hand that are known.[sic] If he sends anymore leave it over until Feb [?] issue.

Yours truly,
JKJ

Dear Smith,

...Tell Pugh to wire me on Monday morning that he is all right – that he has 'enough Ed. Notes and Answers' – that he has received Randolph's letter & "Czar Reminiscences" etc – Post me proof of journals. Post Tuesday to this address.

And a telling off

Dear Smith,

I return quotes etc. Please look at letters before opening them to see they are not marked private.

Yours truly
JKJ

Of course the tone may only reflect the business formalities of the day. Nevertheless there is no mention of Ernest as Jerome K. Jerome's secretary or assistant in either Jerome's autobiography or in biographies. Bramah receives no acknowledgement even in his subsequent role as Jerome's editorial assistant and occasional contributor of short fiction pieces. It is true that there was no reason to believe that Bramah was ever likely to be more than a clerk when he joined the magazine. But it is surprising that by 1926 when Jerome wrote his *My Life and Times* he did not mention that Ernest Bramah, whom he had nurtured and was now famous, was also part of *The Idler* and *To-day* editorial staff.

One possible reason for omitting Bramah from his memoirs could have been that their political views were at the opposite ends of the political spectrum. Bramah's politics and economics were to the far right as clearly set out in his early books and articles. Jerome was a committed socialist and he would have been highly antagonistic to Bramah's political views, which could be interpreted as totally reactionary, although Jerome clearly had no objection to W. W. Jacobs's rejection of socialism. He told Jacobs that he couldn't understand why he, Jacobs, was afraid of Socialism. He said that under Socialism all Jacobs's needs would be supplied. Jacobs retorted, 'I don't want things assured to me. I'd have a lot of clever people fussing about, making me happy and doing me good. Damn their eyes.'[2]

Jerome was certainly Bramah's role model or perhaps even mentor, possibly before he had appreciated the political gap between them and, anyway, Ernest's lowly position was unlikely to have provided the opportunity for the exchange of political views. Nevertheless he was advanced from a mere correspondence clerk to deputy editor under Jerome's tutelage. There is no doubt whatsoever that Bramah learnt his editorial skills in the offices of *To-day* and *The Idler*.

During Bramah's early days in London he decided to exploit his farming career by setting down in a light-hearted way, which belied the losses he had incurred, an account of his experiences. The Leadenhall Press published the book in 1894. A glimpse of the gentle humour of his future writing can be seen in this book as the earlier description of the process of selecting a farm for his pupillage shows. The book, *English Farming and Why I Turned it Up* was well reviewed in the agricultural press and John Carter in an essay entitled 'Off-subject books' described it as one of the exemplary books in that field. Exemplary or not, it was not calculated to lure readers away from the best sellers of the year of its publication – Hall Caine's *The Manxman* and Anthony Hope's *The Prisoner of Zenda* – less than 250 copies of *English Farming* were sold.

In 1894 Jerome K. Jerome was at the height of his career. *The Idler* a monthly magazine was well established and *To-day*, which was produced weekly, was successfully launched. In that busy environment it was not long before Bramah's secretarial duties declined and he took on more and more editorial responsibility with the title of 'Assistant Editor'. His fellow assistant editor was George Burgin who also went on to become a popular writer of humorous short stories although, unlike Bramah, he is now totally forgotten. Bramah's promotion to assistant editorship is hinted at in a letter written by Jerome from the Station Hotel, Newcastle-upon-Tyne dated November 11th 1895[3]

> Re. No. 55. I return model (a good idea) you will see my remarks in pencil on the different pages. Use your discretion over rest of pages. I want to see how long before you will be able to run this by yourself with merely a general talk over with myself once or twice a week.

The next year he is addressed as 'sub-editor of *To-day*' by George Gissing's agent, W. M. Colles, replying to Ernest's chivvying, in true editorial style, to get his copy in. 'I should be glad to have the remainder of the series of sketches by G. Gissing at your earliest opportunity. They are urgently requested for purpose of illustrating.'[4]

The contents of *To-day* were divided between current affairs and journalistic matters and a Magazine section with fiction and literary articles. It was the latter for which Bramah became responsible. Commissioning features now brought him into contact with the leading figures of the time. Among his authors were, George Gissing, Barry Pain, Eden Phillpots, Thomas Hardy, Bret Harte, George Moore, Grant Allen, W. W. Jacobs and Thomas Hardy.

If an extant letter from Grant Allen is anything to go by, Bramah was astute or persuasive in negotiating fees. Grant Allen who had very recently won the *Tit-Bits* fiction prize of £1,000 accepted a mere 1½ guineas (£1.57) for the Australian rights of a story previously published in *To-day* – the condition being it was a cash payment. By 1897, doubtless based on his growing fame, Allen was able to obtain 10 guineas from other publishers for his contributions.

Although both Stevenson and Kipling were among the contributors Bramah only dealt with their agents. These included J. B. Pinker and A. P. Watt both of whom were to become important to him in his later literary activities. With the other authors, his contacts were fairly frequent but he confesses that of all the contributors to *To-day* the only one he wanted to see personally was Bret Harte who he most admired. 'I am afraid I wrote to Bret Harte oftener than was strictly necessary simply to get a reply from him.'[5] Almost all Bramah's contributors were highly successful and some of them wealthy which must have stimulated his ambition to become an established author himself.

♦

His new authority and his association with the great Jerome opened the opportunity for him to appear in *To-day* under his now adopted pen name 'Bramah'. Mark Valentine[6] believes that Jerome K. Jerome, with his wry understated humour, most particularly in *Three Men in a Boat,* may well have influenced Bramah when he later came to perfect the splendidly-polished irony of the Kai Lung tales.

So far Bramah's published work was either journalistic or semi-autobiographical. His position at *To-day* placed him in a position to obtain favourable consideration for publication of his work. There is however no question but that the first stories which appeared were there on their own merit not as the result of literary nepotism. Jerome K. Jerome was far too professional to allow anyone to persuade him to publish material that fell below his own high standards.

The first contribution to *To-day* that can be traced is in July 1894 when he contributed a story of about 1,000 words called 'A bad shot'. It concerned a member of an audience who is humiliated by a conjuror and takes his revenge by volunteering at a later performance to assist the conjuror by holding a watch that the conjuror is to shoot. The offended man pretends to be shot in the head and, by using hidden red paint, simulates copious bleeding. The conjuror faints with shock while the audience storms the stage. When the victim recovers the conjuror is laughed off the stage and never performs again. There is perhaps the faintest trace of the Bramah humour in referring to the act that precedes the conjuror, a Victorian 'sister' act. 'At that period they dressed as their grandmothers. Thirty years later they make up as near as like as their grandchildren. Art demands such sacrifices from its votaries.' While the tale is undoubtedly workman-like its climax could easily be anticipated and there is no feeling of a clever 'twist' to its end.

It was over a year before the next short story was published on June 6th 1895. It was titled 'The people's picnic' it is an account of a Bank holiday visit to Hampstead by a visitor from the provinces whom Bramah calls 'The Provincial'. The observations on the vendors of entertainment are trenchant and amusing.

> Less spiritual food is provided by a telescope through which, on the payment of a penny, you can look at the Abbey of St. Albans – and if fortunate see it... . Down in the valley flutters the white tent of the Ambulance Corps, an object of engrossing interest to a somewhat morbid crew, whose chief hope is that a case will soon be brought in.

There is a reference to 'pallid, small-bodied East-enders' which draws attention to how ill-nourished the working class was at this time – something which would cause concern to the authorities a few years later when recruiting for the army fighting the Boer War. The Victorian Archive in the Royal Archive has a letter from Colonel Wood to the Queen in which he comments, 'These poor young fellows had not the metal nor the health & strength to make them really good soldiers.'

The article was accompanied by a drawing of Lewis Baumer. He was a popular artist whose work also appeared regularly in *Punch* and *The Tatler*. Jerome frequently commissioned him to provide illustrations for his magazines.

The next contribution followed quickly in July of the same year 'From a London balcony'. This was more truly Grand Guignol and foreshadowed the dark streak of sadistic malevolence that sometimes emerges in his later books and which contrasts so strongly with his gentle and kindly nature. The tale has an unexpected climax. It begins very much like a gentle piece of observation with a description of a flower-covered balcony of the neighbouring houses and gardens and the observation of neighbours, most particularly one attractive elderly woman who lives next door. She has befriended a young girl. However noises heard through the walls seem to show a great deal of distress which ends with the girl throwing herself from a window and impaling herself on the iron railings below. The neighbour then seeks another girl. It is left to the reader to decide if she is procuress or just a vicious employer. The contrast between the beginning of the story with its delicate descriptions and the gory depiction of the prone body impaled on the railings produces a frisson in the reader.

In the December 21st 1895 issue there is a feature on Chinese jugglers that is possibly an unsigned Bramah contribution.

I had been there a few moments when the women began exhorting the audience for cash to enable them to carry out such a trick as they contemplated putting before them. This audience just like all Chinese audiences – uninterested, but unwilling to move on any further until they have seen it all. Very little cash rewarded the ceaseless begging of the women.

Did this perhaps foreshadow Kai Lung, the itinerant storyteller soliciting cash from his audience before beginning his tales? Kai Lung would appear for the first time the following year and would be the character most associated with Bramah and on whom his success as a writer would be substantially based.

Bramah's contributions were now appearing among established writers who contributed to *To-day* – Israel Zangwill, William Pett Ridge, Bret Harte, Conan Doyle and, of course Jerome K. Jerome. He could be said to have arrived.

Sources & Notes

1   Undated letters from Jerome K. Jerome to Ernest Bramah held at H.R.H.R.C.

2   Jerome K. Jerome. *My Life and Times.* John Murray. London. 1926 p.134.

3   H.R.H.R.C. op. cit. November 11th 1895.

4   *The Collected Letters of George Gissing.* Ed. Pierre Coustillas. Ohio University Press.1992. Vol. 5. p.307.

5   H.R.H.R.C. op. cit. Autobiographical Note.

6   Mark Valentine. 'Ernest Bramah'. *The Book Collector.* London. July 1997.

CHAPTER FOUR

THE EDITOR

Bramah's ambitions as a writer made his work on *The Idler,* which was in any event becoming increasingly routine, of declining interest. The magazine appeared to have lost some of its vigour and important illustrators including Walter Sickert and Louis Baumer no longer appeared in its pages. Seeing no real future with the paper, Bramah was happy to accept an offer from The Artistic Publishing Company to become the Editor of a magazine – an important career step for him – they had just acquired. He believed the Company had many interesting ideas for publishing books and magazines and for building substantial circulations.

At this time, to meet the demand for recreational reading generated by the growth and spread of literacy, new periodicals proliferated. Writers and journalists who could recognise and satisfy the needs of the enlarged market provided by the newly literate were in high demand and they often came from the same clerkly classes which formed a large part of their readership. This was a situation wholly favouring Bramah.

While the number of new entrants to magazine business was considerable, so were the failures. With the demise of *Punch* at the end of the twentieth century *The Spectator* and *The Illustrated London News* are now probably the only journals to have been published continuously from this period until today.

Being an Editor of a journal was, as Bramah was to find out, a risky business. There are a number of reasons which could account for the turmoil in the magazine market; under-capitalisation, fickleness and disloyalty of readers, poor or non-existent marketing and, particularly affecting the more serious publications, the desire by very many readers for sensation in the form of scandal, violence and sex and preferably all three together.

The world which Bramah now entered as Editor, was one where triumphs were often short lived and failures frequent but it was one in which he had high hopes of financial and literary success. The journal which Artistic Publishing Company had purchased and which he was to edit, doubtless on the basis of his sub-editorship that he had held under Jerome K. Jerome, had been a sixpenny church magazine called *The Minster*. It had been a magazine largely devoted to church matters and had been started with high hopes. An Editorial stated:

> We are told that there is no room for any further 'monthlies' without rivalling one or more of those excellent and attractive publications that are already in existence. With all due deference to our critics, we venture, at the risk of appearing self-satisfied, to believe there *is* an opening.

How wrong they were. It lasted only fifteen issues before being sold. The new proprietors signalled a change in the editorial approach. They declared 'it would be the first English magazine not merely in excellence of its literary and artistic matters but also on the quality of its reproduction and printing'. Moreover it was half the price of *The Idler* and therefore was going to be highly competitive

Bramah took over the Editorial chair in the autumn of 1895 and set out the new policy for the paper:[1]

> Our stories will not rely for their interest on harrowing our readers' feelings; they will not be of a character to frighten folk, and to cause men to look under the bed before putting out the light; nor is it our intention to work so strongly on people's emotions as to make them think that life is a blank, and to make them wish they were dead (like so many of our sad-hearted contemporaries). We do not intend to worry over abstruse questions, nor to decide psychological problems. On the contrary, we shall hold to that cheerful spirit which has made us (as we admit) the first nation in the world; which we will keep us so as long as we cling to it.

They claimed to have lined up a most impressive list of contributors many of them members of that close group that had gathered around Jerome and were known as 'The New Humorists'. These included Barry Pain, William Pett Ridge, J. M. Barrie, Israel Zangwill and W. W. Jacobs. Surprisingly given *The Minster* would be a competitor, Jerome K. Jerome himself was also among those it was announced would be contributors.

The first edition was planned for January 1896. The magazine declared, 'Nothing remains of the old but the name'. That was certainly true. The first edition of the new *Minster* was almost entirely destroyed by a fire at the printer's premises

> The publishers and Editors of THE MINSTER feel that their readers are entitled to an explanation for the late date of publication... . The entire issue which was unfortunately destroyed by fire... . Every effort has been made to reprint the number as promptly and as satisfactorily as possible...

The Magazine now contained, in addition to fiction, sections on sports, health and business. There were many cartoons, perhaps to rival *Punch* and supplements and 'offers' such as discounted accident insurance and books. Bramah was not above copying the idea of merchandise tie-ins first adopted by Wilkie Collins and George du Maurier. They had both exploited their work in this way a few years earlier – *The Woman in White* perfume, *The Woman in White* cloaks, *The Woman in White* quadrilles and *Trilby* lapel pins, *Trilby* ice-cream moulds, *Trilby* hats of course, and even *Trilby* sausages.

For Ernest there were opportunities for him to contribute editorial views unsigned and using pen names. Such features as 'Notes by the way', 'Club notes' and the pseudonym 'Plaudite' gave him a platform to express himself and his ultra patriotic right wing views.

Perhaps to its readers, the first signs of financial troubles for *The Minster* were a reduction in size and in the quality of the paper used. Then without warning or even an intimation of cessation of publication, the magazine closed after the March 1896 edition. Its life had been less than half of is existence under its previous owners. Bramah's disappointment might be imagined. He attributed its demise to a lack of sufficient capital to support the ambitious plans. Two years later

W. L. Wilson writing in the *London Handbook,*[2] which Bramah was then editing, penned a final epitaph. Writing about the poor quality of illustrations in most weekly periodicals he states '*The Minster* made a good attempt but came to an end before it was able to fulfil its expectations.' This is praise indeed because Bramah had little real interest in illustration as his writings and correspondence show quite clearly.

♦

Thus in 1896 Ernest found himself without employment. From Bramah's viewpoint, redundancy had come a year earlier than it might otherwise have done. Both *The Idler* and *To-day* came to a precipitous end the following year; Jerome had to close both periodicals because two libel actions brought him to the edge of bankruptcy.

Some of the now unemployed *Minster* staff, including Bramah, then joined, or more likely took over, another publishing business trading as The Leadenhall Steam Printing & Publishing Company with its registered office in Leadenhall Street, in the City of London. This company had been founded by Andrew Tuer and after his death it had languished. It was known for the high quality of decoratively produced publications. It seemed an ideal vehicle to launch a similar publication to the defunct *The Minster,* although on less ambitious lines. The name of the proposed journal is not known.

Although Bramah claimed in the brief autobiographical note to be one of the new owners of the company his name does not appear either as Director or a shareholder. Possibly lack of funds or even lack of confidence in the success of the enterprise deterred him from taking a financial stake in the company, but this does not explain why he did not hold a Directorship since several of the Directors listed also had no shareholding. It is notable that among both the working directors and the shareholders journalists and printers dominated.

As the Leadenhall Press was the company that had published *English Farming,* Bramah doubtless hoped further efforts would be made to promote the book. Whether this occurred is not known but what is known is that the book still did not sell and the stock was passed back to him. Lacking storage space he perpetrated what, with hindsight, seems to have been an act of vandalism. He tore out the title page of each copy and then sent the books to a waste paper dealer. However, some of the books missed the mutilation. As late as 1964, Bertram Rota, a London bookseller, stated in a letter[3] 'A cache of English Farming was sold as one lot at a sale in London about five years ago and subsequently came into our hands. We have some left and still sell them at 30/-'. They were not missing their title page so clearly not all the copies were in fact defaced. Needless to say, today a copy would fetch several hundred pounds.

In 1897 when the new Journal was still appearing, Bramah decided to sever his full time links with it and become a free-lance 'outside' writer. Clearly he felt sufficiently confident he could earn a living with his pen without having to rely on his father to underwrite his activities as occurred during his farming and early journalistic career. His experience with his first book could not in itself have been very encouraging so that it might be safely assumed that he was depending on his skill as an Editor and feature and short story writer.

♦

William White summarised Bramah's career on the verge of his thirtieth year.[4]

> 31st out of 31 in Classics at the Manchester Grammar School, no matriculation or university, failed at farming, very moderate success as a local newspaper's parish correspondent, dead-end employment in a magazine, a failed book, a member of a bankrupt publishing firm. 'Undistinguished' would be a generous description of his career to date.

On the last day of 1897 he married Maisie Lucie Barker, an extremely pretty woman some six years younger than himself and whom he had met while she was visiting relatives near to his farm. The marriage took place at the Church of St. Andrew in Holborn, a choice perhaps influenced by the association with the church of William Hazlitt and Charles and Mary Lamb, authors whom he admired. Ernest's brother, Charles Percy Smith, then a curate at The Church of St. Chrysostom's in Manchester, officiated. Ernest's occupation was given as 'Editor'.

Although he was probably living with his parents in Muswell Hill just before his marriage the Certificate gives his address as 60 Chancery Lane, in Holborn, which were the offices of The Grosvenor Press. The witnesses were Maisie's brother, Alan, and Ernest's sister, Emily Jane. Maisie's parents did not attend but there could be no question that they did not favour the marriage as a generous marriage settlement shows. Nevertheless there was to be very little contact over the years between Ernest and his in-laws.

Maisie Barker is an elusive figure and little is known about her. She was the daughter Edward Barker, who described himself in his 1874 Will as a draper but on his daughter's marriage certificate twenty-three years later as a wine and spirit merchant. This career change was the result of him going into business with his brother-in-law who was an ex-Gilbey salesman and who had a well-established wine and spirits business.

Maisie was one of the Barkers' two children. The evidence is that they were a prosperous family living in Edgbaston, a suburb of Birmingham. Edward's estate on his death in 1899 was only a relatively modest £1,282 (£80,000). Nevertheless, Maisie brought with her a marriage settlement that appeared to yield about £300 per annum. If, as was usual at the time, it was invested in Consols (a British Government Bond) it implies the settlement was a very substantial capital sum.

The allowance would have underwritten Ernest's income while he developed his free-lance career and nurtured his literary contacts. It was not a fortune but, with his free-lance earnings, the young Smiths could lead a comfortable, but not a lavish, life style. One thing is certain, the marriage settlement was not dissipated since it was returned to Maisie on Ernest's death.

Maisie is almost invisible. Her nephew and niece commented that they never saw any signs of affection between Maisie and Ernest. The only dedication in his books would seem to challenge this. She shared Ernest's enthusiasm for coin collecting which he acknowledged with what can only be construed as a very affectionate dedication. 'To M if only (but not only) for the hours it has given to us.' Other than this shared enthusiasm other details of Maisie's life are fragmentary until her last years and her death in 1957.

The autobiographical information that is available prior to Ernest's marriage compared to the vigorous and successful attempts to protect his privacy after his marriage leads to another speculation. Could it be that it was not Ernest who really wanted seclusion? Certainly the family view was that the Smiths' reclusive life style was due to the eccentric and unpredictable behaviour of Maisie. There is a family belief that it is possible she suffered with an alcohol problem. As will be revealed later, there are some inexplicable acts by Maisie that might be ascribed to 'eccentricity' and which gives the view of their relations a degree of veracity.

♦

In what might have been the lean years before full recognition, Ernest's income was purely from his free-lance and editorial work. William White's bibliography of 1975, admittedly not complete, does not include any journals between 1898 and 1904. There is little doubt however he was writing for the periodicals of the day. *The Short Story Index*[5] although giving some seventy Bramah titles does not unfortunately date any of them so it is impossible to know from this listing which might have appeared at the turn of the century.

Despite his lack of success up to this time Bramah's career was finally beginning to develop. By the end of 1897 he obtained the first of his free-lance editorial appointment. This was *The London Handbook*[6] published by the Grosvenor Press. This Journal combined the features of a Directory and a Review. It contained a mixture of 'Who's Who', travel features, forthcoming events, book and theatre reviews, articles and stories as well as full details of London elections. In a letter to the Librarian of the Hammersmith Library Bramah's widow stated that all the contributions to the Magazines were by the owners of the Grosvenor Press and, of course, Ernest himself.[7] This was not a wholly accurate statement, there were outside contributors.

There is in existence a dummy copy of the *Handbook*,[8] which was doubtless a mock-up used to advance-sell advertising space in the publication in which Bramah writes:

> ...It is safe to say that the Handbooks will possess full attractions for all members of the high-class public at which it aims, and will be preserved as a charming souvenir, always worthy to read

and consulted not merely by visitors but by the whole of the educated classes throughout the country...That is to say, we shall write for the same class of people as ourselves.

The first edition has a Preface simply signed 'B' and an unsigned feature – 'Latter day palaces'. This was a description of two London Hotels, the long gone Cecil and the Gothic Midland Grand at St. Pancras, which now, after many vicissitudes, has been completely renovated and converted back to a hotel. Although the article is unsigned the Contents page does attribute it to Ernest Bramah.

In a breathtaking, by today's standards, piece of intellectual snobbery and patronisation the editorial states:

> ...the book appeals not to any selected circle, but to the whole general public – to town and country, masculine and feminine readers of every intelligent type. With perfect candour, however, it may be added that the lower classes of readers – those who draw their whole mental sustenance and recreation from the less tolerable periodic press – are not aimed at, nor desired.[9]

There is nothing to suggest that Bramah was either a snob or condescending. The statement was probably that of the publishers whose interests were, of course, entirely commercial and who had a very clear idea of what is now called the 'target audience'.

It is the source of much confusion that by the second edition of *The London Handbook* in 1898, the name had changed to *The London Year Book.* The contents were not significantly different so the title change might have been to ensure that readers understood it was an annual production.

It says much for Bramah's skill in obtaining contributors that for the second edition in 1898 he managed to obtain articles from such dignitaries as Joseph Chamberlain, Walter Besant and A. J. Balfour, all of which carried facsimile signatures, the latter idea taken directly from Jerome's periodicals. The *Year Book,* was lavishly illustrated, included an obituary of Aubrey Beardsley which fiercely defended his work, but none of the illustrations used were among those which had caused such public controversy.

The 1898 edition also contains a feature that again illustrates Bramah's leanings towards the macabre. Although apparently very serious it is another tongue in the cheek approach to his subject, this time instead of agriculture it is the more sombre topic of suicide. 'A modest defence of constitutional suicide.'[10] It might have appeared outrageous given the mores of the Victorian period and probably left many readers believing this was a serious suggestion.

It starts in a thoughtful and solemn manner.

There are subjects which the world prefers to ignore because they are, to the comfortable, unpleasant; there are evils which have no place in the agenda of persons or parties, inasmuch as for them no reformer has yet suggested a specific. I am far from classifying suicide, in itself, as either evil or an unpleasant subject...

But what then is reader to make of:

Think you that Signor X., who lately disposed of himself in a London hotel (much to the proprietor's inconvenience and the dismay of visitors), by drinking every liquid particle in the room and then probing his brain, through the auricular aperture, with a pair of scissors, would have selected that exceedingly elaborate and painful manner of exit had he been able to go, armed with the proper credential, to a good hospital, and then flicker out surrounded by every comfort.

Bramah the social commentator and a thinker of the unthinkable? Bramah the humorist? Intriguingly the article is signed 'E. B. Smith'. Just why on this occasion he chose not to hide behind his pseudonym cannot be known since he was given to using his pen name even when replying to personal correspondents.

Both the *Handbook* and the *Year Book* contain several of Bramah's own stories but unsigned. Their authenticity is proved by drafts of these features in Bramah's papers. In one article, 'The fascination of the tragic', he refers to several of his own contributions which must have been published elsewhere. Another feature in the same style as 'Constitutional suicide' is 'The art of perjury'.[11]

I take some honest pride in the act [perjury] to show these inexperienced plaintiffs and defendants how, by the arts of cunning, misrepresentation, and false witness – by all departments, in short, of Perjury – they may hope, with diligent study…to equal or outwit the cleverest practitioner who at present use them as grain to their own mills…

Also among Bramah's papers is a series of short biographies of such public figures of the day as Flinders Petrie, George Goschen, Cardinal Herbert Vaughan, Sir Henry Irving and Lord Justice Rohmer and many others. As they are all in Bramah's handwriting it must be assumed he wrote the pieces himself. It would seem they were intended for publication as part of an ongoing series called 'A Gallery of Londoners'. *The London Year Book* foundered before all the pieces could be used.

There is a long piece of doggerel called 'Flagellum Stultorum [Scourge of the Stupid] by W. Lawler'[12] which is a paean to leading writers including Conan Doyle, Jerome K. Jerome and Israel Zangwill which ends with what ought to have been to Bramah an excruciatingly embarrassing quatrain:

Of thee Bramah, I had an aim to treat
And lay a friendly garland at his feet
But since my spirit's trail elsewhere he has led
Forgo the verse, and take my love instead.

Bramah let it through.

There is no evidence that the publication continued under either title beyond 1898 as they would almost certainly have been in the collection that Maisie donated to the Hammersmith Library in 1944. A similarly named Handbook appeared in 1911 but Bramah was not involved with it.

♦

By now he felt sufficiently sure of his skills to produce *A Handbook for Writers and Artists. A Practical Guide to the Press and Literary and Artistic Publications.*[13] This appeared in 1898 as authored by 'a London

Editor'. There can be no doubt that this was Bramah as his own annotated copy exists.

The *Handbook* contains an amusing list of 'Dos and Don'ts' for would-be writers but substantially it is a media guide. The long Introduction is really a do-it-yourself guide for aspiring authors and journalists with a substantial input of cynicism and flashes of humour.[14]

> ...it does not matter greatly what you write, for it is bound to be amateurish, both in expression and in selection of subjects, and nothing but practice will mend this. No doubt it reads all right now, but in after years the sight of these early manuscripts, which you sent so confidently to the leading magazines will heighten your colour wonderfully for the moment

Advising on plots, he does not spare the presumptions of the author.[15]

> It is a statistical fact that about ten per cent of the stories received from beginners deal with the misfortunate of a young genius who writes wonderful books while starving in a garret. Very often he expires just as the publisher – the only one who ever thought it worth while to read the MSS, we are assured – arrives to offer him a fabulous sum for the book. He dies with a happy smile on his lips and a week later all England is ringing with his name. No doubt very comfortable for a beginner to relieve his feelings in this way but do not follow his example. It has all been done so often, and so much better than you can hope to do it. The "To be returned" coffers of the editorial departments team are filled with pathos and idylls with self-sacrifice and sex problems.

On the mechanics of submission, after advising the aspiring author: 'If you cannot afford this [having the manuscript typewritten] only write half the amount you are now doing and spend the time you save in endeavouring to earn the money to pay for the typewriting.' And, 'Fasten the sheets together with a brass binder in the top left-hand corner'.[16] This is advice that he himself ignored as Grant Richards, his publisher noted. '...it was a careful typescript [*The Wallet of Kai Lung*], sewn bookwise into a brown-paper wrapper, and that every manuscript of Ernest Bramah's that I have since seen looked exactly like it'.[17]

A wry smile might be justifiable when it is appreciated that the advice to authors was written when Bramah had to his name only his own very unsuccessful remaindered and finally destroyed book *English Farming and Why I Turned It Up*.

There have been suggestions that he also edited *The Book & News Trade Gazette* but there is no direct or deducible evidence in the publication that he was the Editor although he could have made non-attributed contributions.

◆

In 1894 Matthew Arnold described the state of the British press as 'the new journalism' which was 'full of ability, novelty, variety, sensation, sympathy, generous instinct; its one great failure is that it is feather-brained'.[18] Bramah's unpublished novel, *The Optimist*[19] which has a strong autobiographical content reflects all these things and, more importantly, tells a great deal about Bramah's attitudes and experience. It was probably written about 1900 and leans heavily and amusingly on his editorial experience when two of his characters start and edit an unsuccessful periodical. Their discussions and decisions on its title, the type of material it was to contain and their target market must all reflect his time as Editor dealing with contributors to his various journals. The manuscript reveals a detailed knowledge of publishing economics. Additionally in the Bramah collection there is also a barely readable draft of a facetious article in which he demonstrates how to pad out a feature.

There is no doubt that Bramah had promotional as well as editorial responsibility for the magazines he edited because he sent copies of the *Handbook* to a number of prominent people including the Duke of York, (later George V) Bernard Shaw, and Lord Wolsley, hoping to get some favourable quotations to use in the promotion of the book. It would seem from correspondence from the recipients that this was a marketing effort that failed. As is shown later he was able to make use of the results of this failure.

The 1890s were perceived as a time of literary and artistic decadence personified by Oscar Wilde, Frank Harris and Aubrey Beardsley. Bramah used some of Beardsley's less provocative drawings, (there are no contributions from Wilde). It has already been shown he was not straight-laced but he was firmly on the sober side of the aesthetic divide with Henry James, Arnold Bennett, Byam Shaw and Gordon Craig. In modern parlance he didn't 'do' decadence. The new realism of Shaw's *Widowers' Houses*, Moore's *Esther Waters* or Zola's *La Terre* had no attraction for him. Just the opposite. He had a totally different idea for fantasy, not realism, in the person of Kai Lung an itinerant teller of tales who would eventually bring him to the notice of the public and fame.

Sources & Notes

1   *The Minster*. Artistic Publishing Company. Vol. 1 London. 1895. The Journal is also listed as published by Periodical Publications. London.

2   *The London Handbook*. Grosvenor Press. London. 1897.

3   Quoted by kind permission of Mr. Anthony Rota.

4   *ULULA*. Manchester Grammar School Magazine op. cit.

5   Dorothy Cooke. *The Short Story Index*. H. W. Wilson Company. New York. 1955.

6   H.R.H.R.C. *The London Handbook*. op. cit.

7   Letters of Maisie Bramah Smith by courtesy of the London Borough of Hammersmith archives.

8   The dummy copy is undated and contains no publisher's name. When it eventually appeared it carried the name of Periodical Publications. London.

9   *The London Handbook*. op. cit. pp.17-18.

10 op. cit. pp.78-81.

11 op. cit.p.73.

12 op. cit. pp.17-18.

13 *A Handbook for Writers and Artists*. Charles William Deacon. London.1898. pp.82-84.

14 op. cit. p.2.

15 op. cit. p.3.

16   ibid.

17   Grant Richards. *Author Hunting.* Hamish Hamilton. London. 1934
     op. cit. p.1.

18   Quoted by Matthew Sweet. *Inventing the Victorians.* St. Martin's Press.
     New York. 2001 p.62.

19   Ernest Bramah. *The Optimist.* H.R.H.R.C. op. cit. Typescript, n.d. but
     probably early 1900s.

CHAPTER FIVE

INVENTING CHINA

My unbecoming name is Kai to which has been added Lung. By profession I am a relater of imagined tales and to this end I spread my mat wherever my uplifted voice can entice a company to listen. Should my feeble efforts be deemed worthy of reward, those who stand around may perchance contribute to my scanty store.

Thus Ernest Bramah's most memorable and loved character, the 'modest itinerant teller of tales' whose only worldly goods are his thin cloak, an empty wallet, his mat and his handstaff, is introduced to the reader, in a style of writing no one else has ever succeeded in copying for more than a few paragraphs. William White claimed that it was impossible to describe it. Doing so can be no more effective than trying to describe the vibrancy and luminosity of a Suerat picture or an eighth-century Chinese temple painting. Bramah developed a highly attractive and total distinctive prose style of the most addictive quality using a super-structure of elaborate vocabulary and circumlocution within a rigidly artificial convention. The writing is flawless and is beautifully executed with a gentle rhythm. He created his own way of depicting Chinese dialect by rephrasing, in the most ingenious manner, English idioms in mock Chinese phrases. It meticulously avoids any ego-display ("this person" not "I"). In fact it could be said that Bramah invented Anglo-Mandarin speech.

The idiom is intended to generate a particular effect of humour by the use of a foreign convention, the Chinese convention, in the English tongue – circuitous. convoluted and mock heroic. It conforms to Fowler's definition of 'pedantic humour' which assumes that if a Western custom is described in ornate Oriental verbiage, the reader will find both the incongruity and the custom funny. They did. In Hilaire Belloc's words:[1] 'It was meant to produce a certain effect of philosophy and at the same time it was meant to produce a certain completed interest of fiction, of relation, of a short epic. It did all these things.'

Bramah himself in a letter to an unknown recipient stated, 'I can only say the idea was in part serious and partly burlesque; but where the one ends and the other begins I cannot always be quite sure myself.'[2]

Every word and phrase is chosen with fastidious care. The literary craftsmanship and extremely subtle humour has been much admired by many writers – Hilaire Belloc, John Buchan, George Gissing, J. B. Priestly, J. C. Squire and Dorothy L. Sayers among others. Dorothy L. Sayers, included a fondness for quoting Kai Lung as one of the signs of discernment of her aristocratic sleuth, Lord Peter Wimsey. In *Gaudy Night*[3] Wimsey says 'My tastes are fairly catholic. It might easily have been Kai Lung or *Alice in Wonderland* or Machiavelli…' Kai Lung is quoted again at some length in *Busman's Honeymoon*.

J. B. Priestley, a great admirer of Kai Lung wrote in his book, *English Humour*[4]

> All is written in a solemn mock-oriental manner and style, the launching pad for innumerable shafts of wit and humour. Either you find this a joy forever – and Bramah has always had his faithful devotees of whom I am one; or you don't care for this kind of elaborate fooling (I have yet to meet a feminine Bramah enthusiast)…

This last statement may be true so far as Priestley was concerned but judging only from the contributors to Mike Berro's website[5] it is a generalisation too far. There are indeed feminine followers of Kai Lung, and there is no reason why there should not be. Claire Rayner in a B.B.C. discussion with John Mortimer made a spirited defence of Bramah's Chinese books.

◆

With *The Wallet of Kai Lung* Bramah first created a Chinese never-never land which is a parody of nineteenth-century stereotypes of the mysterious East but not of the *Chu Chin Chow* or *Turandot* variety or moving further east not even *The Mikado*. This, according to John Connell,[7] in his Introduction to *The Celestial Omnibus*, was:

> ...the China Bramah loved but from which he was cut off by the accidents of geography and economic circumstances. This was deprivation he could not accept. Therefore by the exercise of a strong and disciplined imaginative faculty, he created his own China. For many people, before the advent of mass communication, Bramah's China was probably a reality – a China peopled by Mandarins and bandits, merchants and maidens and poor students, manufacturers and workmen, corrupt officials and artists, fishermen and alchemists all of whom express themselves in a winding, highly stylised and deferential language of the Chinese as it might sound when translated into English. The pretence at over-polite self-deprecation and the externals covering over the sharpest barbs at human weakness appear, to Western eyes, to be a mood that is thoroughly Chinese.

It is virtually impossible to describe or compare the style Ernest Bramah developed for the Kai Lung books. There is nothing similar. The most effective way to convey to anyone who has not read the stories is to quote from them, and no excuse is given for doing so, at length.

But no extract can do full justice to Kai Lung. He must be read in the whole to be appreciated and to understand his true worth but the flavour of the tales can perhaps best be savoured from the aphorisms and maxims which are to be found in every narrative, sometimes several on one page and from examples of the polished, exaggerated, refined and elaborate language.

Here is a declamation from the leader of a band of robbers:

> "It would be useless to conceal from a person of your inspired intelligence that I am indeed Lin Yi" continued the robber. "It is a dignified position to occupy and one for which I am quite incompetent."

One character can be recognised as a shop steward seeking to impose a closed shop on his employer:

"Suitable greetings, employer of our worthless services," remarked their leader, seating himself upon the floor unbidden, "Those who speak through the mouth of the cringing mendicant before you are the Bound-together Brotherhood of Colour-mixers and Putters-on of Thought-out designs, bent upon a just cause."

The negotiations rapidly become bad tempered.

"Know then, O battener upon our ill-requited skill, how it has come to our knowledge that one who is not of our Brotherhood moves among us and performs an equal task for less reward."

The language of course is pure invention because in real life Chinese peasants and artisans were, and are, notorious for their swearing and profanity.

This is a poor student speaking:

"The reason" admitted Lao Ting frankly, "need not be buried in a well. Had I avoided the encounter you might have said among yourselves 'Here is one who shuns our gaze. This perchance, is he who of late lurked within the shadow of our backs to bear away our labour'? Not to create this unworthy suspicion I freely came among you, for, as the Ancient Wisdom says, 'do not adjust your sandals while passing through a melon field, nor yet arrange your hat beneath an orange tree'."

This formal type of delivery does not differ markedly from that of a Mandarin:

"The name has a somewhat familiar echo," interrupted the Fountain of Justice, with a genial interest in what was going on, rare in one of his exalted rank. "Have we seen this ill-conditioned being before?"

Kai Lung can insult his audience with equal elegance.

"In particular, there is among this august crowd of Mandarins one Wang Yu, who has departed on three previous occasions without bestowing the reward of a single cash. If the feeble and covetous-minded Wang Yu will place in this very ordinary bowl the price of one of his exceedingly ill-made pipes, this unworthy person will proceed."

One of the greatest attractions of the stories is the use of aphoristic wit and the rendering of proverbs, many of which are pure invention, expressed in the mannered ornate style that Bramah made his own.

Some of the maxims may have come from Chinese sources. There was no shortage of material to build on. In 1874 W. Scarborough published nearly 3,000 Chinese proverbs[8] and a book *The Middle Kingdom*[9] listed over 100. These genuine proverbs may lack the Kai Lung elegance but the sentiments are often similar. 'Not to distinguish between the beautiful and the ugly is like attaching a dog's tail to a squirrel's body' and 'To instigate a villain to do wrong is like teaching a monkey to climb trees'. It is very likely Bramah consulted these books but there is no evidence that he used them in the form they were given.

A few of the maxims that appear throughout the Kai Lung books will give their flavour.

He who lacks a single tael sees many bargains.

When one is enquiring for a way to escape from an advancing tiger, flowers of speech assume the form of noisome bindweed.

Although it is desirable to lose persistently when playing at squares and circles with the broad minded and sagacious Emperor, it is none the less a fact that the observance of this etiquette deprives the intellectual diversion of much of its interest for both players.

It is a mark of insincerity of purpose to spend one's time in looking for the sacred Emperor in low-class teashops.

He who is compelled to share a cavern with a tiger learns to stroke the fur in the right direction.

Before hastening to secure a possible reward of five taels by dragging an unobservant person away from a falling building, examine well his features lest you find, when too late, that it is one to whom you are indebted for double the amount.

It has been said that there are few situations in life that cannot be honourably settled, and without loss of time, either by suicide, a bag of gold, or by thrusting a despised antagonist over the edge of a precipice on a dark night.

When actually in the embrace of a voracious and powerful wild animal, the desirability of leaving a limb is not a matter to be subjected to lengthy consideration.

When struck by a thunderbolt it is unnecessary to consult the Book of Dates as to the precise meaning of the omen.

In shallow waters dragons become the laughing-stock of shrimps.

It has been truly said that the whole course of an ordinary person's life may be rearranged by so slight a matter as having his gravity displaced at the wrong pause during a speech by a high official.

If to succeed in a business way, sell your sacred books and therewith purchase and display a pretentious banner.

A rock falling outside one's door makes a greater stir than a landslide across the valley.

We think there is nothing so delightful as placing a person of high honourable rank in a ridiculous position.

It is, of course, a simple task to translate many of the proverbs and aphorisms back into their Western original. 'There are times when the classical perfection of our graceful tongue is strangely inadequate to express emotion' – 'Words have failed me'. 'Do not let the rice grow above your ankles' – 'Do not let the grass grow under your feet'. 'He who hires the carriage picks the road' – 'He who pays the piper calls the tune.' 'It is as lengthy as it is far across' – 'It is as broad as it is long.' Perhaps the most well known is 'May you live in interesting times' which occurs in *The Wallet* although there is some doubt if this is a Bramah original.

The adaptation of some of the most quoted Shakespeare lines appear heavy-handed and laboured but to J. C. Squire they are burlesque in an impeccable style. 'A sedan chair! A sedan chair! This person will unhesitatingly exchange his entire and well-regulated Empire for such an article.' 'The object before you is your distinguished and evilly disposed father's honourably-inspired demon.' 'Friends, Chinamen labourers who are engaged in agricultural pursuits, entrust to this person your acute and well educated ears...'

Three of Bramah's aphorisms appeared in the *Oxford Dictionary of Quotations* but were later transferred to *Oxford Dictionary of Modern Quotations.* Which title was more appropriate to include the sayings is arguable but the examples the editors chose, all from *The Wallet,* are by no means the best.

Besides the proverbs Bramah cunningly inserts small vignettes such as:

After secretly observing the unstudied grace of her movements, the most celebrated picture-maker of the province burned the implements of his craft, and began life anew as a trainer of performing elephants.

The manner by which he gained his livelihood consisted in leading a number of blind mendicants about the streets of the city and into the shops and dwelling places of those who might reasonably be willing to pay in order to be relieved of their presence.

When we arrived at a great row of mean green shacks, the cheering might have been by a defeated army at last able to turn brigand and earn an honest living.

By, as it were, extending the five-fingered gesture of derision from the organ of contempt, you have invited the retaliatory propulsion of the sandal of authority.

Although there exist many thousands subjects for elegant conversation, there are persons who cannot meet a cripple without talking about feet.

"Your insight is clear and unbiased," said the gracious Sovereign. "But however entrancing it is to wander unchecked through a garden of bright images, are we not enticing your mind from another subject of almost equal importance?"

The most farcical of situations are described with a straight face and a highly relevant moral:

It is related that a person of limited intelligence, on being assured that he would certainly one day enjoy an adequate competence if he closely followed the industrious habits of the thrifty bee, spent the greater part of his life in anointing his thighs with a yellow powder which he laboriously collected from the flowers of the field. It is not so recorded; but doubtless the nameless one in question was by profession a maker of opium pipes for this person has observed from time to time how that occupation, above all others, tends to degrade the mental faculties, and to debase its followers to a lower position than that of the beasts of labour. Learn therefrom, O superficial Wang Yu, that wisdom lies in an intelligent perception of great principles and not in a slavish imitation of details which, for the most part, are beyond your simple and insufficient understanding.

…an objectionable and excessively round-bodied individual who had amassed an inconceivable number of taels by inducing persons to take part in what at first sight appeared to be an ingenious but very easy competition connected to the order in which certain horses should arrive at a given and clearly defined spot.

The plots of the Kai Lung stories are deceptively simple and picaresque as well as ingenious. They frequently mock modern institutions and conventions: the principle of the 'closed shop', 'life insurance', 'pensions', 'bookmakers', 'casinos', The League of Nations, the seeding of sports men and women in competitions and even the phenomenon of 'vanity publishing'. The last is described in 'The Confessions of Kai Lung' in *The Wallet*.

> At the end of two years this somewhat disillusioned but still undaunted person chanced to hear of a benevolent and unassuming body of men who made a habit of issuing works in which they discerned merit, but which, nevertheless, others were unanimous in describing as 'of no good'. Here this person was received with gracious effusion, and being in a position to impress those with whom he was dealing with his undoubted knowledge of the subject, he finally succeeded in making a very advantageous arrangement by which he was to pay one-half of the number of taels expended in producing the work, and to receive in return all the profits which should result from the undertaking. Those who were concerned in the matter were so engagingly impressed with the incomparable literary merit displayed in the production that they counselled a great number of copies being made ready in order, as they said, that this person should not lose by there being any delay once the accomplishment became the one topic of conversation in the tea-houses and yamêns. From this cause it came about that the matter of taels to be expended was much greater than had been anticipated at the beginning, so that when the day arrived on which the volumes were to be sent forth this person found that almost his last piece of money had disappeared.

This description is almost certainly autobiographical and it is most likely that Bramah's farming book was in fact a piece of vanity publishing. The facts ranging from his father's financial support to the return of the unsold books by the publisher seems to confirm this.

Not all the interpretations of modern institutions were as long. Advertising was covered in a few lines '…it was the cunning and elaborately thought-out method for gaining the attention to certain persons who claimed to vend a reliable and fragrantly scented cleansing substance'.

♦

Most of the Kai Lung books are short stories in which he is simply the narrator. In others Kai Lung's own life and fortunes are interwoven into the narrative. There is however also what might be called the Sheherazade effect where Kai Lung escapes execution by diverting a Mandarin or brigand with a tale – an old device rendered fresh by Bramah's skills and by the language with which the stories are related and embellished. The storyteller is invariably victorious while the grasping and oppressive are defeated.

The elaboration of the prose does not conceal the vanity, deceit, greed and selfishness of many of the characters, which reflects precisely those characteristics to be found in any society. The counterpoint between the loftiness of the narrator's and the baseness of the characters' motives gives the Kai Lung tales their beautiful irony, and rarely has irony been so subtly pointed, nor ever more quaintly entrancing. There are meanings within meanings, rather like the Chinese devil balls with their diminishing series of finely carved spheres within each other. Bernard Levin, a great enthusiast, refers to his 'effortless imagery' 'his almost imperceptible yet very shrewd philosophical stance' and 'his delightful wit' (the barb so carefully concealed that it only begins to sting some after it has been withdrawn).

Behind the entertaining mock Chinese phrasing, with its indirectness and pretence at self-deprecation, the most horrifying events are told with a bland callousness. Individuals veil their actions and their intentions behind the most obvious of lies and sophistry and say the most offensive things in the politest possible way. Characters and situations are honed to a sharper edge of satire, which cuts no less deep for the humanity and benevolence that constitutes one of Bramah's most appealing qualities. It is not every inmate incarcerated in a pitch-dark dungeon who would protest against personal injury and indignity in such a manner as this: 'If it is not altogether necessary for your refined convenience that you stand on this one's face, he for his part would willingly forgo the esteemed honour.'

The artistic exploitation of the hyperbolic was not confined to Bramah. James Elroy Flecker had also used it in his play *Hassan* with great effect. The impact of Bramah's style on a small but influential group of writers and politicians was sufficient to engender a Kai Lung Club. The members wrote to each other in the Kai Lung style. J. A. Spender in his biography of Sir Robert Hudson quotes one of his own letters in which he maintains the style well – that is for the first three paragraphs only. E. C. (Clerihew) Bentley exchanged letters with G. K. Chesterton in Kai Lung style and in his own book *Those Days*[10] pays the most fulsome tribute to Bramah.

> I do not know if Ernest Bramah ever dreamed of the keenness of joy that had been created by him in the bosoms of young men such as ourselves. If the book had not then the fame it deserved, it was no fault of ours: we made no secret of what we thought about Kai Lung, then or ever afterwards. But what we thought did not greatly matter. The Wallet is classic now, and has long been; but at the outset no critic of influence as far as I know, paid it any attention.

♦

There are very few clues as to how Bramah arrived at and developed his unique style. Bramah's own explanation barely provides an answer.[11]

> I suppose if you or I sat long enough opposite a Chinese screen or ivory carving we would write a tale about it...when a satisfactory idea does evolve, its elaboration is more or less automatic though still painfully slow.... I suppose that by now I have assimilated a considerable amount of miscellaneous Chinese literature – at all events all that has come my way, and the only book in which I could find nothing of interest or novelty was one written by a Chinaman who had long resided in America. He seemed to have completely lost every celestial touch and to have forgotten what China was or, perhaps, ought to be like.

The book that attracted Bramah's disdain is more than likely to be *Letters from a Chinese Official*.[12] Its hectoring and censorious views were completely at odds with the gentle, courteous Kai Lung.

> Hitherto they [Westerners] have confined their acts of spoliation to those who they regard as outside their own pale. But always, while they divide the spoil they watch one another with jealous eyes, and sooner or later, when there is nothing left to divide will fall upon one another.

Clearly Bramah was not the only person to have taken a poor view of the book since it appears to be part of a minor literary skirmish instigated by Lowes Dickinson's *Letters from John Chinaman*[13] and *Letters to a Chinese Official*.[14]

One possibly outlandish suggestion concerning the genesis of the Kai Lung idiom was made in 1982 by Nigel Perrin in the *Washington Post*.[15] 'It came about like this. In early manhood Bramah encountered the highly ritualised and super-polite mode of speech employed by well-bred Chinese before the revolution.' There is absolutely no evidence to suggest he met such people and indeed it is extremely unlikely such encounters would have taken place in the countryside of Warwickshire or in Grub Street. Nevertheless it is a pretty conceit.

Also unprovable is the suggestion that if Charles Clement, his father, was indeed a director or the owner of Smith & Crofton, shippers of textiles to China, Ernest's interest might have been stimulated by the China connection.

Even though there is very little information on how Bramah evolved his Chinese idiom, he does reveal that ideas for some of the stories had been stimulated by current events and other sources. He refers to a Chinese Art Exhibition where he was attracted by a picture entitled 'Poor Chinese student, reading by the light of a glow-worm held in gauze bag'. This provided 'The story of Lao Ting and the luminous insect'.[16] 'The story of Wang Ho and the burial robe', Bramah admitted, derives much from Frazer's *The Golden Bough*.[17]

China was very much in the news. For a century or more China had been the plaything of Western and Japanese interests and was now emerging from what Chinese officials called 'the period of humiliation'.

In 1898 the Emperor Te Tsung had initiated 100 days of reform only to have them revoked a few months later by the Dowager Empress of China who seized power. Sun Yat Sen was emerging as rebel leader and America and the other great powers were manoeuvring over the Treaty Ports to prevent further territorial partition of China. At the time of the publication of *The Wallet of Kai Lung* the siege of Peking had just been lifted.

◆

The verisimilitude of some of Bramah's interpretation of modern institutions was enhanced by events in real life China. Compare The Bound-together Brotherhood of Colour-mixers and Putters-on of Thought-out Designs which is to be found in 'The story of Wong Ts'in and the willow plate embellishment' in *Kai Lung's Golden Hours* with the real life Society of Righteous Harmonious Fists – a secret Society which formed the nucleus of the Boxer Revolution in 1900. However, not every reader understands that Bramah was not mocking the Chinese or their customs. His target was Western institutions, mores and ideas.

One of the best summaries was in J. C. Squire's Preface to the Methuen 1923 reprint of *The Wallet of Kai Lung*.[18]

> Mr. Bramah, in his book, has got the Chinese equanimity wonderfully; the most moving and the most horrible things are told with mild deprecation; the most grotesquely farcical situations are analysed and developed with a full sense of their rich ludicrousness but with the very slightest loss of gravity on the part of the narrator. All the characters behave consistently veiling their actions and their intentions behind the most transparent lies and subterfuges...

Squire ends with the encomium:

> But it is not surprising that one who likes good satire, good humour, good romance and good English should find the book worthy of being an inseparable companion.

The Wallet of Kai Lung received very little attention at the time of publication but the Reviews that did appear were mostly very favourable. An anonymous reviewer in *The Athenaeum*[19] wrote '...the book constitutes a refreshing element among the many volumes of short stories that have appeared of late', and concludes with a prescience that took many years to realise, 'It might be popular'.

The reviews of later editions, after Bramah had established his reputation, varied from complimentary to panegyric with just the occasional dissent. The *Times Literary Supplement*[20] found the book 'irresistibly funny...they [the stories] are beautifully executed with a flawless consistency'. It then qualified the comment, 'Today much of the old magic has evaporated: the tales which seemed so delicious and so witty...now seem only terribly long winded and without fundamental point'. *Time*[21] commended the book to those readers who like slyness slow and stately. 'Ernest Bramah is a lordly dish'. G. K. Chesterton'[22] wrote '...it is on the highest level which only English craftsmanship could have attained'. (Doubtless the reference to English craftsmanship appealed very much to Bramah's patriotism.) E. C. Bentley[23] called the book 'a triumph of original humour'. Bernard Levin[24] praises the 'beautiful tailored style'.

◆

The history of *The Wallet of Kai Lung* can be easily traced. In October 1896 there appeared in *Chapman's Magazine,* sandwiched between a story by a John Halles and an episode of a serial by Violet Hunt[25] (both long forgotten Victorian authors), 'The story of Yung Chang as related by Kai Lung in the open space before the tea-shop of the Celestial Principles at Wu-Whei'. This was the beginning, but not a particularly auspicious one, of the character of the itinerant storyteller, who became known and loved by generations of readers. A second story, 'The story of Kin Yen the picture maker' appeared in the same journal in December the following year.

Bramah then prepared a manuscript containing these tales and two others, 'The transmutation of Ling' and 'The probation of Sen Heng' and sent them to eight publishers – Chatto, Heinemann, Constable, Cassell and Macmillan among others. All rejected them, one returning the manuscript the same day as it was received and two sending it back after three days. The reader at Cassell's, A. T. Quiller-Couch, recommended acceptance. When this recommendation was not accepted he wrote to Bramah expressing his disappointment.[26] 'I suppose they [Cassell] had their reasons. But the stories pleased me so much that I am sending this note to make [sic] you with my compliments upon them if you won't think my compliments impertinent." He then offered the disappointed author four guineas to publish one of the stories in *The Cornish Magazine,* rather less than the going rate.

With a negative response from major publishers Bramah, like many authors before him and still today, began to approach smaller firms among which was the flamboyant publisher Grant Richards. Richards's reputation rests on his choice of authors and his willingness to take chances on unknown writers which encouraged a cavalier attitude toward his finances and contributed to his drastic swings of fortune. He thought the manuscript clever, unusual, funny and deserving of publication. This he did in 1900, but it was not a title calculated to compete with the best sellers of the year: Conrad's *Lord Jim* and Colette's *Claudine.* Nevertheless the first Kai Lung book was now on the shelves of a few, a very few, booksellers. Six more stories had been added before the book finally went to the printers. Given that on Bramah's own admission his rate of composition was slow, it is clear that many of the additional tales must have been in an advanced stage of completion.

Unfortunately the public did not share Grant Richards's confidence and enthusiasm for the book. He wrote that the edition, even with its small print run of some 2,000 copies, (figures differ and some give it as 1,000 which is not likely) took 'years to sell out and then only with difficulty'. An American publisher, Page and Company, Boston, took 750 copies from sheets, 'attracted not by the book's literary excellence but the cover design'. It was seven years before the stock was exhausted.

Richards's claim that the first edition took years to sell out is probably an exaggeration because much of the Edition was placed with Brentano in New York. Nevertheless, according to Richards, he still had to remainder a large number of copies. In Bramah's own words '...it [the book] never seemed able to more than just to struggle on. On the other hand it obstinately declined to die outright.'

It cannot be said that Richards did not do his utmost to popularise the book. There was a further edition of 500 using the same sheets but with a different cover in Grant Richards Colonial Library with the prohibition that it was only for sale in India and the colonies.

Over a decade later in 1911 Grant Richards, his faith in the book unshaken despite the slow sales and his own financial problems, in conjunction with Brentano's in New York, produced a luxury limited edition consisting of a single tale from *The Wallet* 'The transmutation of Ling'. This had twelve black and white illustrations by Ilberry Lynch. The future of the book was not assured until finally Methuen included it in their cheap library in 1915 and priced at 1/- (5p).

The book may have been a slow starter but Richards's opinion of the book was certainly justified over time. There have been very many different printings in the United Kingdom. Apart from Richards and Cape, Methuen alone issued the book nine times between 1917 and 1942 and Penguin Books four times between 1937 and 1954. In the United States, where Kai Lung has always attracted an appreciative audience. Mike Berro[27] has identified at least eleven different impressions and editions. Indicative of the popularity of the book is the fact that it was an early choice (number 39) for Penguin Books 6d paperback series. There were also special limited editions. The book remained in print in Britain for nearly seventy years. There is no need to search the shelves of booksellers or charity shops because it is now available, without charge, in electronic form published by the Project Gutenberg[28] as well as reprints from American book and electronic publishers.

Twenty-six years after the first edition a German agent was attempting to sell a translation of *The Wallet* and suggested, 'I shall have a better chance if Mr. Bramah will allow me to publish one or two of the smaller stories of his book first in a German paper.' He suggested 'The probation of Sen Heng' and 'The vision of Yin' from *The Wallet*. He goes on 'I think I can get one of these stories, and perhaps both them, into *Kölnische Zeitung*. You are of course aware of the fact that this is a very high-class paper that has considerable influence in German literary circles.'[29]

The stories appeared in the paper but it has not been possible to confirm whether the book was published in Germany. In September 1929 Bramah acknowledges a copy of the *Kölnische Zeitung* sent to him by his agent. There is no reference to a German edition of *The Wallet* in that letter. In October the same year a translator wrote to Methuen[30] asking if she could undertake the translation. If the quality of the English in her letter were to be used as a criterion for her appointment it would have been just as well if her offer had been refused. Among other translations 'The history of Tung Chang' also from *The Wallet* appeared in a Venezuelan periodical, *Elite*, in 1936.

An additional accolade was bestowed on the first Kai Lung story 'The story of Yung Chang' when it was chosen by G. N. Pocock, Editor of Dent's King's Treasures Series, for inclusion in *Modern Prose* in 1925 as an example of the modern short story – a considerable recognition for what was a very youthful work. The insightful analysis by D. J. Enright[31] concluded that 'Bramah's place is in the more elevated, refined and sequestered reaches of the large and multifarious bazaar in which literary wares are offered for sale', a view with which it is easy to agree.

Unquestionably Bramah's reputation rests on his Kai Lung short stories and books as well as, to a lesser extent, on the blind detective, Max Carrados stories, so the roots of his success as an author can be traced to the very first appearance of Kai Lung in 1898.

◆

William White claims that the Kai Lung character was the suggestion of a fellow author but there is no clue as to who this might be. Nevertheless, strokes of genius do not spring unaided into life. It is known that Bramah studied many English translations of Chinese literature that together may have provoked the genesis of the idea but not the style in which it was written. Among these sources are the *Chinese Biographical Dictionary*[32] compiled by Herbert Giles and published in 1898 just pre-dating Kai Lung. 'You cannot speak of the ocean to a well frog'. 'A battering ram can knock down a wall but it cannot repair a breach'. 'A poor waggoner of the Wi State overheard singing and beating in time on the horns of his oxen by Jung King of the Chi State and was at once taken into his employ where he rose to be privy councillor'. These might be compared with some of the many proverbs and vignettes that Bramah puts into the mouths of his characters.

The two volumes of the dictionary contain many short stories and, none of them is in the Chinese vernacular adopted by Bramah. Indeed many of the characters in the Giles book are addressed or referred to by an honorific 'Mr.' or 'Mrs.' Bramah most certainly did not copy the Giles style but it may well have been one source of the idea for the itinerant teller of tales. Other candidates which have been suggested are perhaps more obvious, Oliver Goldsmith's *Citizen of the World* and Charles Lamb's famous 'Dissertation on roast pig' in his *Essays of Elia*.

For a long time it was believed that Bramah had spent time in China. Claims to this effect appeared in such normally reliable sources as the *New York Times, Twentieth-Century Literary Criticism*. The *Morning Post*[33] wrote Mr. Bramah must have a particularly intimate knowledge of Chinese manners and customs and of the Chinese habit of mind to reveal them so intimately ...' The feature called 'The Chinese Juggler' in *To-day* and referred to earlier, had a footnote describing the author as perhaps the greatest living English authority on China which Bramah said 'sent me hot and cold for weeks'.

There is no doubt whatsoever that Bramah had never been to China. He totally refutes this suggestion. William White discovered a letter to the publisher of the first Kai Lung book, Grant Richards, dated April 27th 1923[34] in which he writes:

> Specifically I have never been to China but I do not know that [to others] it is diplomatic to be specific on the point. It seemed to me that an attitude might be: (a) if I have lived in China then the stories are probably mere translations or at all events not entirely original; (b) if I have not been in China and have no special knowledge then the fabric is imaginary and unreliable as a picture of Chinese life; so that I have in general rather evaded the direct question, desiring personally only that the books should be taken as they stand. However that blameless secret is now in your keeping and I shall not reproach you wherever use you may make of it.

Evidence would suggest that, if he had not visited China, he had studied it carefully as his stories reveal knowledge of many aspects of Chinese life, law and society. Is it pure coincidence that he describes a character's walking pace as that of a 'shell-cow upon two slabs of wood'?

The Chinese term for snail is represented by the ideograms for shell and cow.

♦

While it is difficult to trace a direct connection between Kai Lung and earlier books it is much easier to see how Kai Lung influenced later writers — some of whom were more successful than others. A website[35] with mostly anonymous contributions identifies books by Lily Adams Beck, Barry Hughart, Maurice Magru, Frank Owen, Helen Beauclerk, Manly Hall, Roland Fraser, F. Hadland Davis, H. Warner Munn, Jack Vance and even Rumer Godden's book *Chinese Puzzle* – a goodly mixture of the famous and the obscure. Omitted are Sir Arthur Fraser's *Landscape with Figures* and *The Song Book of Quong Lee of Limehouse* by a poet essayist who styled himself Thomas Burke of Eltham. This last book was published in 1920 and contained pseudo Chinese poems in true Kai Lung-ish vein.

> 'Last week this person desiring it to be made known
> That he was in all ways moving up to date
> Introduced into his insignificant shop
> A machine that counts
> Called a National Cash Register
> Which announced to refined and intelligent customers
> The amount of their purchase'

Burke was clearly inspired by the Kai Lung books even if his Chinese stories bore no relationship to them as they were often brutal, sordid and salacious.

Barry Hughart, an American writer, perhaps comes closest to Kai Lung with his Master Li series of oriental fantasies. His China is perhaps more sentimentally drawn and less ornate than Bramah's but is clearly in the same serio-comic style.

♦

It can be said with certainty that it is not possible to read the Kai Lung books quickly. To really appreciate the humour, the morality of the stories, the many faceted aspects of human nature and the gentle mocking of Western institutions and values, they have to be read slowly and savoured. Readers cannot wallow, they must interpret and compare. 'The China of which they [the Kai Lung books] are so undeviating an evocation lives and glows in your mind for ever once you have encountered it' wrote John Connell[36] again a sentiment it is difficult to dispute.

Some time was to pass before Bramah was to match the success of his close contemporaries who were already established authors. Kipling had his first triumph with *The Light that Failed* in 1890. The following year Arnold Bennett's *A Man from Nowhere* had appeared, in 1895 H. G. Wells's *The Time Machine* and Jacobs's hugely successful *Many Cargoes* in 1897. It was however going to be more than a decade before Bramah was to achieve the sales and readership of these books.

Thus Kai Lung did not bring Bramah instant fame and fortune. Nevertheless, over the years the five books (six, if the posthumous *The Kai Lung Six* is included) sold in considerable number as the different editions and impressions already referred to demonstrates. In addition the inclusion in numerous anthologies and at least three single author volumes (*Short Stories of Today and Yesterday, The Kai Lung Omnibus. The Celestial Omnibus*) and numerous reprints in newspapers and journals together generated a comfortable income. But all this was still to come. Ernest was now an established, if relatively unknown, author with two books to his name; one sank without trace, the other laid the foundation for his career.

Sources & Notes

1   Ernest Bramah. *Kai Lung's Golden Hours*. Grant Richards. London. 1922. Introduction by Hilaire Belloc

2   H.R.H.R.C. op. cit.

3   Dorothy L Sayers. *Gaudy Night*. Gollancz. London. 1935 p.163

4   J. B. Priestley. *English Humour*. Longman. London. 1929 p.106.

5   www.ernestbramah.com

6   'A Good Read'. B.B.C. Radio 4, July 3rd 1994.

7   Ernest Bramah. *The Celestial Omnibus*. op. cit. Introduction by John Connell.

8   W. Scarborough. *A Collection of Chinese Proverbs*. American Presbyterian Mission, Shanghai.1875.

9   S. W. Wells. *The Middle Kingdom*. John Wiley. New York. 1851.

10 E. C. Bentley. *Those Days*. Constable. London. 1940 p.217.

11 H.R.H.R.C. op. cit. Letter to Grant Richards. April 27th 1923.

12 Anon. *Letters from a Chinese Official*. McClure Phillips. New York. 1903

13 G. Lowes Dickinson. *Letters from John Chinaman*. Dent. London. 1901. p.17.

14 W. J. Bryan. *Letters to a Chinese Official*. Harper. New York. 1906.

15 *Washington Post*. Washington. September 26th 1962.

16 H.R.H.R.C. op. cit. April 27th 1923.

17 ibid.

18 J. C. Squire. Preface. *The Wallet of Kai Lung*. op. cit. p.ix.

19 *The Athenaeum*. London. April 1900.

20 *Times Literary Supplement*. London. November 28th 1963.

21 *Time*. New York. September 6th 1937.

22 G.K.'s *Weekly*. London. September 10th 1936.

23 E. C. Bentley. *Those Days*. op. cit. p.217.

24 Bernard Levin. 'Wanted some impeccable tales of Kai Lung' op. cit.

25 Violet Hunt, in the words of Cressida Connelly, is not remembered as the author of thirty books so much as a footnote in the lives of the great; a friend of Oscar Wilde and Henry James and having had affairs with Somerset Maugham and Ford Madox Brown.

26 H.R.H.R.C. November 12th 1898. op. cit.

27 www.mike@ernestbramah.com op. cit.

28 www.gutenberg.net

29 Charles Deering McCormick Collections Library. Northwestern. University of Evanston. Illinois.

30 ibid.

31 D. J. Enright. 'A Chinese never-never land'. *Times Literary Supplement*, London. June 27th 1986.

32   H. A. Giles. *A Chinese Bibliographical Dictionary*. Quaritch. London. 1898.

33   *Morning Post*. London. May 8th 1928.

34   Papers of the Bibliographical Society of America. New York. Vol 87. 1972. pp.511-513.

35   www.mike@ernestbramah.com op. cit.

36   Ernest Bramah. *Celestial Omnibus*. Introduction by John Connell op. cit. p.8.

CHAPTER SIX

PINKER LENDS A HAND

The literary agent had first emerged in the middle of the nineteenth century in a highly amateur form; John Forster acting for Dickens and G. H. Lewes for George Eliot in an informal and unpaid capacity. By the beginning of the twentieth century the literary agency was established although still a pioneer profession. The Society of Authors having decided that their agencies, Authors' Syndicate, was not to be part of their services, gave the opportunity for men like William Colles, who was responsible for it, to develop one of the first independent professional literary agencies. This was to become a valuable service to authors although Colles himself was not successful. The agent in return for a small share of authors' royalties undertook to read manuscripts, find publishers, negotiate agreements collect royalties and generally manage business details.

Bramah acquired an agent in 1905 – James B. Pinker the redoubtable American, who represented H. G. Wells, Arnold Bennett, Eden Phillpotts and Joseph Conrad. He had known Pinker, who had a formidable reputation for negotiating authors' terms and for protecting their interests, for some ten years. As importantly Pinker knew the market and he encouraged his authors to write what would sell and re-sell.

That Bramah was achieving a degree of recognition is evidenced by Pinker agreeing to act for him as he only accepted established authors or those he judged would become so. Bramah only wanted Pinker to represent him for his stories, serials and articles but these Pinker regarded as the less profitable part of his business. Bramah agreed, reluctantly, that Pinker would be his agent for his books too although at that time they amounted to no more than two not very successful efforts.

Nevertheless future success was heralded even at this early period. Requests for alternative features or stories accompanied rejections. Comyns Beaumont, Editor of *The Bystander* writing in 1906 to Pinker[1] explains that although he could not use a submitted manuscript, 'The last Englishman', 'I like his [Bramah's] work very much and I remember in my Christmas number last year I liked the article of his immensely'. He then goes on to offer 9 guineas (about £550 currently) for 3,500-4,000 words for a story for his Worldly series and asks for a piece for his forthcoming Christmas number. This was above the going rate because Bramah only received 5 guineas and 4 guineas for two stories in the *Pall Mall Magazine*. Pinker must have been at his persuasive best as a later letter from Beaumont states that 'The last Englishman', previously turned down, had been accepted 'at the usual rates' of £2.2s.0d per thousand words. The feature was 1,900 words.

Some of the rejected pieces were to appear later, possibly revised to make them acceptable to the different magazines that subsequently published them. There are other examples of Pinker's skills. A letter from Bramah to Pinker dated December 18th[?] 1914[2] accompanied an article rejected by *Punch* but which eventually appeared in the following June.

About this time Bramah decided that 'I am not fond of writing about myself and only to a lesser degree about my work. My books are about all I care to pass on to the reader.'[3] The trail now goes, if not cold, then tepid and personal information becomes more fragmentary. Fortunately much autobiographical material can be garnered from his writings which do reveal a great deal concerning his interests, opinions and attitudes.

It is known that after Ernest left the farm Charles, his wife and younger daughter Rose moved from Knowle in Warwickshire and again followed Ernest, this time to London. In 1896 Ernest was writing from an address of 32 Addison Mansions, (no other location is given) where, judging by the use of the word "we" and the fact he was not married, suggests it was his parents and sister's home. When the first Kai Lung book appeared the family were living at Marsden House, 36 Colney Hatch Lane in Muswell Hill, then a rapidly developing suburban area on what was virtually the outskirts of London. It has been suggested, but it is no more than speculation that the house was chosen because of its proximity to the asylum at Colney Hatch where Rose may have been an inmate at some time. Their home was a large detached Victorian house with an extensive garden. Regrettably the Land Registry has no information as to whether Charles owned or rented the house but, given his prosperous position there is every reason to believe he owned it. Today it is converted into four flats but it is easy to see that the original rooms were spacious and high ceilinged.

At the time of the 1901 Census of Population the only occupants of the house were shown as Charles, his wife Susannah, their daughter Rose and a servant. Ernest and Maisie were living in lodgings with seven other boarders at 50A Haverstock Hill in Hampstead. He was also using as an address the home of his elder sister Emily Jane, Brentholt, 26, Brent Street in Hendon in Northwest London, who lived there until her death in 1939.

♦

Bramah's writing career was now developing quickly. It is no coincidence that after the appointment of Pinker, his name occurs more frequently in periodicals including *Punch*. Uncharacteristically the stories carried his real name, Smith. After 1915 it was to be another twenty-five years before he was to again appear in *Punch*. The cause of the interregnum will never be known.

Developments in the book trade were very much to favour Bramah in his developing career. The three-volume novel had dominated the publishing world for fifty years. The circulating libraries had demanded these in order to tie readers in and to make books too expensive to purchase and – thus encouraging loans. The multi-volume novel was finally killed when in 1904 both Mudie's and Smith's, who together commanded the subscription library business, changed their policy and now refused to buy any fiction except in single volume editions and at no more than half the price of the 'three-decker'. The loss of the lucrative circulating library business saw the end of the three-volume novel. Bramah's fiction neither needed nor was suitable for this format so the change was one that he and his publishers welcomed.

The circulating libraries, such an important part of the publishers' market, were sensitive to the moral susceptibilities of most of their subscribers and their decision on which books were to go on their shelves reflected this. Nothing that offended contemporary mores would be purchased. This was a policy that benefited authors like Bramah rather than the new realist writers.

Despite the initial disappointing sales of *The Wallet* Bramah was not discouraged from his Chinoiserie and plunged into his second oriental book. This time, instead of projecting and disguising Western institutions and mores into a Chinese landscape he brought China to the West in the person of young and innocent Kong Ho. He is exposed to all manner of English activities and many different types of English characters whom he tries to understand and comment on with a naïve charm.

The manuscript was refused by Richards, who was experiencing serious financial difficulties, It was doubtless Pinker who, in 1905 was able to persuade Chapman & Hall to publish *The Mirror of Kong Ho*[4] which is the most neglected of Bramah's Chinese books. *Twentieth-Century Literary Criticism Volume 72*[5] devotes ten pages to Bramah's works in which Kong Ho gets only three lines – more a mention than a review. Nevertheless even if the book was described by one critic as 'a volume frequently found amusing by those who cannot stand Kai-lung genre', it is still a worthy successor to it.

Kong Ho, a young Chinese visitor to London writes fourteen letters to his father in China about life in the West. The book is a whimsical parody of refined oriental circumlocution and gives a satiric picture of English life in the early twentieth Century. Bramah's Introduction is in true Kai Lung style.

In an entirely contrary manner some, who of recent years have gratified us with their magnanimous presence, have returned to their own countries not only with internal fittings of many of our palaces (which, being for the most part of a replaceable nature need be only trivially referred to, the incident, indeed, being generally regarded as a most cordial and pressing variety of foreign politeness)...

Bramah carefully explains why some of the letters are in idiomatic English (or Cockney).[7]

> ...it only remains to be said that in order to maintain unimpaired the quaint-sounding brevity and archaic construction of your prepossessing language, I have engraved most of the remarks upon the receptive tablets of my mind as they were uttered.

Kong Ho comments on the people he meets in and around London who he regards as comparative barbarians. He is puzzled, horrified and amused by Western etiquette, manner, and above all by the devices and machinery of a totally alien civilisation. He attempts to explain such things as indoor games and outdoor sports that baffle him by their complexity or inanity. Here is his description of a Rugby match.[7]

> There is a favourite and well attended display wherein two opposing bands in robes of a distinctive colour, stand in extended lines of mutual defiance, at a signal impetuously engage. The design of each is by force or guile to draw their opponents into an unfavourable position before an arch of upright posts, and then surging irresistibly forward to carry them beyond a limit and hurl them to the ground. Those who successfully inflict this humiliation upon their adversaries until they are incapable of further existence are hailed victorious, and sinking into a graceful attitude receive each a golden cup from the magnanimous hands of a maiden chosen to the service, either on account of her peerless outline, the dignified position of her House, or (should these incentives be obviously wanting,) because the chief ones of her family are in the habit of contributing unstintingly to the equipment of the triumphant band.

And on hockey:[8]

> There is also another type of strife, differing in its essential only so far as that all who engage therein are provided with a curved staff, with which they may dextrously draw their antagonists

beyond the limits or, should they fail to defend themselves adequately, break the smaller bones of their ankles.

Here is his description of the underground railway that in 1905 was still operated with steam engines.[9]

> ...the surroundings are ingeniously arranged as to represent as nearly as practicable the terrors of the beneath world. Both by day and night a funereal gloom envelops the caverns, the pathways and resting-places are meagre and so constructed to be devoid of attraction or repose, and by a skilful contrivance the natural atmosphere is secretly withdrawn and a very acrimonious sulphurous haze driven in to replace it. In sudden and unforeseen places eyes of fire open and close with disconcerting rapidity, and even change colour in vindictive significance; wooden hands are outstretched as in unrelenting rigidity against supplication, or, divining the unexpressed thoughts, inexorably point, as one gazes, still deeper into the recesses of the earth; while the air is never free from sounds and groans, shrieks, the rattling of chains, dull, hopeless noises beneath one's feet or overhead, and the hoarse wordless cries of despair with which the attending slaves of the caverns greet the distant clamour of every approaching fire-chariot. Admittedly the intention of the device is benevolently conceived, and it is strenuously asserted that many persons of corrupt habits and ill-balanced lives, upon waking unexpectedly while passing through these beneath parts, have abandoned the remainder of their journey, and, escaping hastily to the outer air, have from that time onwards led a pure and consistent existence; but, on the other foot, those who are compelled to use the caverns daily, freely confess that the surroundings do not in any material degree purify their lives or tranquillise the nature of their inner thoughts.

Conversations between the characters Kong Ho meets are perhaps closer to those that figure in the Kai Lung books:[10]

> "Say no more about it" urged the first person, and to suggest gracefully that the incident had reached its furthest extremity,

he began to set out the melody of an unspoken verse. "I will say no more then" he replied; but you cannot reasonably prevent my doing something to express my gratitude. If you are not too proud you will come and partake food and wine with me beneath the sign of the Funereal Male Cow"

and[11]

"Why Mr. Kong, you say such consistently graceful things of the ladies you have met over here, that we shall expect you take back an English wife with you. But perhaps you are already married in China?"

"The conclusion is undeviating in its accuracy," replied this person, unable to evade the allusions. "To Ning, Hia-Fa and T'ain Yen, as the matter stands."

"Ning, Hia-Fa An T'ain Yen"! exclaimed the wife of the Law-giver pleasantly.

"What an important name. Can you pardon our curiosity and tell us what she is like?"

"Ning, Hia-Fa *and* T'ain Yen," repeated this person, not submitting to be deprived of the consequence of two wives without due protest. "Three names, three wives. Three widely separated likes."

There is even a Kai Lung-like episode in the book. Kong Ho attending a temperance meeting, which he calls an 'all water diversion' is persuaded to relate a short tale 'The Three Gifts' to the assembly.

Interestingly, ten years later W. W. Jacobs was to use exactly the same confidence trick of which Kong Ho was a victim [Letter VIII] in an identical plot for one of his Night-watchman's tales. ['Sam's ghost' *Deep Waters*]

If the antecedents of Kai Lung are obscure there is a clear affinity between the *Mirror of Kong Ho* and Oliver Goldsmith's *Citizen of the*

World with its subtitle of *Letters from a Chinese Philosopher Residing in London*, first published 1770. While Goldsmith could be said to be seriously whimsical, J. C. Squire thought Bramah, in this book, to be a quiet buffoon creating an atmosphere of muted knock-about. That is a viewpoint but to the modern reader the texts bear a striking similarity whether they are regarded as 'whimsical' or 'knockabout'.

> I have received more invitations in the streets of London from the sex in one night, than I have met with at Peking in twelve revolutions of the moon. Every evening as l return home from my usual solitary excursions, I am met by several of those well disposed daughters of hospitality, at different times and in different streets, richly dressed, and with minds not less noble than their appearances.[12]

Goldsmith's Chinese philosopher, like Kong Ho is duly deceived and robbed.

Of course Bramah rather than basing himself on Goldsmith's book, might well have gone back to the original sources which were traced by Rosalind Vallance. Her Introduction to the Folio Society's 1969 edition of *Citizen of the World* could as easily apply to Bramah as to Goldsmith. She wrote:[13]

> To preserve the convincing fiction of the Chinese authorship of the letters, and to produce such a quantity of material about a country of which he knew so little, Goldsmith had frequent recourse to two books, Louis de Compte's *Memoirs and Observations made in a journey through China* and Du Halde's *General History of China*. He was thus able [and here Vallance quotes from *The Mikado*] to give an air of verisimilitude to an otherwise bald and unconvincing narrative by referring casually to everyday things and customs of China or to the maxims of Confucius, some of which he may be suspected of inventing.

Overlooked as a source is Horatio Walpole's 1757 *A Letter from Xo-Ho a Chinese philosopher in London, to his friend Lien Chi at Peking*[14] which was published twenty years before Goldsmsith. Walpole satirised the politics, the foibles of English society and character, dress and even the weather. The absurdity, as seen through oriental eyes, of having an official opposition party and the method of choosing ministers. While all three books use the same approach, the composition of each is quite different. If Goldsmith could be said to be whimsical and Walpole satirical then neither adjective will fit Kong Ho. It is simply hilarious and doubtless that is how Bramah wanted it to be.

Letters from John Chinaman[15] by G. L. Dickinson published in 1901 may have a closer connection to *Kong Ho* although this was a more serious critical comparison between Chinese and Western Ways. There was also *Letters from a Chinese Official*[16] and the portentously titled *Letters to a Chinese Official: being a Western View of Eastern Civilisation* (A reply to *Letters from John Chinaman*). It can be seen that East-West comparisons were not unique and were attracting serious attention. One earlier but not dissimilar book can be ruled out. *The Tower of London* by the Japanese author Natsume Soseki contained many humorous (and many unhappy) descriptions of an Oriental's experience in London. Although published in Japan in 1902 it did not receive an English translation until about 1954. Bramah certainly did not read Japanese.

♦

In 1923 Grant Richards, who originally rejected the book, expressed an interest in a new edition. He wrote to Bramah that a publisher had remaindered *Kong Ho*. It is not entirely clear who this was, but he was probably referring to Chapman & Hall who were the original publishers.

> The implication is that they have to be sold at a reduced price to bring the agreement to an end. I should not like them to bring the book out again anyhow. I propose rather to read it again myself and then, if I find that I like it better than I did on first reading –well then we might consider reviving it.[17]

He was as good as his word even if it was another six years before it appeared in 1929 followed quickly by a reprint in 1930. The editions had a preface by J. C. Squire who, strangely, damned the book with faint praise by comparing it less favourably with the Kai Lung books.[18]

> *The Mirror of Kong Ho* which first appeared in 1905 is not one of Bramah's major achievements…but had he written no other "Chinese" book it would have been quite sufficient to give him a reputation and keep a modest place on the shelves of the discriminating…. This person cannot but recommend the book which, if not pearl only worthy to be hung upon the pure bosom of the unequalled Hi, is at least better than most.

There were to be a number of books published later using the Kong Ho formula, (or perhaps reverting directly back to Goldsmith). *Letters from John Chinaman* by G. L. Dickinson[19] published in 1901 and referred to earlier, may have a closer connection to Kong Ho although this was a more serious critical comparison between Chinese and Western ways. Perhaps a more direct connection is *Honourable and Peculiar Ways*[20] by Pêh Der Chen published in 1932. The direct link is that it had a Foreword by Bramah.

The Mirror of Kong Ho, unlike the first Kai Lung book, did not attract an American publisher until 1930 and seems to have been largely ignored by the critics with the exception of John Carter who, when the American edition was published, wrote in the *New York Times Book Review:*[21]

> While Kong Ho might be said to be hilarious, this is not an adjective that would readily apply to Walpole or Goldsmith. As always with westernised Chinoiserie, Bramah is on his own. Mr. Bramah is an English savant and philosopher and Kong Ho is a purely a fictitious character. This is a device which recommended itself to the greater satirists, to Voltaire as to Goldsmith …East and West, Mr. Bramah reminds us, are not opposite; they are sideways from each other…The Mirror of Kong Ho is something more than an ordinary production. It is part of a carefully distilled and rarefied humour and wisdom of one of the few modern writers of whom it can be truthfully said they should write far more than they do. Kong Ho takes his place besides, or a little beneath, Mr. Bramah's immortal Kai Lung. This is one of the few books no intelligent man ought to neglect, as it is one of the few every intelligent man will enjoy rereading.

1971 saw a new British printing[22] and in 1997 an electronic version became available on the Internet as part of the Project Gutenberg.[23] Despite past neglect, surfing the Internet will produce many references to the book. The latest edition from the Wildside Press in 2003 was completely taken up. It would appear that *The Mirror of Kong Ho* is at last receiving the attention it deserves.

After *The Mirror of Kong Ho* Bramah concentrated on articles and stories for publication in various periodicals. His book royalties alone would not have been sufficient to live on. Mike Berro in his bibliography[24] has traced stories in *Macmillan's Magazine*, *Cassell's Magazine*, *Pearson's Magazine* and *News of the World* and of course, *Punch*. Doubtless there were others that have not been identified and which appeared in now long forgotten periodicals and newspapers. They stand as evidence of Pinker's success as Bramah's agent.

But Bramah wanted to break away from his Chinese stories and his fertile mind was considering a much more serious work that would combine his interests in science, politics and the future. The parturition of a new Bramah was under way.

Sources & Notes

1   Comyns Beaumont. Charles Deering McCormick Library of Special Collections. op. cit. Letter October 4th 1905.

2   Berg Collection of English and American Literature. New York Public Library. New York.

3   In reply to an inquiry by Howard Hayward and quoted in *Murder for Pleasure*. Appleton Century. New York.1941. p.78.

4   Ernest Bramah. *The Mirror of Kong Ho*. Chapman & Hall. London.1905. Reprinted by Wildside Press. Holicong. Pennsylvania. 2003.

5   *Twentieth-Century Literary Criticism*. Vol 72. Thomson-Gale. Farmington Hills. Michigan. 1984. pp 1-10.

6   Ernest Bramah. *The Mirror of Kong Ho*. op. cit. pp.vi-vii.

7   op. cit. pp.196-7.

8   ibid.

9   op. cit. pp.166-7.

10 op. cit. p.79.

11 op. cit.p.32.

12 Oliver Goldsmith. *Citizen of the World.* Folio Society. London. 1969. p.45.

13 *Citizen of the World.* op. cit. Introduction by Rosalind Vallance. p.11.

14 Hugh Walpole. *A letter from Xo-Ho a Chinese Philosopher at London to his friend Lien Chi at Peking.* Middleton. London. 1757.

15 G. Lowes Dickinson. *Letters from John Chinaman.* op. cit.

16 Anon. *Letters from a Chinese Official.* op. cit.

17 H.R.H.R.C. December 14th 1923.

18 J. C. Squire. Introduction. *The Mirror for Kong Ho.* op. cit. p.v.

19 G. Lowes Dickinson. *Letters from John Chinaman.* op. cit.

20 Pêh Der Chen. *Honourable and Peculiar Ways.* Hamish Hamilton. London.1937.

21 *New York Book Review.* New York. December 14th 1932.

22 Lythway. Bath. 1973.

23 www.Gutenberg.net

24 www.mike@ernestbramah.com op. cit.

CHAPTER SEVEN

POLITICAL FICTION AND
SCIENCE FICTION

Bramah's next book was to be a complete break from his Chinese fantasies. In a letter to Grant Richards[1] he confirms he was a very slow writer and that he was working on a 'modern novel of English life'. Bramah thought that it might be 'more popular than the Chinese stories but less acceptable to the discriminating'. This could have been *The Optimist*, which was never published, or the 400-page political and science fiction book, *What Might Have Been: the Story of a Social War*.[2] The latter was not finished for another five years.

His extensive knowledge of many subjects, but particularly science, begins to emerge in this book. It could not have been acquired during his truncated education in Manchester. It is unlikely he could have mastered so many topics, and in such detail, from the wealth of self-improving and self-educating journals and books, so popular at the time, such as *Illustrated Scientific Weekly*, *Home Mechanics*, *A Dictionary of Medicine Designed for Popular Use*. All were aimed at simplifying and popularising technical subjects. Bramah's reading before and during the writing of the book was unquestionably at a far more scholarly level.

The strongly political content of the book was evolved against the background of the growth of the labour movement which was beginning to terrify the middle classes who believed they and their way of life was menaced by the emerging power of the working classes. The formation of the Labour Representative Committee in 1900 comprising the powerful grouping of most left wing movements including the TUC led to the creation of a parliamentary party and the ending of Lib/Lab co-operation. A resolution declared that 'members are to abstain strictly from identifying themselves with or promoting the interests of any section of the Liberal or Conservative parties...'. The prime co-interests of the new party were ensuring the well-being of labour and, ominously, the ending of the inequality of wealth.

Bramah must have shared the middle classes' trepidation. The result was the socio-science fiction of *What Might Have Been* and its revision, *The Secret of the League*. The book chronicles Britain under a Socialist government in 1916, not of the current but some parallel era. They have such a huge majority it is impossible to dislodge them. They do not introduce a full Socialist economy so much as continue to operate capitalism for their own benefit by raising wages, creating a huge army of bureaucrats and taxing the upper and middle classes out of existence. Pinker summed it up. 'It treats of the time which Mr. Keir Hardie prophesied would soon exist, that is, when there will be only two parties in the country, Socialist and anti-Socialists.'

Considerable nationalisation takes place; strikes are frequent; overseas trade has collapsed; politicians are described as illiterate and incompetent; India and Burma are abandoned; Downing Street is rented to a rich American lady 'who engineered wealthy debutantes from her native land into the best English society', while the cabinet meets in a sordid house in Mornington Crescent.[3] The workers reign supreme anticipating 'We are the masters now' proclaimed by Sir Hartley Shawcross in 1946 after the post-war Labour victory.

The manuscript was offered by Pinker to John Murray[4] but his approach was very strange, if not positively mysterious. In submitting the manuscript Pinker claimed that he did not know the author but that he had received it through a client who was a friend of the author who wished to have the book published anonymously. It is extremely unlikely Pinker did not know that the manuscript was the work of Bramah. More intriguing is why Bramah did not want to be identified.

John Murray raised no objection to the request for anonymity, nor, it would seem, expressed any curiosity, as to who the author might be, but within two months his identity was known. Murray's editor made some suggestions for changes that Bramah must have resented. John

Murray wrote to Bramah directly in December 1906[5] and apologised. 'I am very sorry if I have caused you unnecessary trouble…I much regret it but please understand that all the suggestions I make are made on the understanding that they are to be rejected without hesitation, if you see fit.'

Nevertheless Murray intended to reduce their financial risk. The financial terms agreed were half of the profit, not a royalty. The book was published early in 1907 with a flourish, at a price of 6/-.

At the outset Bramah's prognostication that it might be more popular than the Chinese stories was wrong but in the longer run and for some years he was right. The first edition of 1,525 copies sold poorly. He claimed that he was out of pocket on the first edition on the profit-share basis but that he himself had added considerably to the costs by incessant proof corrections that he said were made to satisfy the publisher.

Very shortly after publication Bramah made the disconcerting discovery that there was another book with the same name by an author, Cashel Hoey, probably as obscure as he was at the time. Her book was priced at 1/-. He was perfectly aware from his editorial activities that there is no copyright in title. Nevertheless, either through an intermediary or directly to Pinker, he asked that this information be passed to John Murray.[6] It was typical of his total honesty that he wanted to send his apologies to Mrs. Hoey and get her permission to retain the title or to change the title in any subsequent reprints. This last course did not arise – there were to be no further impressions with the Murray imprimatur. The book did not sell.

Murray were approached by Nelson to allow them to publish the book in their 7d library. Murray seeking to reduce their losses happily agreed with Nelson that they could publish it using the more commercial title of *The Secret of the League*. The cheap edition that appeared in 1909 must have undermined any remaining sales of the 6/- edition. John Murray calculated that their share of the royalties on the cheap edition would produce a higher return than the slow sales of whatever stocks they still held. They were right. The Nelson edition was successful and the remaining stock of their own edition was pulped. A further printing from Nelson was issued in 1920 and another edition was issued in 1926. It can be calculated from the royalty statements that some

360,000 copies had been sold. The book was re-issued in America in 1995.

William Charlton undertook a detailed textual analysis of the two versions – Murray's *What Might Have Been* and Nelson's *The Secret of the League* and found a number of differences. The latter was some 100 pages shorter than the original partly because there were fewer words on each page. It contained a Preface by Bramah. Chapter titles and order were changed and there are great many minor differences. The later edition appears to have dropped a three-page glossary explaining passages in dialect that might not have been clear to a reader. "I think that our cock-sure kumred has geete howd of another mare's nest" would not be easily comprehensible to a reader in the hoped-for U.S.A. edition (that was not to materialise for ninety years). Sensibly the Glossary was restored in the American reprint in 1995.

◆

Some of the ideas for the story might well have come from a short contribution, 'The rival rain-makers' unsigned but unquestionably by Bramah, published in *The London Handbook*[7] in 1898. It carries all the hallmarks of his interest in science. The action is set in 2153. It involves air motors capable of flying at 10,000 feet, an aerial express train travelling at 100 mph and machines for creating rain and earthquakes.

Predictions of the future, near or far, are as dangerous in fiction as in real life and mostly fail. Surprisingly perhaps, Bramah's are uncomfortably close to conditions as they were to be a century later. The middle class are now heavily taxed and penalised and the civil service has swollen to previously unimagined numbers. There is reference to a special tax to fund pensions 'earmarked' (or in modern politico-managerial speak – hypothecated) to meet growing pension claims because the working class did not think it worthwhile to save.

In the plot the social and political transformation begins with a variety of labour laws and heavy taxation on production and on the rich. Social welfare programs of the type that destroy lives as often as they save them are established. Predictable enough so far. Only later do the Socialists attempt to pass a property tax and the last straw is a minimum wage law. Bramah discusses minimum wage laws as if it was obvious that everyone would agree that they would have a deleterious effect on production and employment which, as it happens, has not proved to be the case in reality. (In parenthesis, new, and some would say insidious, forms of property taxation and minimum wages are very much part of the fiscal structure in the United Kingdom since the end of the twentieth century and all introduced by a Socialist government.)

The middle and upper classes form The Unity League to launch what turns out to be a highly successful economic war against the government. This comprises the hoarding of fuel oil and the conversion of coal burning factories and electricity generating stations to oil burning. Then, without warning, they boycott the coal industry, then one part of the triple alliance (coal, steel, and railways). This results in mass unemployment and distress and, finally, civil war. In the course of conducting their war the League has no reservations about buying off the media, conspiring with foreign powers including obtaining foreign aid and generally destroying the principles of democracy. Bramah clearly believed that the captains of industry are the rightful rulers.

Trade unions were abolished and a form of non-parliamentary regime established which George Orwell[8] described as a form of fascism. He goes on:

> Why should a decent and kindly writer like Ernest Bramah find the crushing of the proletariat a pleasant vision? It is simply the reaction of a struggling class, which felt itself menaced not so much by its economic position as its code of conduct and way of life?

Nevertheless in his letters Orwell does identify this work as being one the formative sources for his seminal *Nineteen Eighty-Four.*

One edition at least of the book had a half-apologetic Preface inserted by the publishers.

> We gratefully admit that this doleful anticipation is not likely to be realised, for, since the book was first published, we have seen Labour advance in education and breadth of vision, and Labour Ministers attain broad-minded statesmanship. The type of labour leader here represented is fast dying out, and it is certain

that the working class would not tolerate a Government of such parochial outlook and mediocre capacity.

Many of the social attitudes look odd from the standpoint of the twenty-first century but viewed in their own time are explicable. The moral values do not change. The conflict between honour and duty deeply exercises Bramah, with honour winning. Sir John Hamden is faced with the dilemma of having promised a dying man to deliver a message to the Home Secretary that would have revealed the plans of the League. He takes the honourable course which places his word above that of the interests of the five million members of the League and passes the information to the Home Secretary thereby disrupting his own strategy.

The book ends with the country restored to its former glory by the repeal of repressive laws and the abolition of universal suffrage. It perhaps throws some light on an issue that Bramah never touched on but was of considerable concern to the public. This was the women's suffrage movement that at the time the book was written and published was daily creating headlines through their acts of violence and defiance. Given Bramah's political views at that time, there is little doubt he was against the enfranchisement of women.

The heroine, to fit the future scenario, is an evolutionary New Woman; self-confident, well educated, sporting, a match for any man but still essentially feminine – but for all her modern ways and defiance of the older generation she never refers to women's voting rights. In fact she is not all that different from the more enterprising ladies of the inner chamber in the Chinese books.

The science fiction aspects of the book are in someway both remarkably prescient and in others, as in all science fiction, frequently just that. His muscle-powered personal flying machine is still fiction but the equivalent of aerial express trains flying at an incredible 100 miles per hour and air motors travelling at 10,000 feet, envisaged in the short story 'The rival rain-makers' published ten years earlier, were to become a reality within a decade. At the time the *Secret of the League* was published the Wright Brothers had just flown their powered aeroplane but the English Channel had not yet been crossed by a flying machine. An airship had flown some fifty miles in three and half-hours. Bramah had predicted a different method of aerial transport from muscle-powered wing harnesses.

He prognosticated a wireless-telegraphy terminal connected to a nation-wide network. E-mail? The telescribe machine was efficient, speedy, cheap 'and transmitted in facsimile'. A proto-fax machine that is mentioned in the plot was in fact featured in many reports, which he must have seen, on the St. Louis World Fair in 1904. Most incredible of all is the 'cipher typewriter' which is uncannily like the Second World War German Enigma machine. While the latter was based on revolving drums, the 'cipher typewriter' operated by the use of a shift key that brought into use four different series of alphabets, the same as the Enigma. Bramah even goes on to explain the danger of the frequent recurrence of certain symbols, by which a code is most usually broken.

The Secret of the League (but not *What Might Have Been*) included a scheme for replacing street names with letters and numbers, not unlike designating roads and routes used in Britain, as 'A', 'B' and 'M' and almost identical to the now ubiquitous postcodes, but with street names retained.

◆

The book attracted many reviews that Bramah called 'loud and lengthy criticism'– running to editorials and special articles, etc.[9] with opinions differing. *The Pall Mall Magazine*[10] believed:

> It gives a striking picture of England of 1916, with an imagined Socialist Government, *sans* army, *sans* navy, *sans* colonies, *sans* everything except rates and taxes; which the upper and middle classes pay, and the rest live on... . The book is extremely well written, it contains some very striking passages and characters.

The *Evening Standard and St. James's Gazette*[11] described it as:

> ...a clever story, abundant in word satire, amusement, excitement and even instruction. ...It is excellent fun and beneath the fun lies meaning. The book should be read. Of its kind it is one of the best that has appeared in recent years.

That there were unfavourable views is barely surprising given there is none of the gentle irony Bramah's readers had already come to expect. He wrote in deadly earnest and the book is savage and angry, even allowing for the occasional apophthegm; 'It is not the young who are curious. They have the fascinating study of themselves.' H. J. Lethbridge[12] in the Introduction to a later Bramah book, criticised *The Secret of the League* as 'gloomy, reactionary and fiercely illiberal', a view which is not difficult to accept. George Orwell[13] considered that 'As a political forecast it is trivial, but it is of great interest in the light it casts on the mentality of the struggling middle class'. He classes Bramah with Gissing as a 'sensitive, idealistic man whose private fear of the mob turned him into a passionate anti-democrat'.

Many contemporary and later critics considered the book as glib and reactionary; championing the interests and attitudes of Bramah's bourgeois readers. Albert Muench, a well-known Bramah collector, wrote in a letter to William White:[14] 'The book itself is God-awful, far worse than anything else of his I have ever read.'

In a B.B.C. talk John Connell compared Bramah's vision to that of H. G. Wells.[15]

> Here is the reverse of the bland, optimistic face which, in those days Wells and his friends put on the Future. …Now Wells, who in 1906 had so rosily and so genially patted the Future on his head was, in old age, embittered, disillusioned and filled with dread. And Ernest Bramah, his contemporary, long ago went out of business as a political prophet and quietly concentrated his genius on Max Carrados and Kai Lung.

It was to be nearly ninety years before an American edition was published under the second title *The Secret of the League* when it received favourable attention not just as curiosity, but in its own right. Latter day opinions of the book are perhaps more favourable than the contemporary ones. For example Sean Haugh, who had not seen Bramah's original Preface, which only appeared in the Murray first edition, assumed 1916 was in the present era whereas the book was set in the fictional era of A.C. (After the Calamity). Writing in *Formulations*[16] in 1995 when an American Edition of the book appeared he stated that:

From Bramah's vantage point in 1906 England, he projects what his country might well be like by 1916 if the Socialist Party took power. From my view here in America in 1995 it seems he has far more hits than misses. Writing about the near future is one of the most dangerous options a writer can take... . Except for a few bizarre wrong turns, if Bramah erred in his predictions of technological advancement, he posited too much too soon.

With minor transformations into current terminology, the conflicts of capital, unions, trade, social values, and so forth within Edwardian Britain look very like our contemporary issues and struggles. Moving forward, the first Labour Party term in office in 1924, the General Strike of 1926 and Labour's second term from 1929-1935 can have come as little surprise to Bramah. Winston Churchill said in January 1924 (thinking of Russia and Germany) "The enthronement in office of a Socialist Government will be a serious national misfortune such as has usually befallen great States only on the morrow of defeat in war." But with historical perspective we see sadly that many of our worst defeats are self-inflicted, in peacetime...?

In another American retrospective review in May 2002 by R. W. Fransen[17] speculates whether the Liberal Party triumph of 1906 led Bramah to imagine what a Labour Party triumph might do for British Society. Fransen believes that not many writers were sufficiently prescient in 1907 to anticipate Britain's socialist progression when such ideas seemed extreme, radical and unlikely of realisation.

But before the Great War, before the Russian Revolution, and long before the first national victories of the Labour Party, Ernest Bramah saw a darkening future. One thing is clear. Bramah, neglected as he is, can be classed with H. G. Wells and George Orwell in his imaginative conceptualisation of the future.

Fransen concludes:[18]

...despite being a prophetic-warning novel, full of social commentary, and rather thin in the departments of characters and plot, The Secret of the League possesses a good deal of witty comment on character types and social issues that are still with us ... . [The book is] rather fun to read for the historically minded and philologists of science.'

Perhaps it was a case of Sir John Adcock's thesis working in reverse. 'If Darwin had followed The Origin of the Species with Three Men in a Boat, I doubt whether the pundits would have taken him seriously.' Perhaps if The Secret of the League had not followed The Wallet of Kai Lung and the Mirror of Kong Ho, the serious book would have attracted more favourable comment but it was not what was expected from an author of humorous works.

Whatever differences the critics may have had, the book was widely and lengthily reviewed and discussed and the later Nelson editions included a preface by John Buchan, who was both a Partner in Nelson and their literary advisers. He would certainly not have added his lustre to a work which was not of literary merit.

There have been suggestions that a short story called 'The war hawks', published in the Pall Mall Magazine in 1909, was originally conceived as a sequel to The Secret of the League. His airships in 'The war hawks', a short tale written just after The Secret of the League, were protected by what Bramah called Lietke-ray emanations detectable only with sensitised glasses – not unlike the infra-red night vision viewers of today. It was rejected by Pearson's Magazine, and Cassell's Saturday Journal in 1909 and did not appear in print for another eighteen years when it was included in the collection The Specimen Case. There is unquestionably some resemblance to The Secret of the League – England under threat, and self-propelled personal flying machines.

Given the infinitesimal sales of English Farming and the slow sales of The Wallet of Kai Lung, The Mirror of Kong Ho and the first edition of What Might Have Been it is incomprehensible why Bramah was 'disappointed' with the Nelson edition of the book. Immediate sales were over 70,000 copies and ultimately, as has already been calculated, more than 360,000 copies were sold. Perhaps later in life a greater disappointment was that both Kai Lung and Max Carrados far outlasted the central characters, John Hampden and George Salt. These were two men who represented all that Bramah admired in the English character – honest, patriotic, determined and effective.

Whatever his views, the royalties opened up new personal possibilities.

Sources & Notes

1   H.R.H.R.C. op. cit. n.d. but the letter can be attributed to 1901-2.

2   Ernest Bramah. *What Might Have Been: the Story of a Social War*. John Murray. London. 1907.

3   Ernest Bramah. *What Might Have Been*. op. cit. p.106.

4   Letter from James Pinker to John Murray. October 10th 1906. John Murray. Archive.

5   Letter to Ernest Bramah from John Murray. December 10th 1906. op. cit.

6   ibid. March 6th 1907.

7   *The London Handbook*. 1898 op. cit. pp.94-103.

8   George Orwell. 'Prophecies of fascism'. *Tribune*. London. July 12th 1940.

9   H.R.H.R.C. op. cit. Autobiographical note.

10 H.R.H.R.C. op. cit. Extract of reviews compiled by Ernest Bramah. n.d.

11 ibid.

12 Ernest Bramah. *Kai Lung's Golden Hours*. OUP. New York. 1985. Introduction H. J. Lethbridge. p.vi.

13 George Orwell. 'Prophecies of fascism'. op. cit.

14 H.R.H.R.C. op. cit. July 20th 1959.

15 John Connell. 'The recluse who created Kai Lung'. *The Listener*. May 29th. 1941. pp.841-2.

16 Sean Haugh. A review. *Formulations*. Raleigh. North Carolina. Autumn 1995.

17 R. W. Fransen. A review. Published on the Internet www.troynov.com

18 ibid.

CHAPTER EIGHT

PROSPERITY AND PRODUCTIVITY

About this time, with *The Wallet, Kong Ho* and *The Secret of the League* in print and selling along with success in finding publishers for his many stories and articles, the Bramahs were able to afford a home of their own. In 1905 they moved to Lothian Lodge, what is now 216 Uxbridge Road, Hampton Hill in West London. This was a large Victorian house, one of about six, in what was then a country lane. It was a typical, highly respectable, middle class dwelling with a large garden entirely suitable for a rising young author and his wife. It appears to be somewhat bigger than what would be required for a couple on their own but doubtless they still expected and hoped to have children. By the time Ernest and his wife moved to Lothian Lodge they had been married some eight years but there were no children nor were there to be. It is doubtful, given their affection for their nieces and nephews, that being childless was by choice.

Within the family there were a number of suggestions as to why there were no children ranging from non-consummation to the concern about insanity on Maisie's side of the family. With Ernest's sister Rose also being mentally retarded this may well have been a basis for the decision to remain childless.

Susannah, Ernest's mother, had died at her home in Muswell Hill in March 1906 at the age of seventy-eight with Ernest at her side. Charles Clement Smith, Ernest's father who had financially supported him so generously, died four years later in May 1910 at the age of eighty-four. Both Ernest's father and mother suffered from severe bronchial trouble and, as is suggested later, one reason for Ernest avoiding meeting people might have been that he himself was an asthmatic.

Charles's estate was over £8,000. A life income was left for his younger daughter Rose, who, unmarried at the age of forty-five and mentally retarded, was certainly destined to be a spinster for the rest of her life. The remaining estate was divided equally between Emily Jane, Charles Percy and Ernest, who were all executors.

The Smiths were a close family and there is no doubt that Ernest would have been very much affected by his parents' deaths – most particularly his father 'surely the most accommodating of parents'. It would have been out of character for him not to have deeply regretted that Charles, who had been so generous and supportive, did not live to enjoy vicariously the successes that were still to come.

Another loss quickly followed when his brother, Charles Percy, died the following year leaving a widow and twins both of whom ultimately became beneficiaries under both Ernest's and Maisie's Wills.

Bramah's literary output at this time was considerable. According to an incomplete listing in *The Short Story Index*.[1] Over seventy titles are identified but, as already noted, the Index gives neither dates nor the names of the newspaper or journals. Some of the stories and features must have been published in the few years before the First World War. It is known that more than a dozen stories appeared in 1913. In 1975 William White[2] compiled and published a bibliography of over one hundred stories and features complete with the name of the publication and date but recognised that there must be many that were not located (as the Bibliography at the end of this book notes).

In addition to that which appeared in print, the Harry Ransom Humanities Research Center at the University of Texas holds a large number of stories and articles in manuscript form, almost all undated and no indication whether they were published or not. Some drafts, barely readable and written into the blank pages of a dummy copy of the *London Year Book*, suggests that many may be of an early date. The subject matter shows an extreme catholicity in the odd choice of subjects. Bicycle tyres, Phonographs (dictating machines), Barrels, Typewriters, Emery Cloth, Toiletries, Gas Light Globes and Bicycles are subjects that attracted his attention. The fact that similar articles appeared in *The London Handbook* and *The London Year Book* is a clear indication that these were the intended media but both collapsed before they could be used.

Each of these types of articles, all written with a light touch, directs the reader to a supplier which makes them exactly like the modern marketing phenomenon of the 'advertorial', that is advertisements written and laid out to look like an editorial or ordinary feature of the publication. In the article on bicycles the reader is gently directed to the Ariel Company, 119 Newgate Street, London E.C. Should he or she want emery cloth then the London Emery Works is the place to go and, for toiletries, the ladies would find John Goswell in Upper Thames Street is the preferred establishment.

It is possible to conjecture that the companies that were mentioned paid for the articles. Indeed, using today's nomenclature, they might have been 'sponsored' or, most likely, they were just the result of primitive but nevertheless successful Press Relations by the companies involved. Yet another possibility is that they were never published at all and were printed and distributed by the businesses mentioned as advertising material to accompany their catalogues. The articles on Bicycles and Gas Lighting Globes actually have space left for an illustration taken from the catalogues of Ariel Bicycles and Holophane Globes. It would be no surprise if copywriting was included among Bramah's many skills and the articles were all written as advertising copy. The material itself shows a skill in identifying features of the products that would attract customers. Moreover it is quite clear that Bramah was aware of that important marketing concept now called 'U.S.P.' (Unique Selling Proposition) which he termed 'Snap cry', a promotional tactic which emphasises benefits not to be found with competitive products.

Among the manuscripts of this period are also a number of 'character' pieces describing individuals and their work. These include a collector of fossils, a waitress, a stationer and a journalist. They too were, in all probability, part of a commissioned series for a publication. There is a faint similarity to some of the *Sketches by Boz*, Dickens's earliest journalistic efforts.

There are also poems. A. E. Housman who was one of Grant Richards's discoveries must certainly have inspired a poem by Bramah that begins:

Nay hie away, arise today,
Too long I've served thy bidding,
Too oft at call, left ox and stall
And braved my master's chiding.

This continues for three more verses and is not so very far from Housman's:

Therefore they shall do my will
Today while I am master still,
And flesh and soul, now are strong,
Shall hale the sullen slaves along.

Perhaps the situation was also reversed.
Bramah wrote:

I'm going to write a poem on
A little girl aged six
Who always did as she was told
And played no monkey tricks.

This continues for some thirty-six lines. Housman who is not well known for his humorous verse produced a short poem to introduce his *More Poems*.[3] His ended:

This is for all ill-treated fellows
Unborn and unbegot
For them to read when they're in trouble
And I am not

A longer manuscript is of particular interest – Bramah as a travel writer. He was far from being a much-travelled man. He referred to himself as 'a most timorous and inexperienced traveller'. However in what is an autobiographical account he described in an article 'From Sydenham to St. Petersburg'[4] his eighteen-day tour to St. Petersburg via Helsingfors (Helsinki) and returning through Copenhagen. Maisie probably accompanied him although there is no mention of her in the article. It can be deduced that it was written about 1910. Clearly Ernest was now prosperous enough to indulge in foreign travel although he was careful to explain just how cheap the basic travel costs were – £30. Possibly the visit was inspired by his ex-employer, Jerome K. Jerome's visits to Russia in 1895 and 1905.

The article, and there is no evidence either way whether it was published or not, is full of Bramah's humorous touches even if the racial aspect would, today, be regarded as unacceptable.

> …its Mongolian waiters would probably be generally considered more ethnologically interesting then personally attractive…a waiter approaches and stands dumbly waiting your order or places before you a hieroglyphic bill of fare from which you may quite reasonably select a box of choice cigars or two portions of Worcester sauce.'

and

> …the Winter Palace where the scale of expected gratuities for being shown over this many-storied building averaged half a rouble for each step of the staircase…

Another interesting manuscript and which Bramah mentions in a letter written in 1912,[5] but which did not go to Pinker until 1915, anticipated the book on coinage some seventeen years later. The article was an account of his first interest in coin collecting. It was called 'Through the eyes of a child'[6] and is unquestionably autobiographical. He relates how a Sotheby's auction catalogue item – 'Lot 647 BATTY. Descriptive Catalogue of the Copper Coinage' poignantly recalled his childhood interest in coin collecting and his somewhat edgy relationship with the eccentric coin dealer called, perhaps appropriately, Batty. The article gives another glimpse of at least one aspect of the author's persona – a consistent interest in numismatics and possibly an obsession in collecting and classifying coins and identifying their origin. The fact, as will be shown, that his wife shared this interest was indeed fortunate.

From all this it can be seen Bramah was far from idle and that his income was rising. Besides the book sales, there was also a flow of articles and stories which appeared in many newspapers and periodicals such as the *News of the World, Bystander, Pall Mall Magazine, Sunday Referee, Everybody's* and *Punch* as royalty statements show.

◆

In May 1909 the Smiths had moved into a flat much closer to London. 10 Ravenscourt Mansions (later renamed and numbered 210 Hamlet Gardens) in Hammersmith, West London. This was to be their home for the next thirty years. It was a comfortable fourth floor flat in what was then a mansion block in a well-to-do neighbourhood and overlooking the pleasant Ravenscourt Park. John Barker, Maisie's nephew described it as 'gloomy'. He recalls the book-lined rooms as being decorated in the style of William Morris. There was a piano as well as a mandolin decorating the wall. Maisie who had some musical training certainly played the mandolin and probably the piano. The block of flats and its location under various disguises appears in a number of Max Carrados stories. 210 Hamlet Gardens is now rundown providing temporary accommodation for the homeless with the Bramah apartment divided into two smaller ones.

Surprisingly, Maisie and Ernest do not appear to have had a telephone installed. Directories up to 1939, when they moved homes again, do not list Ernest Bramah Smith or Maisie or any combination of names and initials. Although an ex-directory service did exist it was rarely used but it would appear entirely in keeping with Ernest's insistence on privacy that he would use such a service if there was a telephone in his flat. None of his letter headings give a telephone number.

In 1911 Grant Richard decided despite the poor sales of *The Wallet of Kai Lung* he would experiment with the book again and in his own words[7]

> ...but I, remembering how difficult it is to revive a book, had but little courage and reprinted only one of its stories 'The transmutation of Ling'. To that, aided by the Riverside Press of Edinburgh, I gave a handsome folio form... . The reprint also sold slowly – so slowly that I was glad to have placed much

of it with Messrs Brentano of New York... . Many copies I foolishly jobbed off in the early days of the [First World]war to one of those English Booksellers who can be depended upon to know a good thing when they have time to learn of its existence. Six years later Messrs. Methuen...thought of adding the book to one of their cheap libraries, and its presence therein is a standing evidence of my own lack of daring.

Taking books, journalism, and editorial work together along with Maisie's marriage settlement and Ernest's inheritance from his father, there is little doubt that the Bramahs, if not affluent, were living in very comfortable circumstances. This gave him sufficient financial security to experiment once again with a story in a different genre.

Sources & Notes

1 The *Short Story Index* op. cit.

2 *Bulletin of Bibliography*. William White. 'Ernest Bramah in periodicals. 1890-1972'. Papers of the American Language Association. Vol. 32. No.1 New York. 1971.

3 A. E. Housman. *More Poems*. Cape. London. 1936.

4 Ernest Bramah. 'Sydenham to St. Petersberg'. H.R.H.R.C. op. cit. Typescript.

5 H.R.H.R.C. op. cit. June 16th 1912.

6 Ernest Bramah. 'Through the eyes of a child'. op. cit.

7 Grant Richards. *Author Hunting*. op. cit. pp.273-4.

CHAPTER NINE

THE CORNERSTONE OF
DETECTIVE FICTION

Bramah confessed to Grant Richards that he had the unfortunate habit of altering each morning every word that he had written on the day before. This alone cannot explain why it was seven years after *The Secret of the League* before Bramah was to publish another book. The new book was the eponymous *Max Carrados*[1] – a blind amateur detective. Twelve Max Carrados stories had already appeared previously in the *News of the World* at intervals between 1911 and 1913. Eight of these stories were now included in the book so in fact only four were written specially for it. His slow rate of composition would not appear to be reasons for the delay. Although Pinker, despite being restricted to stories and articles had the manuscript as early as 1910 it was not until 1914 that Methuen accepted it. It must have been offered to Grant Richards first who rejected it. His views must have changed later since he published the second book in the Carrados series.

The Ellery Queen list of top ten mystery collections of all time includes this first Carrados book and Jessica Salmonson described the Carrados books as a cornerstone of detective fiction.[2] The term 'cornerstone' had been coined earlier by Howard Haycroft who used it to describe collections of the best and most influential writing in the medium. Needless to say Ernest Bramah was included in this category. Unquestionably Max Carrados the blind detective is Bramah's second creation upon which his reputation rests.

The genre of the gifted fictional amateur detective, starting with

Edgar Allen Poe's Dupin, and Emile Gaboriau's Lecoq had long been established; Sherlock Holmes, Dr. Thorndyke and Lord Peter Wimsey are the most obvious examples.

Edgar Allan Poe was almost certainly an author whom Bramah had studied and admired since he was the pioneer of both the detective and science fiction novel, both of which figure strongly among Bramah's work.

Although George Orwell[3] classified Bramah's stories as 'good bad books', which he defined as the kind of book that has no literary pretensions but which remains readable when more serious productions have perished. He placed him in the same class as Conan Doyle but as is obvious, Sherlock Holmes has long outlasted Carrados in book, film, radio and T.V. form.

William Charlton in his Preface to the French translation of *Max Carrados*[4] quotes a letter from Bramah to Pinker. 'Just now I am engaged on a series of detective tales. I dare say you remember Sir Arthur Conan Doyle's anecdote of an author-friend who said to him, "Oh, by the way I'm going to chuck literature. I intend writing detective stories in future." ' This, Charlton felt, displayed Bramah's self-consciousness about entering the field of crime writing.

Authors of detective fiction are no better at resisting the temptation to make their central characters different from previous ones than are classical novelists. This seduction has led to some dreadful results with bumblers, alcoholics, paraplegics and outright certifiable idiots. Fiction is littered with physically disabled detectives – amputees, deafness, facial disfigurement and asthmatics.

Bramah decided his detective was to be blind. But he did not make his hero blind as a tawdry attempt just to be different from all other detectives popular at the time. His was a very serious attempt to show that the blind did not live in total darkness and are as capable in many respects of seeing as well as the sighted. Most frequently the portrayal of the blind in fiction is mawkish, exaggerated and stereotypical. Bramah most certainly did not fall into this trap. He treats blindness without sentimentality and not as a handicap. Indeed in some instances he shows how it can be an advantage.

He went on, perhaps to justify by precedence, the choice of a disability, listing other authors who also endowed characters with physical or mental imperfections – Walter de la Mare, Mary Webb, William Pett Ridge and even Susan Coolidge in her *What Katy Did at School* series.

Nevertheless Max Carrados was neither the first blind detective nor the last. Indeed Baynard Kendrick's blind Duncan MacLain was described as an antidote to what Kendrick saw as the excesses of Max Carrados. Other blind fictional characters are not rare. Elizabeth Gaskell's Margaret Jennings in *Mary Barton* identified the eponymous heroine by her breathing. Arthur Morrison, an exact contemporary of Bramah's, created a blind fiddler in *The Hole in the Wall*, who too accomplished feats it is difficult for a sighted person to accept could be possible, D. H. Lawrence's Maurice Previn in *England my England*, blinded in the First World War, managed very well with only touch. The citizens of H. G. Wells's *The Country of the Blind*, published three years before the first Max Carrados book, were also endowed with strange powers. Henry Green's John Haye in *Blindness*, has especially acute hearing and can hear not only the words of those around him but also their thoughts.

There is nothing in the real lives of authors of detective stories that might relate to or explain the type of fiction they write. Indeed the great writers of detective fiction led very ordinary mundane lives and unquestionably a long way from the violent and sordid scenes of their imagination. In a series called *Meet the Detectives*, Bramah gave one of his only two B.B.C. talks (for which he was paid ten guineas). This was transmitted on the Empire (now World) Service and was not broadcast domestically. In this talk[5] he provided a very positive explanation of how he alighted on the idea of a sightless detective. He attended what he called a 'crook play', which he described as of the type where people drift out of a room about a fifth of a second before the pursuers drift in and where the sleuth turns round to admire a picture on the wall while the confederates pass the jewels. He commented that this action goes on until five minutes before the end of the play then someone suddenly becomes extremely brilliant and then the mystery falls in place.

"If it comes to that" Bramah said, "why not have a blind detective I thought? I mean a really blind one." The incongruity of a man so handicapped taking part in what was generally supposed to be a particularly open-eyed occupation appealed to him. The idea of a man with no blundering self-confident eyes to be hoodwinked and who was flippantly conceived was to become a classic in detective fiction.

In Bramah's own words[6]

> Max Carrados…is blind, quite blind, but so far from crippling his interests in life or his energies, his blindness has merely impelled him to develop those senses which in most of us lie half dormant and practically unused. Thus you will understand that while he may be at a disadvantage when you are advantaged, he is at an advantage when you are at a disadvantage."

Many years later Henry Green wrote about his character, John Haye, that there were more ways of being blind and more than one way of being able to see. He might have been quoting Carrados.

Bramah made Max Carrados wealthy, the legatee of a fortune. He is unmarried so that the tradition of bachelor detectives is not yet broken. He is a round, cultured person with a love of music and sport and his hobby (not surprisingly given Bramah's interest) is coin collecting. After being blinded in a horse riding accident he developed and supertrained his other senses to allow him to do many things as well as, if not better, than sighted people. He can hear a newspaper boy's cry that is inaudible to others; he can read newspapers, in those pre-digital lithography days, through his sense of touch; locate electric light bulbs by their radiation. In one plot his enhanced sense of smell enables him to detect a person wearing a false moustache because of the interaction of perspiration and glue.

Like many other writers of detective fiction Bramah was aware of the seedy reputation of private detectives in real life since most of their commissions were for divorce inquiries which generated salacious press reports. In making Carrados a person of substantial independent means he is able to ignore the cash nexus in selecting the inquiries the detective was prepared to undertake.

♦

E. F. Bleiler in the Introduction to an American anthology *Best Max Carrados Stories*[7] perceives that:

Max Carrados's blindness is obviously a tour de force, since it involves a man who is described as blind, but in actual practice is little less keen in visual perception than most men. Carrados, in short, is a blind man who can see perfectly well. Yet the tour de force is strikingly successful; it develops a facet of interest that shows many planes: unexpected ways of obtaining data, plot situations where a blind man can have advantages over a seeing man (as in total darkness), character subtleties and much else.'

Bramah recognised that that darkness was the only situation where Carrados would have an advantage and he was too clever a writer not realise that the 'advantages' have their limitations too. In his B.B.C. talk[8] he explained:

...you can't go on shutting up bad people in dark rooms tale after tale and chapter after chapter without it getting monotonous. So I had to fall back on Max's superlative acuter perception in the sense other than sight. That simply discounted his blindness. Anyone could endow a detective with abnormally developed sense without him being blind. Still, there he was a poor cod no doubt but yet mine own, and as winning card in any tight corner, I took the liberty of equipping him with the elusive sixth-sense – which of course covers anything and everything. Then I flattered myself that whatever happened we couldn't go wrong.

If Carrados was 'different' because he was blind his creator was also revolutionary in another respect. Holmes and Thorndyke were portrayed as infallible and super-human. No door was closed to them because of their incredible skill and knowledge. They were deadly serious, given to a certain pomposity of speech and axiomatically in command of whatever situation they found themselves in. Thorndyke had no discernible weaknesses or recorded failures. Holmes has his weaknesses and his failures, but none the less the impression which he gives is one of invincibility. The battles he lost seem to be unimportant once he has got even with Moriarty.

Bramah saw no need for all this solemnity or for invulnerability. Carrados is neither solemn nor invulnerable so that Bramah did not have to suppress his wit and humour. William Charlton rightly observes,[9] only the author of Kai Lung could have created Professor Holmfast Bulge with his irreplaceable notes on "Polyphyletic Bridal Customs among mid-Pleistocene Cave Men" who appears in the story 'The last exploit of Harry the actor' in *Max Carrados*. There is also breezy banter between Carrados and other characters in the stories.

Despite the drama, fine characterisations and sometimes devastating irony, it does not take close textual analysis to see the humour of Kai Lung poking through the fabric of the detective stories. Unquestionably Bramah had an impish delight in pulling his reader's leg and indulging in self-parody and in creating ludicrous situations. In 'The last exploit of Harry the actor' a brilliant cracksman who has robbed an apparently impenetrable safe deposit returns his loot.

"Oh my friends, you have had an all-fired narrow squeak, Up till Friday in last week I held your wealth in the hollow of my ungodly hands and rejoiced in my nefarious cunning, but on that day as I with my guilty female accomplice stood listening with worldly amusement to the testimony of a converted brother at a meeting of the Salvation Army on Clapham Common, the gospel light suddenly shone in our rebellious souls and then and there we found salvation. Hallelujah!

"What we had done to complete the unrighteous scheme upon which we had laboured for months has only been for your own good. Dear friends, that you are, though yet divided from us by your carnal lusts. Let this be a lesson to you. Sell all you have and give to the poor through the organisation of the Salvation Army by preference."[10]

Bramah also ignored the limiting convention of the day that almost every investigation must concern a murder. In fact there are only two murders and two suspicions of murder in the whole of the Carrados chronicles and the two murderers or suspects commit suicide. However in 'The tragedy at Brookbend Cottage' it is the wife, the intended victim, who commits suicide. For all his ingenuity Carrados had not allowed for the shock which the apprehension and arrest of her husband while attempting to electrocute her would have. Carrados frankly admits his error – an almost unheard of occurrence in detective stories except perhaps for Georges Simenon's Maigret.

Carrados shows a preference for less spectacular crimes such as jewellery theft, kidnapping, fraud and even a landlord and tenant dispute. His ethics are at times ambiguous. In one story a murderer is ordered to commit suicide.

Unusually for the genre, some of the stories are linked to contemporary events, the suffragette movement, the Irish Volunteers (later the I.R.A.) movement and what has a strongly contemporary ring, terrorism. In 'The Knight's Cross signal problem' Bramah has a character defend his wrecking of a train by an Indian nationalist.

> "You are a very cold-blooded young scoundrel, sir!" retorted Mr. Carlyle. "Do you realise you are responsible for the death of scores of innocent men and women?"

> "Do you realise, Mr. Carlyle, that you and your Government and your soldiers are responsible for the deaths of thousands of innocent men and women in my country every day?"

Precisely the justification used by the terrorists who bombed the Madrid railway in 2004 and the London Underground in 2005.

◆

Making his hero blind might appear perverse or an intention at all costs to be different from past and contemporary literary detectives. Carrados's skills and achievements can stretch believability but because each tale poses a problem, readers develop a compulsive need to resolve it and become convinced despite their reservations.

In his Introduction to the second Carrados book, *The Eyes of Max Carrados,* written nine years later, Bramah passionately advances the need to ameliorate the handicaps suffered by the blind and shows concern that advances should be made to reduce or remove the disadvantages they suffer. He refers to there being a special reason why the exploits of the sightless obtain prominence, and why every inch won in the narrowing of the gulf between the seeing and the blind is hailed almost with the satisfaction of a martial victory. 'That the general condition of the blind is being raised, that they are, in the mass, more capable and infinitely less dependent than at any period in the past, is undeniable, and these things are plainly to the good'.[11]

Given the somewhat outlandish idea that a blind man could be a detective, albeit an amateur one, Bramah justified the apparent uncanny powers of his hero, doubtless in response to the criticisms *Max Carrados* received. Although chronologically it is out of order it is appropriate to refer to it here.

In the long Introduction to *The Eyes of Max Carrados* Bramah demonstrates detailed knowledge of blind people who had accomplished exceptional feats in real life. One of his main sources was an 1820 publication entitled *Biography of the Blind, or Lives of such as have distinguished themselves as Poets, Philosophers, Artists &c* by James Wilson. He also quotes from a biography of the blind Nicholas Saunderson LL.D. F.R.S. Nicholas Saunderson became Lucasian Professor of Mathematics at Cambridge, a Chair now held by another severely disabled genius – Stephen Hawking. Saunderson could 'with great nicety and exactness perceive the smallest degree of roughness or defect of polish on a surface; thus in a set of Roman medals he distinguished the genuine from the false.' This is a skill that Carrados demonstrates in the very first adventure when he correctly identifies a forged coin.

Bramah is concerned to show that being blind from birth or an early age was not a necessary pre-condition for the compensatory development of the other senses. Of the twenty-six blind men in Wilson's book, six lost their sight later than youth. Precursors of Carrados's skills and proof that the character was believable were; a blind Scottish tailor who could weave tartan despite the fact every stripe and colour has to fit with mathematical precision; John Metcalf, better known as Blind Jack of Knaresborough, (to whom Bramah claimed to be distantly related) who was an expert swimmer, hunter and violinist as well as designing and managing the construction of 180 miles of turnpike roads and bridges. He also introduced the use of ditching and sub-bases for marshy areas; Margaret M'Avoy who could accurately describe height, dress, bearing and other characteristics of her visitors; Helen Keller the American author and educationalist who was both blind and deaf and about whom Bramah wrote at length. He could also have mentioned the equally incredible ability of John, the blind brother of the novelist Henry Fielding, of whom it was said that as a Magistrate at his Bow Street court, he could identify 3,000 thieves by their voices.

In total Bramah describes twelve extraordinary examples of accomplishments of blind people including a man who solved the mystery of the Queen bee's nuptial flight, another who could detect blindness in horses and a woman who could discern colour through odours. All of these sightless people provided evidence that although Carrados might be a fictional character, his accomplishments were no more remarkable than those which had occurred in real life.

◆

The blind detective's abilities led some critics to complain he was no different from a sighted person, as he experiences none of the disadvantages blind people encounter. Whether or not these unique abilities were realistic is however of little consequence since the public was willing to believe in outstanding powers which the blind have over the sighted.

Nevertheless some of Carrados's achievements were regarded as extreme, if not impossible. David Langford drew attention to these in a critical review.[12]

> The man who sat with me bit his finger-nails, smoked Algerian cigars and wore an elastic stocking. This time, explanations are not given. Anyone can smell cigar smoke, and Carrados has no doubt written a monograph on it. Perhaps a trained ear might interpret the muffled sounds of nail biting. We're left to puzzle over whether, by walking a little way with an unsuspecting blackguard, Carrados could really make that last deduction from his tread. Thrusting one's hands up his trouser leg however unobtrusively done… . In a similar vein [he] smells an anaesthetic from a drugged posy placed momentarily on the ground out in the open two weeks previously does stretch believability to the limits.

Carrados's abilities, some credible and some, by today's standards at least incredible, create a personality not as well known but as outstanding as Holmes who, by the way, Bramah said in his broadcast would make the world's worst detective. Doyle could be extremely careless. Bramah would not have a character copying out an encyclopaedia at the rate of 33,435 words an hour, nor would Max Carrados, as Holmes was variously described, be both an early and a late-riser. Bramah would have known that Death certificates did not exist in Atlanta at the time one Doyle character received one. Perhaps Bramah's early career in farming put him in a better position than Conan Doyle to know that geese do not have crops.[13] He most certainly, being a coin expert, would not let a client rub his coins with a chamois to enhance their appearance. Bramah was thorough and meticulous and no one has found any significant anachronistic, contradictory or inconsistent statements in the Carrados stories.

As one critic pointed out[14] all the senses – sound, taste, touch and smell – are held in thrall to vision. Blindfolded, a sighted person can easily be persuaded that objects, tastes and sounds are quite different to their reality. 'It is no wonder that Justice herself stands blindfolded to best achieve her aim'. Bramah has Carrados declare, "There are a thousand sounds that you in your arrogance of sight ignore..."

◆

There were widely different views as to the character and personality of Max Carrados. The descriptions included suave, genial, considerate, good-natured, kind and resourceful. Others, as Bramah admitted, described him as dull, austere and forbidding. He favoured the latter view. In a throwaway line he said, "I can't imagine that he [Carrados] would be anything but a deadly heavyweight about the social board..."[15] Rose Macauley described him as 'unpleasantly canine'.[16] Jacques Barzun 'alarming and sometimes farcical'.[17]

The Times Literary Supplement which Bramah quoted in his broadcast, concluded that 'Carrados, with the magical development of his senses, is obviously a fairy tale character'. Bramah did not disagree since he thought all detectives in fiction were merely disguised fairies (in the sense of the nomenclature of the times) and the records of their doings 'represent the pathetic yearning of the grown-ups to cling to the illusions and make-believe of childhood.'

Just as the critics of Max Carrados's character differed so their views on the books were also varied. Joan Seay considered 'the tone is witty, ironic and gently satirical. His gift for expression is reflected in clever dialogue and lively third-person narration.'[18] Julian Symonds, an expert on detective fiction, believed that Bramah showed a distinct originality in creating the blind Max Carrados and admires the construction of the stories and their ability to maintain interest. 'There is no doubt that he demonstrates a considerable skill with dialogue and the blending of tragedy and light-hearted humour.'[19] In contra-distinction *The Spectator*[20] considered 'the stories are not particularly distinguished. Some of the mysteries and their solutions are a little too incredible'. William White in an essay in *Twentieth-Century Literary Criticism* wrote that the stories, from a literary point of view, did not hold up and were 'far below the quality of other authors in the same field'.[21] An anonymous essay in the same publication considers 'some of the mysteries and their solutions are a little too incredible'.[22]

Arnold Bennett, who reportedly was jealous of other authors' success wrote;[23]

> I read several stories in Stories of Crime and Detection. Poe is the best, Austin Freeman next, Conan Doyle is poor. Bramah far-fetched and unimpressive. These people have an idea and seem without imagination or skill to use the idea.' Applying Dorothy Sayers's 'fair play' rule – the essential clues are all collected and set before the reader before the detective makes any deductions from them – reveals a weakness in that the reader cannot make some of the discoveries as is possible with the Conan Doyle stories.

The criticism concerning the unreality of Carrados's enhanced abilities, which compensated for his lack of sight, was one of the factors that influenced Bramah to write the long Introduction to *The Max Carrados Mysteries* which has already been quoted extensively.

◆

Carrados, has the inevitable foil only in his case there are three people fulfilling the role Watson occupied in the Holmes stories. The principal one is Louis Carlyle, a struck off solicitor and now a private detective, but not a brilliant one. Carrados also has his invaluable valet, Parkinson, who, fortuitously, has keen observational powers, mechanical dexterity, a truly remarkable memory and an absence of curiosity, which is no defect in a confidential valet of a detective. He also lacks any imagination or the wish to question any judgement of his master. But as a reviewer in *The Times Literary Supplement* observed 'Who knows but that among the Immortals there may yet be found a place for Parkinson in Detectives' Corner between Argus and Dr. Watson?'[24]

Completing the trio is Carrados's secretary, Anneslley Greatorex. However, and with great skill, Bramah does not allow the sighted members of the team to dilute the overriding detection skills of his hero.

Some critics have seen a difference between the Holmes-Watson relationship and Carrados and his sighted team. Collectively they are perhaps more sophisticated than Watson and are much more characterised although some commentators describe Carlyle as 'naïve' and 'unimaginative'. It is notable that whatever cases Carlyle brought to Carrados he kept the more sleazy ones, which comprised most private detectives' case load, away from him. There was never any prurience in the cases with which he sought Carrados's help.

There are two aspects of *Max Carrados*, and indeed the later titles, which seem to have been overlooked by readers and critics alike. First, there has been little if any comment on the very considerable skill that is required for a sighted writer to put themselves in the position of one who is blind and then avoid any inadvertent errors because, in fact, the writer is sighted. Not once did Bramah fall into this trap and the most perceptive reviewers and readers failed to find a single example of a Carrados deduction or conclusion that could have been achieved only if he had been able to see.

Second, Bramah exhibits a sensitivity that was unusual until the present age of political correctness and was very rare in most of the twentieth century. In his contribution to the B.B.C. series *Meet the Detectives*,[25] he said:"...you cannot associate a comic theme with the character of a blind man. You must at all cost keep him serious. And you have to be very, very careful with the mildest of satires." This, given Bramah's almost irrepressible sense of the ridiculous, must have been a difficult task indeed.

Clearly no blind people felt in anyway offended. The Royal National Institute for the Blind sought and received permission for 'The disappearance of Marie Severe' from *The Eyes of Max Carrados*, two later Kai Lung books and one other novel to be transcribed into Braille. *Max Carrados* was also published in a large print edition, as indeed was *The Wallet of Kai Lung*.

♦

In 1917 Methuen[26] had written to Pinker that their earlier intention to publish a cheap impression at seven pence had to be abandoned because of cost. They proposed a one-shilling edition on which they offered Bramah a ten per cent royalty – the going rate. They hoped 'to bring the book out as soon as possible, but the delays in connection with the production of cheap books are very great just now'. Despite their foreboding a cheap edition was in the bookshops by November that year. There were six further editions of *Max Carrados* between 1915 and 1976 and a German edition in 1973.

Some Max Carrados stories, most particularly *The Game Played in the Dark*, were dramatised and staged many times and produced on radio. That play became a favourite of amateur companies although the *Dictionary of Literary Biography* considered it lacked substance.

In 1997 B.B.C. Radio 4 broadcast two plays based on Carrados stories, one dramatised by Bert Coules and the other by Sue Rodwell. Simon Callow played Carrados and Lionel Jeffries, Parkinson.

Bramah always retained the film rights of his books but neither he nor his agents had any success in selling the stories to filmmakers. Correspondence reveals that some tentative negotiations were conducted but never came to fruition.

Given that eight of the stories in *Max Carrados* had already appeared in *The News of the World*, for which he had received 200 guineas – a very substantial sum at the time – and the other four were included in later titles, they generated a satisfactory income for Bramah. In all there were twenty-eight original Max Carrados stories in three collections and a Bramah anthology as well as a full-length novel. Many of them were also reproduced in two Bramah anthologies. They were to become staples in magazines for many years to come. At least sixteen of the tales have been located in over thirty different publications and there is little doubt that this does not represent anything like the total. A German translation was published in 1973 and the fact there was a French translation in 2004 is evidence that Carrados is not in the mausoleum of long forgotten fictional detectives who were popular in early twentieth century.

The successful entry into crime writing added to Bramah's reputation and to his income. But the comfortable life he and Maisie now enjoyed was about to be disturbed by the political turmoil in Europe that culminated in the declaration of war. In 1914 at the age of forty-six Bramah was too old for military service but, given his fierce patriotism, it is not surprising that he considered it his duty to make a positive contribution to the war effort.

Sources & Notes

1   Ernest Bramah. *Max Carrados*. Methuen. London, 1914.

2   Jessica Amanda Salmonson. 'A delicate bouquet of crime'. www.violetbooks.com

3   George Orwell. *Collected Essays 1945-50*. Penguin Books. Harmondsworth.1968. p.37.

4   William Charlton. Introduction. *La Partie se joue dans le noir*. Translated Anne-Sylvie Hommasel. Tere de Brume. Rennes. 2004.

5   Ernest Bramah. 'Meet Max Carrados' in the *Meet the Detectives*. series. B.B.C. Empire Service May 7th 1935. Published in *The Armchair Detective*. New York. December 1981.

6   ibid.

7   E. F. Bleiler. *Best Max Carrados Detective Stories*. Introduction. Dover. New York. 1972.

8 Ernest Bramah. *Meet the Detectives.* op. cit.

9 William Charlton. Introduction. *La Partie se joue dans le noire.* op. cit.

10 Ernest Bramah. 'Harry the actor' *The Best Max Carrados Detective Stories.* op. cit. p.22.

11 Ernest Bramah. *The Eyes of Max Carrados.* Grant Richards. London. 1923. Introduction. p.11.

12 David Langford. 'Ernest Bramah: crime and Chinoiserie'. www.ansible.dem.co.uk

13 An interesting analysis of errors in Sherlock Holmes books can be found in Leslie Klinger. *The New Annotated Sherlock Holmes.* London. 2004. Vol. 2. Appendix.

14 Quoted by Jessica Salmonson. 'A delicate bouquet of crime'. op. cit.

15 Ernest Bramah. 'Meet Max Carrados'. op. cit.

16 ibid.

17 Jack Barzun. Essay. *Twentieth Century Literary Criticism.* Gale Research. Detroit. 1982.

18 Essay by Joan Seay. *Dictionary of Literary Biography.* Thomson-Gale. Framington. Michigan.

19 Julian Symonds. *Bloody Murder.* Faber & Faber. London. 1972.

20 *Spectator.* London. October 20th 1923.

21 William White. Essay. *Twentieth-Century Literary Criticism.* op. cit. USA 1959 pp.6-13.

22 *Twentieth-Century Literary Criticism.* op. cit.

23 *The Journals of Arnold Bennett.* Viking Press. New York. 1916. p.891. This is also well illustrated in a passage from Bennett's diaries: '…what surprised me most was a statement that W. W. Jacobs (quite a new man, who has published only two books of a quietly humorous nature, but about whom an inordinate amount of fuss has been made) recently refused an offer of £600 for six short stories … .' Quoted by Reginald Pound, *Arnold Bennett, A Biography.* Heinemann. London. 1971. p.114.

24 *The Times Literary Supplement.* September 27th 1923.

25 Ernest Bramah. 'Meet Max Carrados'. op. cit.

26 H.R.H.R.C. op. cit. March 14th 1917.

CHAPTER TEN

THE FIRST WORLD WAR

Given his fierce patriotism it would be surprising if Bramah had not been involved in some way in the First World War. Many of his literary contemporaries, who like Bramah himself at forty-six, were too old for active service, nevertheless made identifiable contributions to the war effort. Conan Doyle served as a Doctor in France, E. W. Hornung, the creator of Raffles, and Barry Pain joined the anti-aircraft section of the Royal Naval Volunteer Reserve. Saki (H. H. Munro) although forty-three years old fought, and died, in the trenches in 1916. William Locke threw all his skills and energies in helping Belgium refugees and wounded soldiers which cost him his health. Jerome K. Jerome enrolled in the Ambulance Brigade in France, William Pett Ridge was a Chief Inspector in the Special Constabulary and Algernon Blackwood was not only a member of the secret service but had attached himself to a front line Y.M.C.A. unit (and he also offered himself to the intelligence services in the Second World War at the age of almost seventy).

When the Royal Defence Corps, was formed from the Home Service Garrisons in 1916 Bramah joined it. Army records, unsurprisingly, show a very large number of 'Ernest Smiths' but none that correspond to both the dates of service and his address. It must be presumed his army records were with those that were destroyed in the Blitz.

The personnel of these units were men unfit or too old to serve overseas. The Royal Defence Corps, unlike the Home Guard of World War II were battalions of regiments of the regular army and also unlike the Home Guard they were expected to serve away from home. Thus

Bramah spent some time out of London on the South Coast, probably Dover which was one of their bases. He served with an anti-aircraft battery. In a photograph he appears to be of non-commissioned rank. While he was strongly opposed to the Boer War as the barely disguised diatribe in Kong Ho[1] reveals and which is quoted later on page 234, the fact that he was a participant in the First World War would indicate that he felt the cause was just.

His army service did not stop his flow of humorous, morale raising stories and satirising political and human failings and he took full advantage of his experiences in the armed forces. Writing stories was important, as Edwin Pugh, who was one of Jerome's 'New Humorists' and a connoisseur of cockney low life, wrote:[2]

> And so I come to the justification of my purpose in projecting this book [*A Book of Laughter*] at such a time of international crisis as the world is now passing through.... . Let us keep our souls alive by laughing when we can. Let us enlarge our sympathies and enkindle our courage anew by looking upon the comic as well as the tragic side of things

In the 'Recruiting eye' which appeared in *Punch*,[3] a platoon of the Royal Defence Corps organises what was to be a recruiting march through the local villages and towns that totally failed. Some of the men were in uniform and with rifles, the majority was not. They are mistaken for a rounded-up band of German spies under escort. "I can see their faces yet. Such looks of malice, vindictiveness, brutal cunning, hopeless despair and baffled treachery," says a villager. It is more than likely this story was based on an actual experience.

When the German High Command issued its order Gott Strafe England, from May 1915 London became a target for an air offensive and by the end of the war it had been bombed in fifty-two raids. Because Bramah was away from home serving in the Royal Defence Corps and Maisie was alone she appears to have temporarily taken up residence near Emily Jane at Egerton Gardens in Hendon. Outer north-west London would not seem to have been any safer or more dangerous than outer south-west London which as it happened was not bombed at all. (Bombing in 1940 destroyed the Hendon house.)

Bramah's response to the bombings is to be found among his papers in his execrable handwriting 'A collateral security against Zeppelin attacks'.[4] No published version of the article has been located. The title appears on an undated manuscript headed 'Short MSS not appeared serially or in book'. He had already anticipated attacks on London in 'The war hawks' and there is no doubt that he considered dirigibles to be a key weapon in war superseding both the army and the navy. Airships occur with surprising frequency in his stories including one in a Max Carrados tale. It is not surprising therefore, in seeing his prophecies being fulfilled, he should return to them even if in a humorous feature.

It is doubtful whether there is any serious intent in the article. The suggestion was that every British city should be 'twinned' with a German city. If the British city was bombed then, when the war was won, the twinned German city would have to make financial reparations. Setting aside the fact that bombing could inflict far greater damage than most towns would have the resources with which to compensate, the theory lacks credibility. In 1916 the Germans were as sure of victory as the Allies were, so as a deterrent, it lacked realism.

William Charlton has managed to unravel most of the manuscript. This short excerpt gives some idea of the tone.

> In the past the little village of, say, Sausagehausen would have joined in this hymn of holy joy as loyally as any [?] in the Fatherland. But today (anticipating a little you will understand) Sausagehausen has some doubts about the usefulness, even the morality of Zeppelin warfare. [In]some ways Sausagehausen has learned that it has 'adopted' Stoke Poges and will at the end of the war be held financially accountable for the inviolability of its ward. The more Sausagehausen thinks about it the less it likes the idea, and it is one thing to rejoice over the destruction, even the insensate destruction, of harmless, alien places; it is perhaps almost the same thing to gloat upon it revengefully when it is vaguely feared that Germany as a whole may have to pay for it in the end; but it is a very different thing when it is grasped that little Sausagehausen will have as a first charge on its already burdensome local rates whatever damage Stoke Poges suffers from that date forward...

Airships appear yet again in 'Wireless whisperings' where he devises a German communiqué on the success of the Zeppelin attacks on London. It includes statements such as claiming the destruction of a super-dreadnought, hidden in the Regent's Park waters. This is one manuscript that can be dated as there is a reference to the 'recent disastrous encounters off the Dogger Bank. The Battle of the Dogger Bank took place in January 1915.

Another wartime contribution[5] deals with censorship. The article purports to show what the censors might permit to be published. Of course, it contains no information at all. With typical humour he first raises readers' expectations:

In view of recent visits of Zeppelin airships to the England districts of Great Britain many of our readers are doubtless consumed by a healthy curiosity to know more about these formidable engines of destruction. This very natural craving we will proceed to satisfy.

He intends no such thing.

During the summer the Count [Zeppelin] generally resides at his villa in Friederichshavn, a town of 5,000 inhabitants on Lake Constance, or, say of about 4th same size as Shepton Mallett in Somersetshire. Speaking of Somerset reminds us that Gloucestershire, an adjoining county, provides, in the romantic district of Mangotsfield, an appropriate setting for Miss Amelia Scraggs' forthcoming novel…

'How to brighten warfare',[6] again evidence of publication has not been found, is a farcical suggestion for the training of animals to defeat the enemy. Included is a parrot which, having ingratiated itself within a German army unit, is trained to give contradictory orders during a battle to confuse the troops and a mouse that will gnaw away tent ropes.

Stories also appeared in *Punch*[7] without Bramah's name but are accredited in their archives to E. B. Smith. 'The super saleswoman' is concerned with war charities and 'Phases of the war – a patriot's notebook'[8] ponders on the contradictory nature of the Government's exhortations to the civilian population.

◆

One strange item among Bramah's papers is a very full, highly technical training manual written, uncharacteristically, in perfectly readable handwriting. This was 'Musketry course'.[9] Membership of the Royal Defence Corps. would not seem to qualify him as an expert in rifle use and maintenance. So out of keeping is this manuscript with everything else in Bramah's output it was necessary to seek the opinion of a handwriting expert to ensure that the manual was indeed his creation as it proved to be. The National Army Museum confirms that the manual refers to a Lee Enfield type rifle in use from 1900 and narrows the date to 1907-1916. The ability to master and then to create a training manual on Musketry is yet another indication of his outstanding ability to master a subject.

An incident in a Kai Lung plot also reveals his link with military procedures. He was obviously familiar with the duty of an Orderly Officer and Sergeant visiting the other ranks' messes and calling for 'Any complaints':

> Those in authority over themselves, he added, were so solicitous to secure a life of luxurious ease for all within their charge that during every midday rice one of high standing passed among their ranks and besought that even if the lowliest should have any cause for dissatisfaction for complaint he would openly express it.

There is also a reference in a Max Carrados story to the deficiencies of musketry training in the British Army.

The spy mania that overtook so many civilians during the war came very close to Bramah when Maisie, walking alone on the Yorkshire Moors in 1917 was arrested as a suspected spy. It was said that she adopted a rakish style of dress and women on their own on the Moors at that time would have been a somewhat unusual sight. This might well have drawn the attention of the authorities to her. It took some effort by her Mother, (Ernest was away serving in the Royal Defence Corps) to convince the authorities that Maisie was the innocent victim of an over-enthusiastic official's attention.

What ever else Bramah was involved in during the wartime period there can be no doubt that his literary output continued along with his own and his agent Pinker's efforts to secure reprints of earlier books. A letter from George Allen & Unwin[10] expresses doubts about a hardback reprint of *The Wallet* because of the impending Methuen 7d edition, that is unless they could have the original printing plates and then 'although we doubt whether we should feel disposed to proceed except in conjunction with a new book by Mr. Bramah.'

An immediate post-war typescript[11] written in the euphoria of victory was 'Let money talk' which was an impassioned plea for issue of commemorative coinage as a tribute to the heroism of the armed forces. It brings together his patriotism and his interest in coins.

> An enduring memorial of the Great War is wanted – why not embody it in a commemorative issue of the coinage of the year succeeding the declaration of peace? In the ordinary course of things it would remain in circulation and act as a continual reminder and warning for about a generation as an enduring testimony it would stand as a record as long as the world lasts.

Pointing out that Ancient Rome understood the value of propaganda by this medium, he suggested a number of designs including the Battle of Jutland, women munitions workers and the execution of Nurse Edith Cavell.

The idea was never taken up. Perhaps this was because, in his enthusiasm for coins, he had not allowed for the fact that the general public, unlike collectors, does not study, even momentarily, the pictorial aspects of coins, except when they are very new. Thus as a memorial they would hardly have compared with The Cenotaph. The commemorative value would be very short-lived and, if the number of coins produced were great, it would have little collector value

After the war ended Bramah's stream of short stories and articles continued and there is ample evidence of this in such periodicals as *The Windsor Magazine, London Mercury, Living Age. The Story-Teller,*

Argus, Land and Water (later re-titled *The Field* and edited by the great Bramah enthusiast J. C. Squire) and other periodicals and newspapers.

'The dead march', a serious story of time travelling, was written in 1919, but was not published until 1924 in *The Specimen Case*.[12] It contains a reference to the heroic stand and retreat of the British Expeditionary Force at Mons and is a touching tribute to a bravely fought and lost battle.

Bramah was clearly sceptical about the peace process. In a story, 'The simple law',[13] written from the vantage point of 3001 and reviewing the past millennia he wrote:

> A Herr Bernhardi was in favour of a smoking hecatomb being made immediately of all weapons and armaments and the formation of a permanent Hague Conference which everyone in the world would be compulsorily bound to attend. But a Mr. Woodrow Wilson discredited this proposal by pointing out that every Hague Conference up to that time had not discussed peace but how to carry on War and thus brought it appreciably nearer. A universal peace gathering he therefore concluded would probably end in universal war.

Although neither the date nor publication is certain there is also a short series related by another storyteller – a Mr. Magg. He is more like W. W. Jacobs's night watchman than Kai Lung. Three stories exist 'When Mary went dead' 'Silas Parker and the penitent' and 'Treasure trove'. After these there is no further traces of Mr. Magg.

The demand for more stories was continuous and the *News of the World* was particularly pressing for more Max Carrados tales. Bramah, who was always reluctant to accept deadlines, refused to commit himself He wrote:[14]

> If I undertook a commission and especially if it was defined as to time the thing would be an incubus to me. As time went on I should be paralysed by the thought that I might not finish it within the date. Consequently I would finish it somehow, anyhow, and he [the editor] would be dissatisfied with the thing.

This ties in closely with the words he put into the mouth of a character in *The Optimist* written long before Bramah was a successful author, who says:

"I would never contract in advance to work, for that makes it necessary to write whether I feel like it or not sometimes, and means bad work, and I wouldn't have a fixed high price because that only tempts one to write too much and to rely on a large income; and I would never accept a commission for a story but always insist on sending them out on approval for then if they were bad they would be sent back and that would keep me up to the mark."[15]

In a letter to Grant Richards he admitted that he had never been in a hurry to publish anything and he did not think he had suffered as a result.

When the war ended in 1918 Bramah was fifty years old, an accepted author approaching the height of his success and clearly was carefully considering new plots for his old characters and new ideas for himself and the future direction of his work.

But the post-war world was not to be the land fit for heroes that had been promised and certainly no return to the summer of the Edwardian period; a break down of discipline among the impatient troops wishing to return to civilian life, followed by high unemployment and its inevitable concomitant bitter of strikes, rebellion in Ireland and the Asian flu epidemic killing swathes of people. This then was the new environment into which Bramah had to project his writing.

Sources & Notes

1   Ernest Bramah. *The Mirror of Kong Ho.* op. cit. pp.64-67.

2   Ernest Pugh. *A Book of Laughter.* Palmer & Hayward. London. 1916.

3   *Punch.* June 23rd 1915.

4   H.R.H.R.C. Typescript. op. cit. n.d.

5   ibid.

6   H.R.H.R.C. Typescript. op. cit.

7   *Punch.* August 14th 1915.

8   *Punch.* op. cit. August 25th 1915.

9   H.R.H.R.C. Manuscript. op. cit.

10 The Berg Collection of English and American Literature. February 25th 1915.

11 H.R.H.R.C. Typescript. op. cit.

12 Ernest Bramah. *The Specimen Case.* Hodder & Stoughton. London. 1924.

13 H.R.H.R.C. Typescript. op. cit.

14 Quoted by William Charlton. Introduction to *La Partie se joue dans le noir.* op. cit.

15 H.R.H.R.C. *The Optimist.* op. cit.

CHAPTER ELEVEN

THE CRAFTSMAN AT WORK

In the conditions that prevailed Bramah may well have felt that Pinker was not producing the results he desired. Thus three years after the war had ended Bramah terminated the agreement with Pinker who had represented him for more than twenty years. True to Bramah's nature the break was made in the most restrained and courteous terms:

> Your reference to the time over which our transactions has carried (not either many or as extensive as you say, and, I must add, alas, now, I am conscious, very profitable to you) strikes a sympathetic chord. If you carry your mind back to so trivial an incident twenty years ago, you might remember that when I first saw you in connection with [a] literary agency I wished (having already published two books,) to restrict it to short stories, etc., and to serial-rights generally: but you pointed out to me that as this was the more troublesome and unremunerative part of the business it would put you at a disadvantage, and to the justice of this I acquiesced ...I have now to see to the troublesome and unremunerative details justice seems to require that the books (if any) should come my way also...If however (as would seem to be the case from your now returning the MSS), you think it more convenient to end it [the contract] now by mutual consent, this will be equally agreeable to me if you will send me a line to that effect.[1]

The contract with Pinker only had a year to run but it would seem that Bramah was anxious to appoint the equally formidable A. P. Watt agency for his books and journalism. Bramah had of course known Watt in his Editorial capacity at *To-day*, *The London Handbook* and *The London Year Book* and was doubtless impressed by his negotiating skills, acumen and client list which included Rider Haggard, Rudyard Kipling, Thomas Hardy and Algernon Blackwood. As events turned out the relationship was a happy one over the years and Watt's youngest son, Peter, was the somewhat surprising recipient of the Bramah copyrights under Maisie's Will.

There might have been reconciliation with the Pinker agency when, after J. B. Pinker died in 1922, his son took over the business. The agency was still offering Bramah's writings and received their share of royalties until at least 1929. It was perhaps as well that Bramah had, by then, changed his agent to A. P. Watt since the Pinker organisation crashed during the 1930s taking with it many authors' royalties.

Bramah published no books between 1914 and 1922, but three books – *The Wallet of Kai Lung*, *The Secret of the League* and *Max Carrados* – were all well-established, bringing in substantial royalties. There had been nine printings of *The Wallet*, three of *What Might Have Been* and two of *Max Carrados*.

He was indisputably successful with his short stories and features, four of which were published in *Land and Water* between March and August 1919. Among these was 'Smothered in corpses' which was also included in *The Specimen Case* anthology in 1924 and was re-written as a one-act play much favoured by amateur theatrical companies. It is pure nonsense of the very best sort and he partly parodies his own Max Carrados stories. The plot bubbles with Bramah humour but it was of the same type that was to be later criticised in his full-length novel *A Little Flutter*. The critics, if not the readers, preferred irony and wit to slapstick. '...a driver wearing a crimson opera hat that being the badge of the male member of our society'... . 'There was only one possible place of concealment there. I snatched the coverlet that hid the stark outline on the dissecting table. Imagine my surprise to see before me the corpse of the elderly Italian anarchist who had offered me a throat pastille on the grand-stand at Hurlingham a month ago.'

'Smothered in corpses' was prefaced with a statement by Bramah that the original, almost completed work, was 120,000 words and that he had reduced it to one-thirtieth for the article. It must be presumed he was joking but with Bramah it is hard to be sure because there is evidence of him scaling down larger works. William Charlton discovered that 'The Emperor who meant well' was condensed to less than 6,000 words from 'The Romance of Kwang the fruit gatherer' which ran to 13,500 words. Charlton is of the opinion that the longer version was never published since in a letter to Pinker[2] Bramah tells him to put the manuscript on the fire and replace it with 'The romance of Kwang the fruit gatherer'.

It is doubtful if the increased income that Bramah was now receiving was the reason for no longer writing books. A contributing factor may have been that the public's reading tastes had changed during the rigours of the war. A best seller during the war was H. G. Wells's *Mr. Britling Sees it Through* and no writer of humorous fiction appears among the most popular titles.

As early as 1901 Bramah was writing to a correspondent, a Mr. Charles Gatley,[3]

> ...Richards has spoken to me once or twice e.g. another series
> of Chinese stories, but I do not think that I shall be able to get
> these together before next spring–possibly autumn.

How wrong he was. More than two decades were to pass before Kai Lung again appeared in a book. Grant Richards had been writing to Bramah at least twice a year for a follow up to *The Wallet*. In 1921 he was replying to Richards using his work on his coinage as an excuse for delay.[4]

> I am writing to you first, not because I think you the likeliest
> publisher to consider it, [English Regal Copper Coins] but because
> you were good enough to write to me about a second Kai Lung
> book, and as that has necessarily hung up for some time, this
> will explain to you the reason.

The following year he wrote:[5]

In the meanwhile, with his [Richards] interest in Kai Lung unshaken, in spite of the unsatisfactory results of that wandering minstrel's first appearance, Mr. Richards never ceased to press me for a successor. On average he wrote to me twice a year on the subject. But it was not until last year [1921] that I began to see before me something like sufficient material for a second volume.

By 1922 *The Wallet,* despite its inauspicious start, had been in print for twenty-two years. This doubtless was part of Richards's motivation in seeking to persuade Bramah to write another series about his Chinese 'incapable relater of imagined tales'. It was nearly ten years after his previous book, *Max Carrados,* before it appeared.

♦

China was again attracting attention when the second Kai Lung book finally appeared. An agreement had been reached by the major powers for securing China's independence and maintaining an open door for trade. Sun Yat Sen launched a military attack on the government and the Chinese Communist party was formed. All this was a long way from the mystical land that Kai Lung inhabited.

The new book, *Kai Lung's Golden Hours,* was described as a model of the storyteller's art. Hilaire Belloc, provided the Introduction, in which he declared it to be worthy of its predecessor. 'There is the same plan,' Belloc wrote,[6] 'exactitude, working-out and achievement; and therefore the same complete satisfaction in reading, or to be more accurate, in the incorporation of the work with one-self.'

Bramah had again created an almost hypnotic atmosphere capable of persuading the reader that he or she is a temporary inhabitant of the world being described, however remote in time and space that world was from the reader's own experience. The *Golden Hours* shows clearly that it was not necessary to have travelled to China or to learn the language. His time was better spent developing his unique style. The book demonstrated yet again Bramah's great talent, his observing with an artistic sympathy, his painstaking work and his inventive powers.

Perhaps reflecting on the slow appreciation of *The Wallet* or anticipating no great rush to purchase the new offering Belloc continued;

In the best of times (the most stable, the least hurried) the date at which general appreciation comes is a matter of chance, and today the presentation of any achieved work is like the reading of Keats to a football crowd. It is of no significance whatsoever to English letters whether one of its glories be appreciated at the moment it issues from the press or ten years later or twenty or fifty. Further, after a very small margin is passed, a margin of a few hundred at the most, it matters little whether strong permanent work finds a thousand or fifty thousand or a million readers. Rock stands, mud washes away.[7]

The most telling factor of all is that the *Golden Hours* was Bramah's own favourite in the Kai Lung series. He had taken a great deal of trouble in deciding, with Richards, on a title. Some fifteen ideas were considered including 'Deeper into the Wallet of Kai Lung' and 'The Obsequious Kai Lung' and 'The Golden Hours of Kai Lung' before settling on *Kai Lung's Golden Hours*.

The *Golden Hours* is the book from which enthusiasts quote most frequently and which, unlike the previous book, is a single narrative which follows the Scherharazade concept of postponing punishment by a series of stories. Kai Lung is imprisoned by the Mandarin Shan Tien and escapes torture and death time after time by diverting the Mandarin with a tale.

The book opens explosively with one of Bramah's best jokes. Waking from sleep in a wood Kai Lung sees two maidens approaching.

> Kai Lung rose guardedly to his feet, with many gestures of polite assurance and having bowed several times to indicate his pacific nature, he stood in an attitude of deferential admiration. At this display the elder and less attractive of the maidens fled, uttering loud and continuous cries of apprehension in order to conceal the direction of her flight.

The tales include the one that is generally regarded as the finest in the Kai Lung chronicles. This is 'The story of Wong Ts'in and the willow plate embellishment'.

For the millions of owners of articles, mostly pottery, displaying

133

versions of the Willow pattern this narration placed a new and comical light on the meaning of the design which, by the way, is as authentic as Kai Lung himself. Although based on Chinese patterns in fact it was designed in Shropshire in 1779 by Thomas Turner.

The generally accepted interpretation of the pattern is one derived from a story that appeared in *Family Friend*[8] in 1841 by an unknown author and is a sad tale of thwarted love and death. Bramah's version is a hilarious satire, far divorced from the original that was not, of course, Chinese either.

The narrative tells how the hero by accidentally sitting on the still wet and unfired piece of pottery and then on an undecorated piece transferred the design and thus discovered a method of mass production, although it was to be many centuries before it was appreciated it was not actually necessary to sit on each plate to transfer a design. (Charles Lamb's roast pig again where the peasant found it was not actually necessary to burn down his hut in order to savour the delicacy.) For the pattern itself Bramah dispensed with the Turner version, which included a pair of lovers transformed into swallows, in favour of a very modern interpretation.

> The pagoda-like building on the right is that erected by this person's venerated father, its prosperity indicated by the luxurious profusion of fruit-trees overhanging it. Pressed somewhat to the back but of dignified proportion, are the outer buildings of those who labour among us.... The three stunted individuals crossing the bridge in undignified attitudes are the debased Fang and two of his mercenary accomplices. They are as usual bending their footsteps in the direction of the hospitality of a house that announces its purpose beneath the sign of a spreading bush. They are positioned as crossing the river to a set purpose, the bridge is devoid of a rail in the hope that on their return they may fall into the torrent in a helpless condition and be drowned, to the satisfaction of the beholders.

The three men on the bridge are shop stewards in the Bound-together Brotherhood of Colour-mixers and Putters-on of Thought-out Designs seeking a closed shop in a passage already quoted. The discussion continues "...in place of one tael every man among us shall now take two and he who before laboured eight gongs to receive it shall henceforth labour for four."

Later, their demands having been refused, they form a picket line.

> Thenceforth these men, providing themselves with knives and axes, surrounded the gate of the earth-yards and by the pacific argument of their attitudes they succeeded in persuading others who would willingly have continued at their tasks that the air of Wong Ts'in's sheds was not congenial to their health'.

Anyone seeking to pass through the picket was a 'dark leg'.

The ten tales that comprise *The Golden Hours* include the memorable one of Hien who fails the literary examinations eleven times running, and of his rival Tsin Lung, whose livelihood comes from:

> printing out the more difficult Classics in minute characters upon parchment so small that an entire library could be concealed among the folds of a garment, in this painstaking way enabling many persons who might otherwise have failed at the public examinations...to pass with honourable distinction to themselves and widespread credit to his resourceful system.

♦

John Connell[9] perceived in the first Kai Lung book, a macabre, almost angry, streak in its author most particularly in one tale of treachery and betrayal, 'The vengeance of Tung Fel'. Connell draws attention to the haunted if muted sadness which is frequently recognisable through all the fun and wit. The older Bramah in *The Golden Hours* and the subsequent Kai Lung books was far more genial and tolerant and the few darker passages were there for 'decorative contrast' and were not a fundamental part of the tale to be told. An unnamed reviewer asserted, '...reading Mr. Bramah still yields more pleasure than 20 solemn books about politics and industry in the emerging Orient.'

It would perhaps be going too far to call the stories moral but, as in all good fairy stories, the righteous as personified by Kai Lung, invariably triumph and the wrongdoer is defeated. As Bernard Levin emphasised in his article,[10] the plots have a mock cynicism woven into them and the wit hides the barbs but does not blunt them.

Levin's enthusiasm was matched by one American critic, Mary Siegrist who in the *New York Times Book Review* wrote of 'seasoned utterances and artistic achievement', 'sustained humour', 'sparkling irony' 'as smoothly finished as polished jade' 'hall mark of genius' then, perhaps fearing all this might sound over-enthusiastic states 'All this seems to be out-blurbing the blurb. And yet it is not much to say about this book...'[11]

The *Golden Hours*, unlike *The Wallet* was an immediate success and is still far from forgotten. It rapidly went to three impressions within a year, each one over 2,000 copies. Over time, there were some six Editions by different publishers. At least half of the stories were reprinted in different magazines including The *London Mercury*, and *Argos* and many were widely anthologised. As late as 2004 one tale – the famous Willow Pattern Embellishment was chosen for inclusion in a Portuguese translation of an anthology of British short stories.

Again there is evidence of Bramah's re-use of material. 'The story of Wang Ho and the burial robe' had appeared in *The London Mercury* in 1920 and was then anthologised in *The Best Short Stories of 1928*.

Nine years after publication the male students of the Old Vic presented in London and Glasgow a programme entitled *Kai Lung's Golden Hours* which comprised one story – an adaptation of the Willow Plate Pattern. The dramatisation was by Allan D. Mainds and had Bramah's approval. The play appears to have comprised Chapters One, Two and Twelve of the original book. Richards, who attended, did not think a great deal of it. He felt the adapter realised less than twenty per cent of the essence of Kai Lung on the stage.[12] 'I prefer my Kai Lung within the pages of a book' he wrote. The adaptation substitutes 'The Property Man' played by Richard Riddle, a son of the great Shakespearean actor Henry Ainley, for Kai Lung in a Chorus role and provides continuity for the action but frequently speaking Kai Lung's words.

The Property Man exclaims: "Wei Chang, with protests that it was scarcely becoming to sit repeatedly in her presence nevertheless complies, and upon her further insistence impresses himself upon a succession of plates." This is almost word for word of Kai Lung's narrative but there are differences from the book. In the book Fang, the militant worker, while in a drunken sleep beside the river over which the willow pattern bridge crosses is pushed into it by 'a devout ox, an instrument of high destinies' and perishes. In the play his end is a grisly decapitation with his severed head displayed in a basket by the Property Man.

♦

Given the triumph of the reappearance of Kai Lung, Bramah decided, to revive his other successful character, Max Carrados. It would have been unlikely, given his slow rate of composition, that he could have produced another book so soon after the *Golden Hours*. Both the *Golden Hours* and *The Eyes of Max Carrados* must have been in preparation during the previous decade and indeed some of the stories had been previously published in newspapers and periodicals.

There is no doubt Bramah had spent the intervening period between books writing large numbers of articles and stories. It is unfortunate that not one of the many extant drafts carry either a date or, even more regrettably, any indication if they were ever published. Thus it can only be speculation that free-lance writing and the writing of the next adventures of Max Carrados largely occupied the long period between books. Thus, just as there had been a gap of many years between the two Kai Lung books, despite the very favourable reception of *Max Carrados* it was to be another ten years before the second Max Carrados book appeared in 1923.

On February 6th 1923 Grant Richards[13] wrote to Bramah that he very much wanted to publish the new Max Carrados book. His reader had expressed great enthusiasm.

> They [the stories] seem to me to be on a very much higher plane than Sherlock Holmes stories – much more ingenious and infinitely better written. I can say no more save that if the manuscript had been sent to me as that of an unknown writer I should have urged publication.

The Eyes of Max Carrados[14] was the new book – a title that seems to have been decided almost casually. In a letter to Grant Richards on May 12th 1923 six titles were suggested. The one Bramah preferred 'Call in Max Carrados' was rejected.

Richards felt that a newcomer to the stories would need an explanation about Carrados, his history and his entourage. Bramah disagreed and believed Richards's point could be met by including the first story from the previous book. Richards did not like this idea and suggested instead that rather than ask Methuen's permission to reprint the first tale that there might be a description of some of the actual achievements of the blind. Clearly this idea appealed to Bramah. The result was the long and meticulously researched Introduction that has already been quoted extensively in Chapter Nine in explaining the structure of the first Max Carrados book.

Aside from the Introduction, one story, 'The Eastern mystery', provides Carrados with the opportunity to claim the superiority of the blind over the sighted. He says to a man he is trying to help "If you were blind it would be all right, but your credulous, self-opinionated eyes will lead you into further trouble."

However, it was felt that new readers could not just 'begin here'. There had to be some concession. Bramah realised the dilemma and solved it with a paralipsis explaining, with his usual irony, what it was he could not set out for anyone coming to Carrados for the first time. This stretched to four and half pages!

There was some speculation as to whether one tale 'The Kingsmouth spy case' should be included. The decision was left to Richards who decided in favour of leaving it in. Bramah wrote on April 27th 1923:[15] 'Thanks for deciding about the Spy story. It occurred to me afterwards that it was too bad to put this off on you, but that's done now.' Just why Bramah had reservations about its inclusion is not clear. Even allowing for the five years since the armistice making a suspected spy a German and the real spy French could hardly be attributed to what now would be called political correctness – a credo which not even his most severe critic would ever accuse Bramah of encouraging.

The story had first appeared in *The News of the World*, under the title 'The Kingsmouth German spy case' so it might have been Richards who had the reservations about the title. There is always the possibility that the purist in Bramah may have raised doubts about the quality of the tale. It does appear to have some loose ends and it is one of those where, to many, the story lacks credibility. A reader, not wholly convinced of Carrados's powers, could lose patience. Some of Carrados's feats in this book surpass many of the documented ones in the Introduction and thus perhaps some conviction is lost. Successfully shooting an attacker by firing at the source of the sound of a single word is, for some readers, stretching believability in the uncanny skills of the blind too far. Bramah's enthusiasm, but somewhat limited knowledge of chemistry, led him to introduce into the stories non-existent substances that affronted some purists. In 'The mystery of the poisoned dish of mushrooms' there is a fictional poison called Bhurine, found in an equally fictional mushroom called Amanita Bhuroides. For the sake of verisimilitude Bramah refers to this mushroom as having many of the characteristics of Agaricus Campestris which is the common mushroom. Another plot includes an anaesthetic that is as unreal as his mushroom.

The plot does however include another remarkable piece of Bramah prescience. He equips his torpedo with a direction-finding system. Unlike conventional torpedoes of the time that only moved in the direction they were aimed, his torpedoes had a device that enabled them to home in on targets.

As with the situation of John Hamden in *The Secret of the League*, the issue of honour versus duty again arises. In 'The Kingsmouth spy case' Mr. Hosier, a curate, has been told in confidence by a dying woman about the theft of the plans of the new torpedo. He refuses to divulge the information.

"You are an Englishman, Mr. Hosier, and you know what this might mean in a conflict – you know that one of our most formidable weapons has been annexed."

"My dear Sir!" rapped out the distressed curate. "Don't you think that I haven't worried about that? But behind the Englishman stands something more primitive, more just – the man. I gave assurance as a man, and the Admiralty can go hang."

For Bramah this ethical conflict between patriotism and honour must have been a formidable paradox to resolve – but honour won however uncomfortable such a decision might have been.

◆

The reviews of the book were mixed. The unnamed critic in *The Spectator*[16] believed that:

> Some of the mysteries and their solutions are a little too incredible. Mr. Carrados is more than once a little too clever to carry belief and there is an absence of psychology and characterisation due to the author's preoccupation with his plots rather than with his people.

He, or she, concludes that those who were delighted with the Kai Lung books would most likely find the book disappointing

Nevertheless, and much to Bramah's and the publisher's relief, despite this type of less-than-favourable criticism, the book was well received by the public even though it is generally accepted that there is some unevenness in the stories. This stems from the cross-genre nature of the book including, as it does, supernatural and science fiction along with the detection elements. This mixture may well not have been acceptable to the enthusiasts for the individual genre. Indeed E. F. Bleiler, the expert on detective fiction, considered that invoking of the supernatural violates the essence of a detective story and the Dorothy L. Sayers rule of 'fair play'.

The Eyes of Max Carrados contains perhaps the two most anthologised of all Bramah's stories 'The ghost at Massingham Mansions', and 'The disappearance of Marie Severe'. In the first of these there is a trace of autobiographical material in that the Massingham Mansions topography is similar, if not identical, to Ravenscourt Mansions where Bramah was living at the time he was writing the book. The second story was described in *Twentieth-Century Literary Criticism* as 'not only an excellent puzzle but its motivation, besides being plausible, seems distinctly novel'.[17]

There is also a personal aspect to this particular story. Maisie had become interested in a movement called The Science of Thought that was closely aligned with Christian Science. Maisie's enthusiasm for the Movement was such that she offered to pay for her nephew, John, to attend their school. In the story Bramah makes a bitter attack on Christian Science which implies that he disapproved of his wife's adherence to the movement.

'The ingenious Mr. Spinola' is one of the plots which perhaps sits uncomfortably, between science fiction and the supernatural. It concerns an automatic card-player that could apparently out-play the most skilled players and which was operated by a calculating machine similar to the one designed by Charles Babbage very many years prior to the time in which the narrative is set. However the dénouement is that Mr. Spinola, who claims to be more than 100 years old is mad and believes himself to be Charles Babbage who was born in 1792 and whose analytical engine was never completed. It is also possible to interpret the ending in a different way. Spinola *was* Charles Babbage and Bramah was adopting a super-natural conclusion to his story by resurrecting Babbage.

More interestingly Bramah was prepared to poke fun at his own editorial skills.

> Does anyone read the old-fashioned unpretentious Guide-Book to London still? One would hardly think so to see how the subject is cut up. We have 'Famous London Blind-Alleys'. 'Historical West-Central Door-Knockers', 'Footsteps of Dr. Johnson between Gough Square and John Street', 'Adelphi', 'The Thames from Hungerford Bridge to Charing Cross Pier', 'Oxford Street Paving Stones on which De Quincey sat' and so on.

None of these nonsensical subjects are that far away from some of the features in both *The London Handbook* and *The London Year Book* which Bramah had edited and for which he commissioned articles and stories. Compare them with 'Latter day palaces', 'London outlets', 'Amaryllis in town' 'Spring in the Strand'.

There is an interesting parallel between the story 'The Eastern mystery' and what is perhaps the best known tale of his contemporary, W. W. Jacobs, 'The monkey's paw', published some twenty years earlier. Both stories have an amulet, and both from India. In the Jacobs's tale it is a monkey's paw while in the Carrados plot a monkey's tooth which in the end turns out to be a nail from the Cross. Bramah's amulet with such divine antecedents protects its owner from harm and saves its unwitting possessor from assassination, a road accident and a gas explosion. All this is quite unlike 'The monkey's paw' that wreaks havoc on its unthinking owners.

Clearly Bramah was not wholly happy with the book despite its success. In a letter to an unknown recipient,[18] he stated that in choosing one of his books to send to someone 'it certainly would not be *The Eyes of Max Carrados*'. Whatever his reservations were, stories from the book were highly praised and widely reprinted in periodicals and anthologised.

Despite strong competition in fiction in 1924 – Dorothy L. Sayers *Whose Body?* and Arnold Bennett's *Riceyman Steps* – the first edition of *The Eyes of Max Carrados* was quickly sold and second printing followed immediately. A year later it was published in New York by George H. Doran and the accolade of success was the inclusion in the Penguin Books catalogue in 1940 – fortunately before paper rationing had really impacted on the printers. Thirty-three years later, in 1973 another reprint was issued by Lythway Press,[19] which unlike the other editions had an illustration of Carrados on the cover.

◆

In 1926 Bramah's financial position again improved through the unfortunate death of his sister, Rose. She had been left an annual income through a trust set up by Charles Clement for both his wife and for Rose. His wife, Susannah, having pre-deceased him, the monies went entirely to Rose and on her death reverted to Emily Jane and Ernest. It is certain that in such a close family he would have happily forgone the additional capital given the circumstances under which it came to him.

This improvement in his financial position may well have influenced him not to start another book immediately, Bramah decided the time had come for what might be termed a 'retrospective'. There were two reasons for this. First the desire to exploit his earlier work many of which would not have been seen by his public as they were written or published before he had achieved his fame and success as a writer. But there was another reason. He wanted a single author anthology that contained a mixture of stories in a number of genres, but most particularly he wanted Kai Lung and Max Carrados between the same covers. This was to dispel a damaging myth that had been circulating and which, according to Bramah, was originated by the critic Edward Shanks and circulated by Rose Macaulay.[20]

Sources & Notes

1   H.R.H.R.C. op. cit. June 14th 1905.

2   Rare Book & Special Collections Library. University of Illinois, Urbana. op. cit. June 14th 1905.

3   H.R.H.R.C. September 19th 1901.

4   H.R.H.R.C. op. cit. April 18th 1921.

5   Quoted by Grant Richards in *Author Hunting*. op. cit. p.ix.

6   Ernest Bramah. *Kai Lung's Golden Hour*. Grant Richards. London. 1922. Introduction by Hilaire Belloc. op. cit. p.4.

7   ibid.

8   *Family Friend*. London. 1849. Reprinted by De la More Press. London. 1957.

9   John Connell. 'The recluse who created Kai Lung'. op. cit.

10 Bernard Levin. 'Wanted some impeccable tales of Kai Lung'. op. cit.

11 Quoted in *Contemporary Authors*. Vol. 156. op. cit. p.44.

12 Grant Richards. *Author Hunting*. op. cit. p.273.

13 H.R.H.R.C. op. cit. February 6th 1923.

14 Ernest Bramah. *The Eyes of Max Carrados*. Grant Richards. London. 1923.

15 H.R.H.R.C. op. cit. 27th April 1923.

16 *The Spectator*. February 20th 1923.

17 *Twentieth-Century Literary Criticism*. op. cit. Vol. 72. p.6.

18 H.R.H.R.C. op. cit. September 26th 1931.

19 Lythway Press. Bath. 1973.

20 Ernest Bramah. *The Specimen Case.* op. cit. p.18. Also Edward Shanks.
    'The Chinese Humorist'. *The Queen.* October 4th 1922.

CHAPTER TWELVE

"REMEMBER THE MAN WITH THE HOE"

Bramah was well aware that his avoidance of any personal publicity had shrouded him in mystery – something that he found amusing. There had been much controversy in literary circles as to whether Bramah was the author of two such different genres as Kai Lung and Max Carrados. There was even the suggestion that all the Bramah books were by a syndicate of authors perpetrating a literary hoax. In the Preface to his next book, *The Specimen Case* Bramah mockingly refers to the mystery he had created about himself by his aloofness from the literary scene and from shunning all personal publicity. He writes:[1]

> Turn to "N.G.R-S." [letter]in the *Westminster Gazette*. "He [Grant Richards] assures us that there is such a person as Ernest Bramah. Well, there may be! I myself still believe ...(This break does not represent omitted matter, but N.G.R.-S.'s too-sinister-for-words private belief). Anyway you can now buy *The Wallet* for seven-and sixpence and form your own opinion of the reasons which keep the author of such a book so closely mysterious behind his unusual name." ..."N.G.R.-S." surrounds his innuendo with a compliment. Miss [Rose] Macaulay wraps up hers in – well, in something quite different: "The crude, stilted, Conan Doyleish English of his detective stories certainly goes far to bear out the common theory that Mr. Bramah has a literary dual personality."

He ends:[2]

> Apparently, for me there is no simple middle way, no sheltered, obvious path. Either I am to have no existence, or it must be that questionable thing, a double life. I doubt if I am even given the choice. But there is one thing that I still can do and thus confound the non-existers and dualists alike – I can produce both a "Kai Lung" and a "Max Carrados" between one pair of covers and here they are.

Three books in three years would seem to be quite out of keeping with Bramah's normal rate of writing. While the previous two in 1922 and 1923 were probably gestating for some ten years *The Specimen Case*[3] required very little preparation as all the stories had appeared previously in books, periodicals and newspapers. In Bramah's own words:[4]

> It is not…intended essentially as a collection of quite the best stories I might perhaps have chosen, nor is it, I am more than sure, a collection of anything like the worst; it consists rather of a characteristic example taken at convenient intervals over the whole time that I have been engaged in writing stories – a span of some 30 years.

The Specimen Case contains one Kai Lung and one Max Carrados story as some sort of proof that Bramah was the creator of both, although any cynic might well have considered the whole book could still be the work of more than one author. The collection covers a span of thirty years, the oldest pieces dating back as far as 1894. Oddly enough the stories are in reverse date order of their being written, not necessarily published. Thus, far from seeing how the author's writing and style had developed, it is necessary to view his output backward and perhaps judge if the later work is significantly better or worse than the early writings. Just why he chose to present his work backwards is an enigma although as he points out in the Preface '…you may estimate your author's progress – and progress along a road, it may be seemly to premise, can be implied in more than one direction'. Thus he did not rule out, although he did not expect, that some readers might think his early work was better than his later tales.

Some critics have written that the juxtaposition in the book of the Chinese style narrative, 'Ming Tseu and the emergency' with the Max Carrados story 'A bunch of violets' shows the superiority of the former. It might well be the nature of the two stories rather than that of the whole canon but there are enthusiasts who would argue the opposite; the Max Carrados books display a technical proficiency and writing skill of a higher order than Kai Lung.

In writing the Preface to *The Specimen Case* Bramah might well have introduced, perhaps unconsciously, an autobiographical element. Half the Preface is taken up with a description of a conversation with a highly successful author of 'pretty hopeless tripe' he called Melwish. Visiting his apartment he notices a hideous inkwell engraved with the words 'Remember the man with the hoe'. Melwish explains he owes every ounce of success to the stand which he regards as an 'eyesore in a pig-sty' and an 'incredible abortion'. "I've used that metallurgical atrocity for nearly twenty years, four days a week, six hours a day..." He then reveals the secret of the inscription. This explanation is a moral tale of how Melwish retired to the country to write his masterpiece. He watched a simple farm labourer with a hoe thinning a line of turnips and taking out the most flourishing and tallest plant.

> " 'Why man alive!' I said, 'you've done for the most promising of the lot.' " 'Yes,' he replied – I won't attempt the barbarous idiom: I never trouble about dialects myself – 'it was a likely enough young turnip, but don't you see, master, it was out of line with the rest? Even if it didn't get cut off by hand among the weeds one time or another, the horse-hoe would be bound to finish it when once it came along.' And then, B., the hob-nailed philosopher uttered this profound truth: 'An ordinary plant where it's wanted has more chance of coming to something than a giant where it isn't.'

> "I walked on with my ideas suddenly brought out into the clear light of day, and perhaps for the first time in my life I really set before my sober judgement a definition of what I wanted

to do and what were the chances of ever doing it... . After dinner I burned the manuscript of the masterpiece so far as I had written, with all the notes and jottings I had made. Then I sat down to write a short story for the magazines."

Melwish urges Bramah to "think it over and remember the man with the hoe". Could this then be the book in which Bramah does remember the man with the hoe and he is offering his short stories in place of some unaccomplished masterpiece he hoped to write one day? Certainly these stories are all 'ordinary plants where they are wanted'. Would the world have seen the later Kai Lungs and Max Carrados if he had been engaged on some more exalted enterprise? This is something else that will never be known.

The first edition of *The Specimen Case* has the title of the book and the author's name stamped into the cover in relief as if the lettering formed by the raised areas was designed to be read by Carrados himself.

Melwish's comment that "I never trouble about dialects myself" might well have referred to Bramah's own view of using foreign dialects. Most of his characters do not have any identifiable accents. His German airship crews in 'The war hawks' manage only one "ach" in their otherwise fluent English. Lizzie Simpson a waitress speaks grammatically and with no perceptible accent and of course Kai Lung's English is impeccable. American accents, when they occur, are mostly travesties of the way Americans speak. In 'Hautepierre's star' he does not even attempt to give French accents to the characters.

However, closer to home, Bramah was perfectly capable of representing dialogue. The conversations of his country characters can be compared favourably with Hardy. Bramah's time as a farmer made him familiar with bucolic accents as is evident in his book *English Farming*, "I dunno know what things be a' comin' to, Marster. ... It ain't enough Marster, whatever it be."

His use of a Cockney idiom was as good as Jacobs', Barry Pain's or Arthur Morrison's. This is Jacobs's Nighwatchman. "They 'ad a pint each to 'elp them to fink wot was to be done. And, arter a lot o' talking and quarrelling, they did wot a lot of uver people 'ave done when they got inter trouble: they come to me." And this is Bramah's William Grice. "Wha'd d'yer expect me 'ands to be when I've been art o work these

six monfs?…Don't be 'ard on me, laidy, sein as I'm dahn and 'elpless"
in *Behind the Wall* which is as good a Cockney representation of the
period as Jacobs's whose use of the Cockney idiom was said to be
phenomenally accurate.

Other accents proved more challenging for him, perhaps because
of a lack of exposure to them. His Scottish dialogue appears a little
strained. In 'Fergurson' he has him declaim "Aa went back and leestened
to a' the fulihsness recht to the end. Then in the dark I just slippit
under the seat and, after bidin' there a wee bit hour twa, aa comes oot
unpairceeved an saw it a' over again for naething."[5] Mr. Tubes Secretary
of State for the Home Department in *The Secret of the League*, manages
a few north-country 'Kumred's [Comrades] but then drops back into
the same accent as the aristocratic Sir John Hampden.

Like his previous books *The Specimen Case* was extravagantly praised,
mildly criticised by some reviewers and ignored by others. The most
effusive review came from *The New York Times Book Review* in May
1925 – 'A very interesting volume…, on its own account, as well as
through its connections with other much-praised work by its notable
author… . The very dextrous, entertaining manipulation of characters
and events one expects to find in a Kai Lung story are all here… . They
are both [Kai Lung and Max Carrados stories] in their unlike ways,
altogether satisfying.'

Less flattering were the comments of the reviewer in *The Times Literary
Supplement*[6]

> Pleasant as they [the stories] are, they come as a disappointment
> from the author of 'The Wallet of Kai Lung'… . They are all
> competently written – one or two with distinction – but the
> themes are for the most part either melodramatic or flimsy

Was there an another Bramah book written about 1924 that has
been lost and which would have been his eighth? Grant Richards in a
letter dated April 24th 1924[7] refers to returning a typescript for a book
called *Sir or Madam* because Bramah's agent, presumably Watt, was asking
what Richards regarded as an excessive advance payment and gave him
no interest in the American rights. As Richards had been largely
responsible for selling other American rights he felt, justifiably, that

he was being treated unfairly. There is no trace of the book among the Bramah papers.

♦

In April 1924 Richards is writing to Bramah '…In regard to the "Kai Lung" books, and particularly in your treatment of me for years in the question of the Wallet, you have been the soul of generosity.'[8] But this 'generosity' was to be severely tested. Disastrously, a few weeks later the rapport and amicability that existed between Richards and Bramah was suddenly ruptured. Richards, not for the first time as he was declared bankrupt in 1905, had again run into financial difficulties. In a handwritten letter dated July 6th 1924[9] Richards seeks Bramah's understanding but ends with a threat. Later in the correspondence the 'My dear Smith' changed to 'Dear Smith' perhaps indicative of the changed relationship.

My dear Smith

A month ago – more really – a large sum on which I thought I had the right to count for that particular period failed to arrive. This upset my plans and arrangements and although every day, so to speak, I have been hoping to come to an end of the delay. I am in the position still of having to be patient. May I ask you to be patient a little longer too? I am very sorry to ask it.

And then in a PS the threat.

It would of course prejudice the matter rather if you had anyone else collect your account until this sum is out of the way but I must leave that to your good will.

The financial problem was not resolved and Richards's business was reconstructed as The Richards Press with a new Board. Richards remained with the company although no longer owning it. He made strenuous efforts to ensure the new firm met its commitments to the authors.
On November 2nd 1926 he wrote to Bramah:[10]

Dear Smith

...Some time ago, before these troubles – and I do, believe me, hope that they may be arranged so that you will not suffer...I feel it would be a feather in my cap to have, under the reconstruction of the business, a book of yours.

Although Bramah was not a man to hold grudges, judging by a letter from Richards it would seem, not surprisingly, that the warmth had gone out of the relationship. He was clearly trying to heal the breach both from a personal and business point of view. He writes to Bramah on May 5th 1928[11]

Dear Mr. Smith [sic]

If, in spite of all the trouble that I have given you, you feel that our association, so happy for me from one point of view, should so suddenly be cut off, especially now, when I gather from a review that Kai Lung will tell stories no more – if, I say, you have any goodwill left to me, then you will make me an inscribed copy of "Kai Lung Unrolls his Mat". Our names have appeared so often on the title page that I have a great wish that they should appear together on the title of his last book.

Bramah relented. A few days later Richards received the copy he asked for duly inscribed. He acknowledged it on May 9th 1928 with a self-justifying explanation of what had been happening.[12]

Dear Bramah Smith [sic]...I do not think that if you had known how hard I worked to secure that neither you nor any other authors lost by the failure of Grant Richards you would [not] feel so angry with me. One of the things that I was assured by Sir Joseph Dobbie and his associates as an inducement to go on with the new business was that the authors at least would be properly dealt with. I strove hard, as My.(?) Field Roseve[?] & Co [probably Richards's solicitors or accountants]could tell you, to secure this. The fact that the authors were not to be considered was the first of a series of differences, and perhaps the most important, that ultimately decided me to resign.

All that exists is one side of the correspondence and from reading this it can be deduced that Bramah was not placated. It is doubtful if he ever did get his royalties. Grant Richards, who was a man of good faith, resigned from the company 'owing to differences of opinion which are clearly irreconcilable'. The firm eventually collapsed. He complained of 'complete subordination to a Board whose literary and publishing experience is necessarily very much inferior to my own'.[13]

◆

By 1929 Richards was back in business again and asking if a previous attempt to get Chapman and Hall to release their rights in *Kong Ho* in his favour could be revived and he gave assurances '…and that should it chance that any ill fate should come upon the house, all rights in the book would more or less automatically revert to you.'[14] He succeeded in obtaining the rights to reprint for the new partnership with H. Toumlin under the imprimatur of Cayme Press with editions both in 1928 and 1929. This indicates an impressive reversal of his views since he turned down the original manuscript two decades earlier.

By 1933 the relationship was sufficiently thawed for Richards, now embarked on the second volume of his memoirs *Author Hunting,* to write to Bramah that he will be saying something about him and the Kai Lung books and asks permission to reproduce an autographed photograph he had given him.[15] As it was used it can be deduced that Bramah agreed despite his reluctance to do anything which might threaten his privacy.

Richards comments to Bramah that his Preface for the 1936 edition of *The Wallet* had been omitted from some later edition and questions Bramah's role in this decision. Again, from one side of the correspondence, it can be seen that Bramah was not responsible for the omissions for which Richards was grateful.[16] Two days later Richards again writes to Bramah thanking him for a copy *The Kai Lung Omnibus* which 'I have added with some pleasure – a melancholy pleasure – to my Bramah shelf' and 'The graceful things you write in my book make me sigh*. Thank you very much. (*Because they are no longer on my list of course!)'[17]

The reconciliation was complete. Bramah has forgiven him even if he had not forgotten.

◆

Apart from the 'lost' novel there exists in manuscript format at the Harry Ransom, Humanities Research Center, three completed novels, undated, which have never been published. *Behind the Wall*, 350 pages (later sketched out as a play) and *Youth at the Helm* with the alternative titles of *Hunchback of Grace à Dieu* and *The Optimist*. The one draft of *The Optimist* is some 400 pages long but in another version it has been reduced to about 300 pages. It is most certainly autobiographical in the sense that it leans heavily on Bramah's journalistic and editorial experiences.

Also among the unpublished manuscripts is one that is a visionary series of eight articles, all looking back from a distant, sometimes far distant, future to the twentieth century. It is a substantial typescript (about 100 pages), possibly written 1907 and appropriately called *In Future*. The stories are set in a parallel era that Bramah calls 'AC' as opposed to 'AD'. 'AC' it would appear is 'After [the] Calamity'. 'The last Englishman', written in 1900, first introduced this abbreviation to designate an undefined cataclysmic event which wiped out the A.D. civilisations.

Bramah's intended Preface provides little guidance to the reader.[18]

> As it may possibly occur to some reader to enquire whether the book is intended as a joke or as an earnest contribution to the restless problem of the age, the author desires to explain in advance that the humorous portions are intended to be taken seriously and the serious portions to contribute matter for quiet amusement. But which is which must – unfortunately – be left entirely to the personal standpoint of the individual reader.

Interestingly Bramah rejects devices for getting the observer into the appropriate age such as machines, (Wells's *The Time Machine*), magic potions or amulets (Anstey's *Vice Versa*) or supernatural creatures (Dickens's *Christmas Carol*).

He wrote:[19]

> In the case of most stories of fiction dealing with chronological impossibility, presented either as books or upon the stage, it has hitherto been customary to offer to the reader's or spectator's instinctive sense of outraged credulity, some grotesque and transparent solatium, generally in the form of a magic potion, an enchanted stone, a wonderful machine or a scientific discovery. As such devices persuade no-one, but are much more likely to offend the discriminating (as they undoubtedly should if advanced seriously) by the utter subversion of intelligence which their acceptance demands, the author has, on reflection, spared himself the effort of inventing any new lie, or appropriating an old one, to give a meretricious air of reality to these pages.

He was as good as his word. In 'Excavating' he simply drops his observer straight into the future. "I had launched myself into Futurity while sitting on a chair in the south-east corner of Hyde Park. The next minute I had found myself on a rock in the middle of a sandy desert [in the year 5000]."

Then, in his typical humorous style, concludes the Preface:

> ...whatever interest the series may possess is entirely made up of plagiarism, distortion, paradoxism, exaggeration, irresponsibility, uncalled-for personalities, bad taste, false sentiment and cheap humour. In return for this admission, he [the author] desires, as a like concession on the reader's part, a broad-minded acceptance of the principle that no article is intended to have any connection with other article in point of time, fact, method or consistency. Once say "But this doesn't seem to fit in – " you are lost. What is worse, your money has been wasted.

Possibly these novels would have been no more successful than any of his longer works. But history shows that posthumously published material often detracts from an author's reputation. (Examples are the release, by Hemingway's heirs, of an early manuscript and Truman Capote's literary executors publishing juvenilia described by one critic as 'embarrassing and a little sickening'.)

It cannot be known if Bramah had decided that he was dissatisfied with the material and never offered it. Nevertheless, together these Bramah manuscripts were the result of a very considerable creative effort. It would have been strange if there had not been either great dissatisfaction or great disappointment at having completed so much work to so little purpose. Perhaps, as William Charlton conjectured, he preferred the creativity of writing to the drudgery of selling. Bramah exhibits no trace of bitterness nor are there any recriminations with agents or with publishers. The disagreement with Grant Richards appears to be the only occasion when Bramah was in dispute with the many publishers of his works.

But now Bramah was on the verge of confirming his position as a leading writer of detective stories with Carrados ranking with Sherlock Holmes (and indeed out-billing him in the *Strand Magazine*), Dr. John Thorndyke and Father Brown and, later, Hercule Poirot, Inspector French and Dr. Gideon Fell. Max Carrados was entered in the American detective stories Roll of Honour. Unsurprisingly a third Carrados book was gestating.

Sources & Notes

1   Ernest Bramah. *The Specimen Case*. op. cit. Preface p.17.

2   *The Specimen Case*. op. cit. p.20.

3   *The Specimen Case* op. cit. p.17.

4   ibid.

5   *Punch*. December 29th 1915.

6   *The Times Literary Supplement*. October 16th 1924.

7   H.R.H.R.C. op. cit. April 24th 1924.

8   H.R.H.R.C. op. cit. April 30th 1924.

9   H.R.H.R.C. op. cit. July 6th 1924.

10   H.R.H.R.C. op. cit. November 2nd 1926.

11   H.R.H.R.C. op. cit. May 5th 1928.

12   H.R.H.R.C. op. cit. May 9th 1928.

13   H.R.H.R.C. op. cit. April 24th 1929.

14   H.R.H.R.C. op. cit. September 11th 1936.

15   H.R.H.R.C. op. cit. November 29th 1933.

16   H.R.H.R.C. op. cit. September 16th 1933.

17   H.R.H.R.C. op. cit. September 18th 1933.

18   Ernest Bramah. 'The last Englishman'. H.R.H.R.C. Typescript.

19   ibid.

CHAPTER THIRTEEN

MASTER OF THE GENRE

It was to be another four years before Bramah completed the third Max Carrados book. The intervening period, as with previous gaps in his writing, was filled writing stories and articles and perhaps some editorial work. Both his Kai Lung and Max Carrados stories were appearing in many anthologies in Britain and America and the English speaking part of the Empire. Judging only from the number of stories, plays and features in the Bramah papers, he was far from idle.

The *Max Carrados Mysteries* was published in 1927 by Hodder & Stoughton. The book comprised eight stories and the consensus among Carrados enthusiasts and critics is that the best are 'The Holloway flat tragedy' which contains one of the only two murders in the Carrados canon and 'The mystery of the vanished Petition Crown'. In the latter Bramah's expertise, experience and knowledge of coin dealers, numismatics and journalism (and perhaps larceny) are combined. This last plot might well have been used as a blueprint by the perpetrators of a real-life coin theft from the London dealers, Glendinning in 1977. Peter Gaspar a leading American expert also points out that a similar technique to that described in the book was adopted to steal a Vermeer from a private museum in Boston.[1]

Bramah also uses the narrative to explain at least one secret of Carrados's success as a detective. Carrados states:

"...there is no form of villainy that I haven't gone through in all its phases...when ever I fail to get to sleep at night...I commit murder, forgery a robbery or what not with all its ramifications…the criminal mind is rarely original, and I find that in nine cases out of ten that sort of crime is committed exactly as I have already done it."[2]

At least one of the tales again revealed Bramah's weakness in attempting to use foreign accents. While he excelled at producing elegant pseudo Chinese dialect he failed miserably with his American characters. In 'The ingenious mind of Mr. Rigby Lacksome' and in other stories, he has Americans' talking as they never do outside most English fiction written before 1930. Since films up to that time were silent he was certainty not influenced by accents heard in the cinema. The same misjudgement is repeated in *The Bravo of London* ten years later by which time he would have been exposed to genuine American accents in the cinema.

Anthony Trollope, despite his familiarity with Americans, avoided the problem of reproducing their accents. In any event at the time of the original publication of his books and the later editions, well into the twentieth century, overwhelmingly his readers had never heard an American accent. In a short story 'Miss Ophelia Gled'[3] he wrote:

"Well!" – I scorn to say that the Boston dandy said "wa'll," but if this story were written by any Englishman less conscientious than myself, the latter form of letters is the one which he would adopt in his endeavour to convey the sound as uttered by Mr. Hoskins.

Isabel Boncassen in *The Duke's Children* declaims: '…"long enough to have heard about you and your father" she said, speaking with not the slightest twang'. This solved the problem of accents. Then, sprinkling a number of 'I guess-es' and 'Sir-s' into conversations suffices to convey the speaker was an American.

◆

'The strange case of Cyril Bycourt' is substantially a ghost story into which Bramah introduces the science he respected and with which he loved to flirt. The plot could as easily fall into the 'fantasy' category as 'detection'. The denouement is that an underground electricity cable has disturbed an old plague pit and transferred the emotions of the plague victims to the eponymous Cyril Bycourt and to another character. In fact a plague pit was discovered in Muswell Hill where Bramah had lived at one time and might have contributed to the idea for the plot. Carrados's explanation was that 'a dynamo designed to transform mechanical force into energy, has here in some obscure way, also changed physical effect into psychological experience'. It is a matter for speculation whether or not Bramah actually believed this was a ghost story or that what occurred could have happened without supernatural interference. Erik Routley in *The Puritan Pleasures of the Detective Story*[4] comments:

> It is not the scientific implausibility of the of the plot that makes it remarkable: it is the fact that its author had the notion of bringing a detective tale so close to what was to him the imponderable world. "We know so lamentably little of electrical energy yet," says Carrados. Exactly. There was one per cent science and ninety-nine per cent superstition in most educated men of letters in 1920.

In this book Bramah leans heavily on the willingness of his readers to suspend belief which, for the most part, they do. Without this, it is asking a great deal of the reader to accept that Carrados could tell from a woman's voice, not heard for twenty-five years, that he knew her sister had died. "You heard?" "Not until now." "Your voice told me that." Again, 'By this time his hand had gone unerringly to the book he sought, and he was turning pages among the Tragedies.'

Howard Haycroft[5] observed that

> Occasionally the tales lean a little too far in the direction of intuition, and at other times they partake of the monotony of the arm-chair method; but for the most part they have a basis of sound investigation and deduction, imaginatively set forth.

J. C. Squire,[6] one of the most ardent of Bramah enthusiasts felt compelled in 1929, when the third Carrados books had been published, to comment that Bramah had:

...sunk beneath his own highest level: he has not maintained that standard of scrupulous perfection in his kind of prose as has been maintained by A. E. Housman in his kind of verse. The adventures of Max Carrados, the blind detective, are amusing and exciting and would have been quite sufficient to make the reputation of a good commercial writer, but it is difficult, when reading them to believe that they are by the same hand as "The Wallet of Kai-Lung".

Fortunately Squire was in a minority in the sense that for readers of detective fiction, who were not necessarily devotees of Kai Lung, Max Carrados stories were as highly regarded as Sherlock Holmes and other great fictional detectives.

At this time Bramah was attracting serious critical attention from the leading reviewers and authors; Desmond McCarthy, Edwin Pugh, Rose Macaulay, J. B. Priestly, L. P. Hartley and Frank Swinnerton among many others. Reviews and comments appeared in quality periodicals and newspapers including *New Statesman*, *Spectator*, *Observer*, *Manchester Guardian*, *Times Literary Supplement* and *The Times*.

The German rights were sold to Lutz and later transferred to Neufeld & Henius but in November 1929 Bramah was writing to Pinker, who must have negotiated the rights rather than Watt, to find out what had happened to the German edition which had already been given an extension. Publication had been due in October of that year. Whether it ever appeared is not known but a second hand German edition, published by Wilhelm Heyne of Munich under a more descriptive title *Max Carrados Detektiv* was found in New York in 2004. What ever happened to the first attempt at a German publication this at least proves that *Max Carrados* was indeed published there eventually.

In 1934 Penguin Books bought the rights for seven years for which they paid Bramah £250 plus a 7½ per cent royalty for a run of 30,000 copies. Assuming this was completely sold it would have produced nearly £500 or approximately £19,000 in early twenty-first century values – a respectable return. In 1956 a Penguin Books internal memorandum suggested that there should be 'serious consideration for republishing'. The decision was not to re-publish.

In all Bramah wrote some twenty-six Max Carrados stories in four collections and one novel. The stories also appeared in many anthologies and in periodicals and newspapers. *The Max Carrados Portfolio* published in 2000 includes all *The Eyes of Max Carrados*, *The Max Carrados Mysteries*, two stories from *The Specimen Case* and the only full-length Carrados novel *The Bravo of London*. In 1997 there were three B.B.C. radio adaptations of the adventures taken from each Carrados volume.

By 1929 Bramah had again assembled a collection of his earlier works and recycled them into a single-author anthology. *Short Stories of To-day and Yesterday*. The book comprised four episodes from *Kai Lung's Golden Hours*, three from *Max Carrados Mysteries* and four from *The Specimen Case*. Harrap which published the book appear to have issued three separate, differently priced editions, each in a different binding. (One of them was produced specially for Selfridges, the department store and has its name stamped on the spine.) It is doubtful if the task of preparing this book interfered with his other writing.

♦

Nevertheless after the *Mysteries* Bramah abandoned his detective for seven years and returned to his Chinese stories. There had been a gap of twenty-two years between the first and second Kai Lung book but only six years before the third book, *Kai Lung Unrolls His Mat* was published in 1928.[7] This relative speed maybe because three of the stories had already appeared in a series commissioned by *The Story-Teller* in 1927 called 'Celestial nights', or perhaps because the very slow composition of the Kai Lung idiom was becoming easier to accomplish. Another reason could well have been that the publisher's pressure for another book gave it priority over other speculative writing. Publishing it simultaneously in London and New York would have justified Bramah's decision to give priority to the new Kai Lung stories.

In fact two of the stories 'The story of Wan and the remarkable shrub' and 'The story of Ching-Wei and the destinies' were both published in New York as chapbooks (small booklets usually containing a single popular story) in the year before the book itself appeared.

Unlike its two predecessors this book has no Preface or Introduction by a prominent personality. The book really comprises a Novella of some 160 pages Part I entitled 'Protecting the Ancestors'. Part II 'The

Great Sky Lantern' and Part III 'The Bringer of Good News'. Only the last contains three typical Kai Lung short stories.

The Novella wrests the storyteller away from Kai Lung's 'small but seemly cottage' and his vivacious wife, Hwa-mei, of *Kai Lung's Golden Hours*. She has been kidnapped on the instructions of an old enemy the malignant Mandarin Shan Tien. In the course of a successful rescue Kai Lung encounters angry villagers, kindly peasants, an army captain reluctant to fight bandits and others. By reciting one of his tales in these various encounters, he avoids injury or death or repays hospitality. The framework of the rescue provides the background for the relating of the chronicles.

Parts II and III find Kai Lung in old age still relating his stories and still artful enough to avoid the stratagems and wiles of others. In 'The bringer of good news' Kai Lung has been awarded a distinction that he treats with great caution. "What," he inquired, with rather a narrow minded precision, "is the nature of the title and are the initiatory expenses set forth in detail?" "The latter part of the subject would appear to have been overlooked," replied the other.

The book commences with a poem. Its resemblance to authentic Chinese poems is very close indeed. Comparison with the translations by the eminent Sinologist Sir Arthur Waley (who too had never visited China) confirms this. As an erudite person Bramah would have been familiar with Waley's work particularly his translations of Chinese poems. To say that Bramah may have been influenced by Waley is not to suggest that the poem itself is not original and a credible composition. Some small credence can be given to the view that Waley did influence Bramah. A poem in *The Wallet*, published sixteen years before the Waley book which itself appeared ten years before *Kai Lung Unrolls His Mat*, lacks the consanguinity with Waley's Chinese poems. Another poem in *Kai Lung's Golden Hours* might be seen as a bridge from his own original style to the similarity and purity of Waley's.

Perhaps the book is best summed up by a critic who described it as '...subtle, suave and intrinsically satirical. We only refrain from saying these books [Kai Lung] are the best of their kind because we know of no others that are at all like them. They are really unique.'[8]

The reviewer in *The Times Literary Supplement*[9] bemoaned that this was to be the last Kai Lung book:

It is good news that *Kai Lung Unrolls His Mat*: less good that it is to be inferred that he will not be persuaded by Mr. Ernest Bramah to unroll it again. For it cannot be without significance that so conscientious an artist in analogies, before telling his last story, pressed upon his guests the few shrivelled fruits remaining in his orchard. "Had we been earlier the fare might have been more full-flavoured," was his mild extenuation, "but who shall blame the tree that has already of its nature yielded crops when autumn finds it wanting?"

Kai Lung Unrolls His Mat might well have been the last of the storyteller according to Bramah and in a letter to Robert Hudson[10] quoted by Richards:

Another? Well, I don't know. When I published the third last year I left KL an old old man. Possibly it was for this reason that four out of five of the notices that resulted said definitely (if occasionally politely regretful) that this was to be the last Kai Lung book. I had never said anything of the sort and I don't know if I ought to regard it as writing on the wall.

Fortunately he didn't.

Penguin Books produced their edition in 1937 with five or six further impressions. There is however some doubt about the size of each one.[11] Judging by correspondence between William White and Penguin Books in 1964 the *Golden Hours* was sufficiently popular, to justify a printing of 250,000 copies with similar quantities for the later reprints and books. However, Bramah in a letter to Allen Lane[12] dated May 31st 1939 twice refers to editions of 25,000 – a considerable difference. Penguin Books can throw no light on the discrepancy. They state that it is possible that both figures could be correct inasmuch as a typical print run at that time would have been in the order of 25,000 but the total sales of all reprints that were made could well have brought the sales up to 250,000. But all this was far in the future.[13]

The now growing band of enthusiasts eagerly awaited the new book. *The Morning Post* (later merged with the *Daily Telegraph*) was enraptured.[14]

Anyone who has once made acquaintance with the inimitable Kai Lung will rejoice to know he has returned among us, and no higher praise can be given to this third incarnation of Mr. Ernest Bramah's creation than to say it is entirely worthy of its delightful predecessors. He must be read as a whole to be appreciated at his true worth; and once read, he will be read again and again. For both on account of his stories and his manner of telling them, Mr. Bramah is always fresh and still enjoyed, There is nothing quite like these tales in English Literature.

The Manchester Guardian[15] found: 'There are splendid stories in this book. The sense of leisure and culture, the sense of adventure and of a bland humour are all here...'the old floweriness of the Kai Lung series is maintained'. Nevertheless the reviewer also felt that the book is '...not quite so well sustained as the author's previous works had led us to expect'.

The new book brought one paean of praise in the form of a poem published in the London *Evening News* entitled 'To Ernest Bramah by Algol'.[16] It ends:

so to the world of your creative mind
Bramah, you summon us to meet anew
The poor, the brave, the courteous and the kind;
Li-loe, the greedy, the malign Ming-shu,
And the brave- Golden Mouse, desired Hwa-mei –
Once more the golden hours pass swiftly by,
Once more the bowl of praise is filled for you.

The low keyed humour of Kai Lung, as *Time*[17] noted, is at '...chess game pace and subacid satire gives them an effect somewhat less than side-splitting, but for readers who like slyness slow and stately, Ernest Bramah is a lordly dish'. There is little doubt that this Kai Lung book lived up to the expectations of the many enthusiastic followers of the Chinese storyteller and who all dined well on this 'lordly dish'.

In 1927 Kai Lung tales were appearing in many journals. There were at least six in *The London Mercury* and The *Story-Teller* alone. Tangentially, it was an Ernest Bramah story from this book, 'King Weng and the miraculous tusk' that the Birmingham School of Printing chose to be produced as a fine edition as an exercise for the pre-apprentices.

With his comfortable financial position and his reputation firmly established, Bramah could at last indulge in writing about the topic which interested him most, and his public not at all.

Sources & Notes

1   Letter to the author from Peter Gaspar. March 20th 2005.

2   'The mystery of the vanished petition crown'. Reprinted in *Best Max Carrados Stories*. Dover. New York. 1972. p.5.

3   Anthony Trollope. *Courtship and Marriage*. Trollope Society. London. n.d. p.217.

4   Erik Routley. *The Puritan Pleasures of the Detective Story*. Gollancz. London. 1972.

5   Howard Haycroft. *Murder for Pleasure*. op. cit. p.75.

6   Ernest Bramah. *The Mirror of Kong Ho*. op. cit. Preface J. Squire p.v.

7   Ernest Bramah. *Kai Lung Unrolls His Mat*. Richards Press. London. 1928.

8   Quoted by William White in an essay in *Twentieth-Century Literary Criticism*. op. cit. Volume 72. p.10.

9   *The Times Literary Supplement*. May 3rd 1928.

10 Society of Authors. Grant Richards. Archive. Chadwyck-Healey. London. n.d.

11 H.R.H.R.C. op. cit. September 3rd 1964.

12 University of Bristol Library. Special Collections.

13 There is considerable confusion over the size of Penguin Books editions. A biography of Allan Lane states categorically that no Penguin Book fiction editions were less than 50,000 copies. Jeremy Lewis. *The Life and Times of Allen Lane*. Penguin Books. London. 2005.

14 H.R.H.R.C. op. cit. Extracts of reviews compiled by Ernest Bramah. n.d.

15 *Manchester Guardian*. June 1st. 1928.

16   *Evening News.* London. April 20th 1928.
17   *Time.* New York. September 6th 1930.

CHAPTER FOURTEEN

NUMISMATICS

B ramah's interest in coins had been manifest since his school days in Manchester. His encounters with the irascible dealer David Batty and the wonders of his dark mysterious shop in the alley beside the Cathedral have already been related.

Bramah had been gathering material seriously on his hobby, numismatics, from about 1910 and had had one or two articles published. There is a highly specialised feature. 'Tokens of the Southern Hop Gardens' in *The Antiquary*. Vol. 50 1914 and there are equally specialised typescripts such as 'The evolution of the humble penny' in the Bramah Collection at the Harry Ransom Humanities Research Center. It is of course conceivable that they did not appear in the numismatic press because at the time of their composition Bramah's reputation as an expert was not really recognised before his book was published in 1929. There is ample evidence that he wrote about coins and tokens in popular journals for example *Exchange & Mart*.[1] There are also a number of other articles in typescript that are of such a general interest they could have easily appeared as features in the popular press. 'An incident at Wethebey's' and 'Let money talk' are two examples. The typescript of the second piece ends intriguingly 'The article can be suitably divided at this point'. The rest is lost.

His boyhood hero, David Batty, had written what, up to that time, was the most extensive work on copper coinage. *Descriptive Catalogue of the Copper Coinage of Great Britain*[2] about which Bramah, in a rare moment of critical disparagement, wrote:[3] [It is] 'a monument of specialisation carried to excess' and 'This is surely specialisation run riot.' '…It is impossible not to respect the intention but it is hopeless to attempt to distinguish the results', and in a moment of sympathy; 'Literary history, especially in the by-paths of research, presents many tragedies, but few among them deal with enterprises so hopeless, so bravely persisted in, and so consistently the sport of adverse circumstances as this'. The way seemed open for a much improved and more easily assimilated guide and for Bramah to combine his hobby and enthusiasm for the topic with his skills as a writer.

From about the end of 1919 Bramah had been devoting a considerable amount of his available time to writing and illustrating the tome but it was not until 1921 that he approached Grant Richards with the suggestion for a book on the topic of coin collecting. As he rightly stated[4] 'one page would bore an ordinary sane person into hysteria but it aims at being useful to the general collector and essential to the specialist' and it being 'of such proportions and detail that at the sight of it no English publisher can repress a shudder. I wonder if any American millionaire would be interested?' Bramah undertook to list every issue of copper coinage by denomination, date and the major varieties. There is no question but that the book was regarded then and for many years later as the most authoritative work on the topic and, at the time, covered much new ground.

Not surprisingly, Richards did not consider it a suitable title for his catalogue but it did eventually find a publisher. Methuen, who had turned down the first Kai Lung book, accepted it, and in 1929, published *A Guide to the Varieties and Rarity of English Regal Copper Coins*.[5] Whether it was modesty or an editorial decision the verso only lists two previous books although by 1929 Bramah had published ten, most of them still in print. This book, perhaps, not unsurprisingly, never went to a second printing.

In the long and highly technical Introduction Bramah expressed the belief that the book would appeal to the general collector 'as being an exact catalogue of types and dates, while for the benefit of the specialist it carries arrangements further…and suggests lines of search and classification.' In a series of extensive footnotes he meticulously acknowledges earlier authors on the subject. Professor Peter Gasper who considered Bramah was ahead of his time, wrote in 1980 that all numismatists owe Bramah a great debt of inspiration.[6]

It has taken a very long time to recognise that the publication in 1929 of Ernest Bramah's only numismatic book was an important milestone for the study of modern coins...it is for the understanding of die varieties and their significance that Bramah was a pioneer... . The descriptions are so clear and vivid however, that the adage is reversed, and one may say truly that a few of Bramah's words are worth many pictures.[7]

The book drew favourable critical attention in the U.S.A. 'This is really a model of its kind, rather technical but extremely fine study of the series' *The Numismatic Review,*[8] New York noted in 1943.

It also stated that they had received a rare letter from Bramah in 1932 in which he informed them he was collecting material for a supplement to his book of varieties that had escaped him when he wrote the book. The Supplement was not completed but the *Review* was delighted when, in 1944, Maisie sent them Ernest's notes found loosely laid in his own copy of the book. It was clear from the notes that it was his intention to update the books. They gave precise indications where each new item was to be inserted.

The *Review* concluded 'English Regal Copper Coins has long attracted advanced and competent scholarly attention. The additions are of real significance.'[9]

Although perhaps of major interest only to coin collectors, it is worth pointing out that, according to Professor Peter Gaspar, the essential merit of the book is the provision of a reasoned framework within which die varieties could be classified. It was Bramah who first turned attention to the question of how they originated.

Among the Bramah papers at The University of Texas is a typescript of the book noted as 'with illustrations'. The published work had no illustrations so presumably it was agreed with the publishers not to include them – a cost saving measure doubtless. Peter Gaspar however believes that the descriptions are so brilliantly written that the loss of illustrations is not important. The Harry Ransom Humanities Research Center also holds several articles, almost certainly not published, on coins and tokens.

It is totally characteristic of Bramah's personality that, despite his enthusiasm for numismatics, he was never a member of the British or Royal Numismatic societies and never wrote a paper for their journals.

A letter printed in an unidentified source commenting on his death, stated, 'He must have been a retiring person, and is not listed among the members of societies one would have expected him to join,' a fact confirmed by their Secretaries.

◆

Bramah's addiction to coin collecting and his expertise can be found in a number of stories, sometimes essential to the plot. A character in a play for radio says, "Carrados has one weak spot, his passion for collecting rare and beautiful Greek coins." Max Carrados is a coin expert and a specialist in Greek tetradrachms. 'The secret of Dunstan's tower' in *The Eyes of Max Carrados* begins:

> It was a peculiarity of Mr. Carrados that he could drop the most absorbing occupation of his life at a moment's notice if need be... . On the morning of 3rd of September he was dictating to his secretary a monograph to which he had given the attractive title, "The portrait of Alexander the Great, as Jupiter Ammon, on an unedited octadrachm of Macedonia", when a telegram was brought in.

There is no doubt that in titling this monograph Bramah was demonstrating his own very great expertise.

Numismatics in one form or another appear in 'The great Hockington find' in *The Specimen Case* (1924), 'The disappearance of Marie Severe' and 'The Kingsmouth spy case' in *The Eyes of Max Carrados* (1923), 'The ingenious mind of Mr. Rigsby Lacksome' and 'The mystery of the vanished petition crown' in *Max Carrados Mysteries* (1927). The jacket of *Max Carrados Mysteries* features a coin. 'The game played in the dark' which was also a radio play, and 'The coin of Dionysius' both appeared in *Max Carrados* (1914) and the latter is praised for its accuracy by one very knowledgeable critic who wrote:[10]

> The details surrounding the event were so detailed that readers to this day feel that they were participating in a rare coin auction much as it must have been in the early part of this century.

There is also a reference to rare coins in the full-length novel, *The Bravo of London*, which in an arcane way is extensively numismatic. The story concerns forged high value notes on genuine Bank of England paper. But it was not only in Max Carrados stories where coins appear. A short story, 'A domestic drama', possibly unpublished, involves Georgian sovereigns. The feature 'Griffiths, the fossil man' finds 'early British gold coins and Roman coins in various metals'. There are references to Imperial aurei in the unpublished *Behind the Wall*. It also uses the auction of an Imperial aurei as the link to the heroine's father. In 1957 a talk on coin collecting transmitted on the B.B.C. German service paid tribute to Bramah's pioneering cataloguing of English copper coinage.

English Regal Copper Coins is a long way from the mainstream of Bramah's writing but does show another aspect of his abilities which clearly included classification. It also adds evidence against those doubters who believed that the authors of Kai Lung and Max Carrados were different people because the styles were so different. *English Regal Copper Coins* is different again.

The vast majority of Bramah readers were, for very obvious reasons, not attracted to the book but numismatists world-over owe a great debt of inspiration to Bramah, as Professor Gaspar has pointed out. 'While others lose their childhood enthusiasms and abandon their collecting activities, Bramah maintained his from childhood to old age.'

Unsurprisingly, given the narrowness of the interest and the world economic crisis following the Wall Street crash, the book was not financially successful for either the author or the publisher.

John Barker, Bramah's nephew, did not think that Maisie shared his pleasure in numismatics. The simple dedication already quoted implies quite the opposite. "To M if only (but not only) for the hours that it has given us." It is of course more than possible that this reflects Bramah's loyalty and generosity rather than any real interest but it is the only dedication in any Bramah book.

But away from his addiction to numismatics, Bramah's short stories continued to attract a wide audience. *The London Mercury* was virtually pleading for contributions "Is there any chance of getting anything, however short, from you," wrote J. C. Squire the Editor.[10] However flattering this invitation was Bramah very much wanted to be recognised as a novelist, despite the critical failure of What *Might Have Been.* He had forgotten or was about to ignore his advice to authors in the Preface to *The Specimen Case* and the moral of the incident of the man with the hoe. An idea was blossoming for yet another genre – a full-length comic novel.

Sources & Notes

1   Ernest Bramah. 'Medallions made by gaol-birds'. *The Bazaar. Exchange & Mart.* London. February 4th 1936. This article was published as a contribution from Ernest B. Smith not Ernest Bramah.

2   David Batty. *Descriptive Catalogue of Copper Coinage of the British Empire.* op. cit. 1868. p.11.

3   H.R.H.R.C. op. cit. 'Through the eyes of a child'.

4   H.R.H.R.C. op. cit. April 18th 1921.

5   Ernest Bramah. *A Guide to the Varieties and Rarity of English Regal Copper Coins Charles II –Victoria 1671-1860.* Methuen. op. cit. p.11.

6   Peter Gaspar makes the important distinction between a 'collector' and a 'numismatist'. The latter extends beyond collecting coins to their serious study.

7   Peter Gaspar. 'On the fiftieth anniversary of Bramah's Regal Copper Coins'. *The Numismatic Circular.* Spink. London. January 1980. p.4.

8   Obituary. *The Numismatic Review.* New York. September 1943.

9   ibid.

10 Edward Rochette. 'Blind detective had a real feel for his work'. *Numismatic News.* January 14th 1997.

11 H.R.H.R.C. August 1st 1929.

CHAPTER FIFTEEN

PUBLISHING SUCCESS AND CRITICAL FAILURE

Bramah's stories continued to be widely and frequently anthologised. For example, in 1927 there had been the two Kai Lung stories published in America as stand-alone books and in the 1929 Harrap Bramah anthology *Short Stories of To-day and Yesterday* where they, rather than the author, probably selected the stories as none of the tales came from the books that he had identified as his 'best'. There were three anthologies edited by Dorothy L. Sayers, that all included Carrados stories. Stories also appeared in the *News of the World*, The *London Mercury*, *The Story-Teller*, *Argosy*, *Strand Magazine* and many others. The *Strand Magazine,* which first appeared in 1891, was the periodical that had the highest prestige and paid the highest rates. To appear in it was the ultimate accolade of literary recognition. Although the Magazine gives Bramah's contributions a by-line, their Index lists him under 'E. B. Smith'.

There is no doubt that Bramah had consolidated his position as an important and successful author and in the 1920s reached the peak of his success. No one has produced a definitive bibliography of all Bramah's published works although both William White and Mike Berro have made the most substantial contributions to date towards achieving this.

Apart from journals William White[1] identified forty-one anthologies that included Bramah stories and this, he emphasised, was not a complete bibliography as his correspondence shows. For example, later he identified two editions of *Argosy* with Bramah tales in them and held at the then Leeds Polytechnic. The bibliography at the end of this book attempts to update earlier lists.

In 1930, the year of publication of *A Little Flutter*,[2] his full-length comic novel, the world was gripped in deep depression and the public wanted escape from the miseries of daily life. The cinema, now ubiquitous talkies, provided this with slick Hollywood comedies and musicals. The theatre offered the Aldwych farces of Ben Travers. The gentle satire of E. M. Delafield's *Diary of a Provincial Lady* and J. B. Priestley's warm-heated *The Good Companions* were in popular demand. Bramah sought to join those who were seeking to dispel the gloom with their light-hearted novels.

The plot for the book dates back to 1909 when Bramah had sent a play *The Great Groo-Groo* to Pinker. It was a fully developed script contained in five notebooks. Pinker did not wish to handle it. Yet again it is not known if the play was ever produced. However the following year Bramah wrote to Pinker to say that he was going to write a book based on the play. Twenty years were to pass before the book appeared. However among Bramah enthusiasts there is general agreement that his success as a writer of short stories, features and articles did not extend to his full-length works where his inspiration flags and the standard of the writing falters. This was perhaps something already portended in *What Might Have Been. A Little Flutter* is of a totally different character to his previous books. When it was published in 1930 it received very little critical attention. The few reviews that did appear were mostly unfavourable. One reviewer wrote 'the yarn isn't up to the standard of Bramah's two best-known series…'. It is described in one bibliography as 'nonsense'. E. F. Bleiler refers to it 'as rather a pointless novel'. The criticisms are harsh and unjustified. The book is omitted from the Bramah bibliography in *Contemporary Authors* and *Twentieth-Century Literary Criticism*. Taken on its own terms the book sets out to be amusing, light reading, and it is. Whatever the critics felt the public bought it.

The plot of *A Little Flutter* concerns a substantial bequest on condition the beneficiary, Peter Coppinger, continues his uncle's interests and research into ornithology and that he maintains his uncle's collection. If he did not do this, the bequest reverted to The Institute of

Ornithological Research. Coppinger knew nothing about ornithology and cared about it even less but was determined to put on a show in order to keep the legacy.

Life becomes complicated when he receives the five-foot corpse of the last Pantagonian giant Groo-Groo bird that had died en route to his home. At the same time an escaped convict hides in the grounds of the house and avoids re-capture by disguising himself in the skin of the Groo-Groo bird. He does however in return for Coppinger providing sanctuary, forge a will that releases Coppinger from the conditions of the inheritance.

The idea of a five-foot Groo-Groo bird, an important part of the plot, might well have been a legacy from the Victorian ornithologists who were excited by the hope of finding the last living specimens of the Great Auk, officially declared extinct in 1844 but with reported sightings as late as 1870. Expensive expeditions were mounted. Not that the Victorians wanted a live specimen. A stuffed Great Auk was worth far more than a living one. By the time Bramah wrote *A Little Flutter* – an Auk's skin and egg fetched nearly £1,000 at auction.

Coppinger is 'an unpretentious figure, with the docile, tacitly resigned expression of the middle-aged underling who has been doing much the same sort of routine work all his life and who sees very little chance of ever doing anything else either in this world or the next'. He is completely lost in a conversation with his bird-keeper.

Pooterish-like, in this confrontation he mistakes the Latin name, Otus Vulgaris, for a plant and then has to wriggle out of the situation.[3]

"Nothing exactly wrong, sir. But that new Otus Vulgaris that came up last week seems to be drooping a bit. I thought you might like to know." Not that he thought any such thing, of course. No man likes to be told that any of his cherished possessions is drooping: What Job really meant was that he hoped it would redound to his credit to have been so observing. Mr. Coppinger's eye wavered in the direction of the nearest bookcase, but the impulse went no further.

"Ah, Otus Vulgaris drooping a bit?" he repeated with nice discrimination in his voice. "Well Job, you had better keep the glare of the sun off it for the next few days and-er-perhaps spray it occasionally with soap-suds."

"Soap suds?" reiterated Job, after considering this course of treatment for a baffled half minute. "You said spray it with soap-suds, sir?"

"...Weak soap-suds of course I meant...just the merest trace of..."

"You understand, sir, that it's the long-eared owl what I am referring to..."

Then, struggling to extricate himself from the embarrassment of ignorance, Coppinger digs the hole deeper when the bird keeper suggests that the correct treatment is Veronica.

"Certainly, Job. Give Otus Vulgaris a ..." But at that point a realisation of the ambiguities of his position warned the unlucky Peter. What in heaven's name, did one give Veronica as – a pill, poultice, injection, powder, or would it be expedient to fall back upon the familiar phrase "A good stiff tumbler?"

◆

This is vintage Bramah humour of the type that can be found in his numerous articles. It is not less amusing because it is not couched in the circumlatory style of Kai Lung or the innocence of Kong Ho.

Bramah names the private inquiry agent in the book 'S. Holmes', perhaps a sly dig at Carrados's competitor. He makes his Mr. Holmes say[4]

"...but life has been embittered by a combination of circumstances over which I have no control. When people hear my name they look to me to do things that are more like conjuring tricks than anything else. I have had an evening party sit around and expect me to produce a burglar that they'd had as if he was a rabbit out of a hat. Ah, you don't know what it is like to have to live up to a reputation that somebody else has made for you!"

There is another cross-link with an exact contemporary author, the Canadian, Stephen Leacock. 'The awful fate of Melpomenus Jones' recounts how the young curate perishes after months confined to the house of a courteous and well-meaning parishioner. He was too shy and nervous to refuse the socially correct and courteous invitation to 'stay a little longer.' Thus he stays with only the family photograph album to divert him until he dies in a raging delirium. Bramah introduces Legge Moon who explains he was 'graciously pressed to take a cup of tea. I stayed and in some inexplicable, I assure you, but natural and un-designed way I seem to have stayed ever since.'

The farcical events of the book might have been acceptable had they been written by Ben Travers but Bramah devotees, whether Kai Lung or Max Carrados, expected something different.

The reviewer in *The Times Literary Supplement* wrote[5] 'What is left is the ragging of Peter: (the hero of the story) and the ragging without any ulterior purpose of an inoffensive little man does not much appeal to onlookers unless – as with Dickens – it is done by someone who likes him.'

Despite being largely ignored or unfavourably commented on by the few critics who chose to notice the book it was sufficiently successful for Cassells to reprint it in 1932 as a 'Popular Edition' priced at 2/6. Priestley's caustic comment that popularity can be a short cut to critical oblivion certainly applied to *A Little Flutter*.

Whatever view is taken of the book it is highly valued as a collector's item. A first edition is now offered at $2,500; however, this could possibly be a special binding with Bramah's signature in the book.

Bramah must have realised his second full-length novel, so different to the first, was also an artistic failure and that to restore his confidence he should return to the ever-popular Kai Lung. He still wanted to write full-length novels so the obvious solution was a compromise – his Chinese storyteller in a full-length novel.

Sources & Notes

1   William White. 'Ernest Bramah in periodicals 1890-1972'. *Bulletin of Bibliography*. Westwood. Massachusetts. 1974. Vol. 32. No. 1.

2   Ernest Bramah. *A Little Flutter*. Cassell. London. 1930.

3   Ernest Bramah. *A Little Flutter*. op. cit. pp.70-71.

4   ibid. pp.72-73.

5   *The Times Literary Supplement*. August 28th 1980.

Chapter Sixteen

RETURN TO THE CHINESE NEVER-NEVER LAND

As when the previous Kai Lung books appeared, China was dominating the news again in 1932. Japan had invaded China and had reached Shanghai in May, the same month as *The Moon of Much Gladness*[1] was published. It had been six years before Bramah had yielded to the persuasion of his publishers and presented them with the manuscript. The gap between the previous Kai Lung and Max Carrados books had been much longer. But with three previous Kai Lung books and a number of short stories already published Bramah had complete mastery over the style. This would have enabled him to compose this book in a shorter time than its predecessors.

He did so without compromising or mechanising the result. Every word is considered, every sentence polished to flawless consistency and the rhythm of the prose never broken. The reader has only to attempt to copy the style to appreciate just how formidable a task it is to maintain it over even a few pages as members of the Kai Lung Club found out.

In this book Kai Lung is no longer confined to the limitations imposed by the short story. Neither the lack of critical success of *A Little Flutter* (which had just been re-published in the Cassell's cheap Popular Editions series) nor the change of format diminished the enthusiasm for the book. The three previous books had all included 'Kai Lung' in the title but his name was missing from the title originally because he is not in the story at all. After consideration it was decided with the publishers that Bramah's name as the author was not sufficient to convey to the reading public that this was another Chinese tale. There was to be no chance of misidentification. Thus it was decided that the precedent must be followed and the book appeared as *The Moon of Much Gladness as related by Kai Lung*. This ensured the enthusiasts would be in no doubt that this was another book in the series.

The reader is plunged straight into the tale and the fact that it is related does not emerge until the last two pages. Nevertheless Bramah perceived Kai Lung as a teller of this tale and therefore justified his name in the title. One result is that the delicious interplay between the storyteller and his sometimes reluctant audience of villagers, peasants and various layabouts is missing.

There are no clues as to why Bramah abandoned the highly successful technique of interweaving the relater into the plot unless it was that his desire to write full-length novels led to a compromise of a Chinese book without Kai Lung, but in a full-length format. This might explain why the original title did not include Kai Lung's name.

Despite these differences the book has all the Kai Lung qualities. It ends in true Kai Lung style with a diatribe by the teller of tales against the 'printers of leaves':

> The essential story of Chin-tung and Haw-che, even if written in this ill–equipped relater's usual bankrupt style and with no particularly improving reflections drawn from each event, would fill seven and thirty volumes of a really distinctive size, but, alas towards this attractive plan they who send forth the printed leaves have turned a wholly repulsive ear and extended hands from which it is impossible to interpret a blessing.

and the last words of the book:

> ...nothing remains for an admittedly tedious and obsolete deliverer of unvarnished facts but to roll up his threadbare mat once more, bow right and left with an ingratiating submission, and not, perchance without an inoffensive glance at his ill-lined collecting bowl – await your distinguished judgement.

The book does contain some of Bramah's most captivating aphorisms put into the mouths of the various characters, ostensibly intended for the moral edification of his listeners: 'To regard all men as corrupt is wise. But to attempt to discriminate among the various degrees of iniquity is both foolish and discourteous' and 'It is possible to escape from an enemy carrying a two-edged sword but not from the interference of a well-meaning woman'. The tales abound with aphorisms and proverbs, real, disguised and original – sometimes as many as two or three on a page:

A single date consumed in peace is better than a basket of figs beneath the shadow of affliction.

Large ears and a well-retired mouth compensate for many obvious failings.

It is inept to glue a boat together to save the price of iron rivets.

She who draws her bow at a twinkling star may perchance hit the eye of a passing bullock.

Although Kai Lung is absent, institutions and conventions are set in the Kai Lung idiom. A leap year; "Owing to the misdirected energy of an inauspicious planet it has been necessary to modify the Calendar, and the First of Much Gladness will this year fall upon the Second in order to restore the harmonious balance of the Upper Spaces," declares Ching-tung, Secretary to the Mandarin.

Kai Lung bemoans the frustration of the Malthusian principle by development of skills to cure what would have been fatal illnesses.

...now by the effervescing of a grain of magic powder on the tongue or the scratching of a cryptic emblem about the forearm even a river-pirate or a hungry beggar might not unreasonably cherish the ambition of outliving those so careful of their skin as even to hire others to perform their recreations for them...

The narrative is really detective fiction in Bramah's Chinese idiom. The profession is referred to as the 'Barbarian sages'. It concerns the loss of a mandarin's pigtail – a deprivation that is synonymous with loss of face and indeed dignity as well as impotence. The heroine, Hwa-che, recovers the pigtail, in what in opera would be called a 'breeches role'. This is the Rosenkavalier stratagem of a girl pretending to be a boy pretending to be a girl. She has studied the methods of the barbarians of the outer-lands and by deduction identifies the miscreant.

Clearly Sherlock Holmes is the detective she admires and emulates. This is her description.

> "The foremost of the band…whose mere name has now become a synonym for alertness, inhales the acrid fumes of smouldering weeds and wraps about his form a flowing robe of talismanic virtues. He it is who also calls up Shapes by means of forbidden drugs and restores the harmonious balance of the Spheres with a machine of wood and string that in his hand produces music."

Of course Hwa-che has to have her Watson (or in Carrados's case, Carlyle). This role falls to Chin-Tung, the secretary to the Mandarin T'sin Wong and in love with Hwa-che, who asks the appropriate questions on behalf of the reader and of course provides the opportunity for the explanation.

> "He [her father into whose mouth she puts words] has now indicated a desire to follow to their source this double line of sandal prints, leading from the outer-garden wall to the Mandarin's shuttered window, and thence back in like progression. Therein, superfluous to explain, resides the answer to the mysterious happening of the First of Much Gladness."

> "Yet" questioned Chin-tung, whose training had not extended beyond the Classics "why should not the sandal-prints have proceeded from the shuttered window to the wall and thence back in strict reversal, whereby the outcome assumes an inverted sequence?"

> "To one versed in the deeper culture of the sleuth-hounds of the West that is transparent", replied Hwa-Che, indicating the

various signs as she described them. "He who sets out to achieve a crime steps lightly on his toes in caution, but the purpose once fulfilled, his only thought is towards swift retreat. Thus and thus. The one who came with stealth returned in extended order."

"What is there to show, however, that the object of this intrusion may not have been based on some variable ambition" persisted the scrupulous Chin-tung, "and how, in any case, do these footprints lead to a definite disclosure?"

"If the one who came stealthily to this neglected spot by night and stood beneath the window did not come for the only thing that has since been missing, how is his action to be accounted for and thereby the whole fabric of argument is menaced?"

There are even stories within the story. Two members of a secret anarchist society who accompany Hwa-che like the band of Canterbury pilgrims each tell their tales.

◆

The book, while enthusiastically embraced by Kai Lung devotees, did not meet with universal critical acclaim. 'With this equipment, and with considerable effort he does manage to squeeze a number of laughs out of the old topsy-turvy joke,' wrote Mary McCarthy in *The Nation*.[2] David Langford[3] was even crueller.

…is definitely too much of a good thing, the anachronistic jokes sometimes found in the short stories here take the form of gags about Western ("barbarian") detective stories, and indeed a great deal of the book is detective pastiche.

John Connell[4] in his B.B.C. Third Programme talk on Bramah omits any mention of *The Moon of Much Gladness*. Possibly the profusion of characters, some twenty in the first sixty pages alone, with names difficult to remember, proved frustrating to some readers and critics.

Nevertheless, John Connell's interrogative summary is apposite for this book as the previous ones.[5]

> It [the writing] is as obvious in its beauty as a butterfly's wing; you can analyse it and you can parse it, just as you can pin down a butterfly and painstakingly count the number of colours in its wings. You can list its careful cadences, its balanced irony, its withholding of that jab to the last twist of the sentence. But when you have done that, have you, in fact added anything to the fun or even enriched your own appreciation of it?

The book again offers evidence of Bramah transferring ideas from one plot to another. William Charlton's detective work has found that Chapters XII and XIII of the book have jokes and ideas transferred from a story written about thirty years earlier – 'The destiny of Cheng'.

The Moon of Much Gladness was published in America by Sheridan House. They clearly did not like the title. When the book appeared some five years later, in 1937, they changed it to *The Return of Kai Lung* thus causing some confusion among readers and later among book collectors.

The humorous interpretation of one Western profession [private detectives] did not add anything serious to the knowledge of how the East regards Western institutions and its peoples. This topic had not received very much attention in the early part of the twentieth century. Bramah's *The Mirror of Kong Ho* took a satirical look at the West through oriental eyes. A more serious approach was *Letters of a Japanese Schoolboy*[6] published in 1909 and severely criticised by Bramah.[7] Apart from its content the author, Wallace Irwin, uses pidgin English, something Bramah eschewed in his Kai Lung books.

◆

In the same year as *The Moon of Much Gladness* was published there appeared a book by Pêh Der Chen entitled *Honourable and Peculiar Ways*[8] which avoided the serious reservations Bramah had previously expressed on other books purporting to comment on the West.

Honourable and Peculiar Ways was a collection of sketches that had appeared in *The Graphic* and *Daily Express* but, most importantly, it had a Foreword by Ernest Bramah in which he praises the author.

> In the following pages Mr. Pêh Der Chen tells us exactly how we strike him – or if not exactly – as near so as one who belongs to the most courteous nation on the earth can bring himself to disclose in a medium intended for publication ...I will only say, therefore, that I have read all these pages with pleasure and many of them with that joy that comes when the prospector sees sparkle and realises he has touched precious metal.

Some knowledgeable Bramah devotees, including Christopher Morley have expressed doubts as to the identity of Pêh Der Chen. Hamish Hamilton his publishers could not find any mention of him in their archives. Was he perhaps no other than Ernest Bramah himself? *The Times Literary Supplement*[9] reviewer commented

> '...one might doubt his (Pêh Der Chen) Chinoiserie, for he writes English as idiomatically as Mr. Bramah writes Chinese'. Certainly the writing styles differ but then it is only necessary to read Max Carrados stories or *The Secret of the League* to see Bramah was perfectly capable in achieving a diversity of style. Moreover he had previously written a number of stories using the pen name "M. B. Packwood". ("Packwood" was both the area where he had rented his farm and the name of his sister's house.)

If Bramah was the author why should he want to use another name? Trollope hid his authorship on two occasions, although the critics soon identified him. Trollope wrote[10] 'I determined...to begin a course of novels anonymously, in order that I might see whether I could succeed in obtaining a second identity.' More than likely Trollope wanted to exploit new themes that might have alienated his faithful readers as in his *Nina Balatka*. It is unlikely either motive could be ascribed to Bramah whose fame at this period of his life was hardly that of Trollope's in his prime and neither was *Honourable and Peculiar Ways* so very different from *Kong Ho*. John Buchan wrote and published his *Lady in the*

Wilderness anonymously. This was largely a political book and possibly he did not wish to expose his views. This might have been the reason for Buchan's unaccustomed reticence.

Whatever the explanation the Foreword is sprinkled with Bramah's humour. 'You probe the dark mystery of what you are really asking for when you order "chop suey" in London'; 'Much water has flowed down the Hoang Ho (and not infrequently out of it over the surrounding country)'; '...although Mr. Pêh in dutiful compliance with his traditions, affects to despise the lily-footed sex and is all for putting women in their proper place (three paces behind men when walking together); '...Can it be that there is an analogous custom [pressing cups of tea on a stranger] among the literati of inviting [the contribution of introductions], but that it is the height of ill-breeding to do anything but profess an entire unworthiness to accept so marked an honour'; 'a British Plenipotentiary, on being slyly invited to sit during a palace conference, naturally inquired – as no seats were available "On what?" and received an obvious but gravity-removing rejoinder'.

The book purports to provide comment on serious matters but Bramah urges the reader 'do not conclude that gravity is the only, or even the predominant, note of the volume'.[11] There are both hilarious descriptions of Parliament at work and serious political comment on for example, the Kellogg Pact, The League of Nations and China's growing role in world affairs – humour and politics both figure in Bramah's writing.

Passages from both the Pêh Der Chen book and Bramah's second Chinese book, *The Mirror of Kong Ho* do show a similarity for example in their refined display of filial disrespect. Pêh Der Chen writes[12]

My adventures had begun and on the waters of the Thames are now floating the two letters of introduction given by my father that I cast overboard. I seek no privileges. I am now a man of 17 summers, old enough to have started a family...

My honoured father from 10,000 miles away did not look upon my proud ideas of adventure with approval. Now five fresh letters of introduction have come by post accompanied by the delicate point that if they were not presented by a reasonable time I would one day find my bank presenting me, not with the usual drafts, but a return ticket.

Kong Ho writes[13]

Can it be that the incapable person whom, as you truly say, you sent "to observe the philosophical subtleties of the barbarians, to study their dynastical records and to associate liberally with the venerable and dignified" has, in your own unapproachable felicity of ceremonial expression, "according to discreet whispers from many sources, chiefly affected the society of tea-house maidens, the immature of both sexes, doubtful characters of all classes, and criminals awaiting trial; has evinced an unswerving affinity towards light amusement and entertainments of no-class kind; and in place of wise aloofness" …He [Kong Ho] is impelled to take a mild and tolerant attitude towards the momentary injustice brought about by the weaknesses of approaching old age.

The book's alignment with Kong Ho makes the suspected link. Bramah himself especially warns the readers; '…as to his [Pêh Der Chen] national bona fides, I (who have been admitted just a step further into whatever secret there may be) would warn you not to be too knowing'.

Besides his slow rate of composition Bramah also disliked deadlines as his letter to Grant Richards already quoted shows quite clearly. He preferred to work to his own timescale. It might thus seem unlikely that he could have produced another full-length Chinese style volume in such a short period after *The Moon of Much Gladness*. However as the work is substantially reprints of sketches that had appeared elsewhere there would have been no problem in assembling the book quickly and providing the Foreword.

The author claims to have fought in the trenches in 1915, which most certainly Bramah did not as he served in the Royal Defence Corps that was based in the United Kingdom. The weight of evidence against Bramah being the author lies in a copy of *Honourable and Peculiar Ways* having the author's signature in both English and as a Chinese ideogram. A note in White's handwriting scribbled on a letter to him from Charles

Yenter[14] suggests that the author was in fact an English journalist, William Christian Peterson. The Foreword may then have been less an act of friendship and regard for the author as a paid commission. The case for Bramah as the author is far from proven.

Bramah still wanted to be a novelist. By his own standards, irrespective of the sales achieved, neither *The Secret of the League* nor *A Little Flutter* had been critical successes – the full length Kai Lung story had. Perhaps if he wove a plot around his other well-known character, Max Carrados, he could achieve the triumph he sought. Bramah had yet again forgotten the man with the hoe.

Sources & Notes

1   Ernest Bramah. *The Moon of Much Gladness as Related by Kai Lung*. Cassell. London. 1932.

2   Mary McCarthy. Book review. *The Nation*. New York. October 23rd 1937.

3   David Langford. 'Ernest Bramah: A delicate bouquet of crime' op. cit.

4   John Connell. 'The recluse who created Kai Lung'. op. cit.

5   ibid.

6   Wallace Irwin. *Letters of a Japanese Schoolboy*. Doubleday. New York. 1909.

7   H.R.H.R.C. Letter from Ernest Bramah to Grant Richards. April 27th 1923. The relevant extract is quoted on p64. (Chapter Five).

8   Pêh Der Chen. *Honourable and Peculiar Ways*. op. cit. p.11.

9   *Times Literary Supplement*. October 30th 1932.

10 Quoted by Angela Thirwell in the Introduction to *Nina Balakta*. Trollope Society. London. 1996.

11 Pêh Der Chen *Honourable and Peculiar Ways*. Ernest Bramah. Introduction.

12 Pêh Der Chen *Honourable and Peculiar Ways*. op. cit. p.19.

13 *The Mirror of Kong Ho*. op. cit. pp.118-119.

14 H.R.H.R.C. July 26th 1973.

CHAPTER SEVENTEEN

'A VICTIM OF THAT MANIA'

W. W. Jacobs, whose full length novels also never achieved the success of his short stories, had remarked that every humorous writer should occasionally try to write a more serious work since otherwise he gets stale: rather like changing the crop on the land, something Bramah would have known about. It is more than likely that this was one of the motives for the next book – *The Bravo of London*[1] published by Cassell in 1934. This was also the year of Robert Graves's *I Claudius*, Mikhail Sholokhov's *And Quiet Flows the Don*, Dorothy L. Sayers's *Nine Tailors*, Scott Fitzgerald's *Tender is the Night* and P. G. Wodehouse's *The Inimitable Jeeves* – five books that remain better known than any of Bramah's work. There is no doubt whatsoever that *The Bravo of London* is not among Bramah's more enduring works and definitely not the best Max Carrados adventure. It was, even for its day, a somewhat old-fashioned thriller and the thrills, such as they are, do not appear until the end of the book.

Critical opinions of what was to be the last appearance of Max Carrados were largely unfavourable. Later views were even harsher. William White[2] wrote that 'it is worth little comment' – so he didn't. Jacques Barzun[3] thought it 'an unconvincing thriller'. David Langford[4] called it 'A disappointing performance whose most memorable section turns out to be a recycling of one of the short stories'. Even favourable reviews damned it with faint praise. E. F. Bleiler considered it 'is an occasionally brilliant performance with fine characterisations, devastating irony, and a great deal of amusing self-parody'[5]. 'While characterisations are excellent and there are some delightful episodes, the pace is tedious, the telling is at times ponderous, and the key elements of the plot unconvincing' wrote Joan Seay.[6]

Arnold Bennett considered all Bramah's detective books 'far fetched' but then Bennett thought Conan Doyle was 'poor' too. If *The Bravo of London* compared less favourably with the previous Carrados books it is nevertheless highly regarded by book collectors when over £1,000 is being sought for first editions – perhaps because there was never an American edition.

The use of 'Bravo' in the title is puzzling and it is a mystery why Cassell agreed to such an apparently un-commercial title. It is an unfamiliar term in English in the context in which it is used. In any event few readers were likely to have known what a Bravo was unless they had read Manzoni's *The Betrothed*. It is explained in Manzoni's text that 'the intolerable affliction in which this City of Milan has lived and still lives on account of bravos and vagabonds'. Obviously Bramah was also aware that the term would not be generally known so at the outset of the book he explained that it is an Italian word meaning a hired assassin. Interestingly, W. W. Jacobs had used the title 'The Bravo' in a *Strand Magazine* story published seven years earlier.

◆

The tale concerns Julien Joolby, the owner of a shady antiques shop with a 'monstrous distortion' of a face, bloated and crippled, who devises an elaborate counterfeiting scheme which involves stealing special bank note paper from a mill and printing and circulating high denomination notes.

The plot is based on a real life incident that has been confirmed by the Bank of England. In 1862 a large quantity of paper, specially manufactured for the Bank of England, had been stolen from Portal's Mill at Laverstock in Hampshire and was used for the fabrication of forged notes. The Bank issued a notice offering £500 reward for the apprehension and conviction of the thieves and a further £1,000 for the apprehension of the forgers. Later four men were charged and convicted. It appears that a master key duplicate had been made which enabled the robbery to take place and one of the convicted men was an employee of the mill and had taken paper at various times.

In the story, Bramah reveals the same streak of anti-Semitism that was common among his contemporaries. One of the plotters is Bronksy – a Jewish Soviet agent – who intends to use the forged notes to undermine or destroy the British economy. Bronsky is however a dupe and Joolby intends to keep the notes himself. There is an element of prescience here since this is what the Germans attempted to do during the Second World War. More recently North Korea, using a Russian K.G.B. agent, was found to be involved in a global plot to forge currency.

Joolby has a Chinese servant Won Chou who Bramah has speak in Pidgin English in most of the book but in colloquial English in the latter part since Won Chou was educated at a mission school.

> "He much plenty busy now" persisted Won Chou, faithfully carrying out his instructions, "Me makee show carpet, makee show cabinet, chiney, ivoly, picture –makee show on ting, two ting, any ting."

Bramah's sudden descent to Pidgin English makes it impossible not to compare unfavourably the style of this conversation with the elegant, delicate and elaborate language of Kai Lung. In this instance, unlike his other non-English accents, they seem very accurate. It is a tribute to Bramah's meticulous working methods that in a dummy copy of *The London Handbook* there is a short lexicon of Pidgin with English meanings. The phrases were, in all probability, taken from some sort of guidebook or dictionary that may well have also given pronunciation. Many words given in this vocabulary can be found in the text of *The Bravo of London*.

Won Chou's part in the plot is significant. It is however asking a great deal of the reader to accept the coincidence that Carrados had previously encountered Won Chou in Shanghai where he had tried to sell his sister to him.

In this book Max Carrados is without his usual foils. His niece, Norah Mellhuish, (the name another version of Melwish in the Introduction to *The Specimen Case*) fills that role and manages to get him into serious trouble which his usual associates and his employees would have helped him to avoid. Nora is a feisty young lady but not always either very sensible or practical. She does not contribute to the plot or enliven the narrative in the same way as do Carlyle, Parkinson and Greatorex. There is no love interest to justify Nora's inclusion so it is hard to understand the thinking behind dropping the established characters. It appears to have been a creative mistake.

Carrados, of course, thwarts the plot but not before he is captured with his niece by the plotters, at which point the reader has to totally suspend belief. The detective shoots out the gaslight, so that as a blind person he then has advantage over the others in the room – a stratagem Bramah used in another plot – and then as one of the criminals attempts to re-light it, he shoots the match out of his hand. Nevertheless, captured and abandoned and locked in a cell-like room he manages to effect a rescue by tapping out an S.O.S. in Morse code on a water pipe and, incredibly, a Water Board inspector happens to be nearby checking on the unauthorised use of water and, even more incredibly, can read Morse code!

There is an interesting reference towards the end of the book. "Nickel will never make a reliable shot," confided Max Carrados to the little band of paralysed listeners, "He always takes sight too low – fault of British musketry training." This is again evidence that Bramah was knowledgeable about using firearms and was the author of the musketry course manual referred to in Chapter Ten. The skills of 'sighting' were written up in the manual.

Moments of high drama unfortunately become melodrama of the sort associated with barnstorming companies and early silent films: "Oh you fiend" she flung back, "you unutterable brute. You would never dare."

Bramah's willingness to re-cycle and build on earlier works is evident throughout his career. There is some similarity between 'The Missing Witness Sensation' in the *Max Carrados Mysteries* and *The Bravo of London*. He also adapted the book as a play called *Adventure*, a draft of which exists but it is not known if it was ever performed. Given the popularity of Bramah's dramas with amateur companies there is every possibility it was staged although no published copy has been found. Samuel French, who had and has the largest catalogues of plays, had no knowledge of it.

As with *A Little Flutter*, Bramah's previous full-length novel, his imagination sometimes deserts him. While there are flashes of the earlier skilful Carrados writing, with its characterisations and humour, it does not, for the most part, compensate for a story which is at times leaden and, in places, the plot unfolds at a snail's pace.

The Bravo of London finally confirmed to even the most enthusiastic of Bramah's readers that his métier was indeed the short story. Dorothy L. Sayers was right that there is a difference between a short story writer and a novelist.

♦

Whether Bramah originally intended this to be the last appearance of Max Carrados cannot be known but neither the critical reviews nor its sales would have been an encouragement to write again about the blind detective. Nevertheless the reviews, contemporary and later ones, should not be allowed to detract from the very high overall reputation of the Max Carrados series. S. S. Van Dine's[7] (the creator of Philo Vance) assessment must stand that 'Carrados must be given a place in the forefront of famous fictional sleuths'.

As with *A Little Flutter* which was either ignored or denigrated by the critics but went on to achieve good sales, *The Bravo of London* was sufficiently popular with the public to justify a cheap edition in 1932. It was also sold to a Canadian publisher. Penguin Books considered it for their catalogue in 1957 but they did not proceed with it. There has never been an American edition.

Despite this, as late as 1941 there was still £106 of unearned balance from his advance. Without knowing what that advance was it is nevertheless obvious that seven years after it appeared the book had not attracted a sufficient audience to clear it. The book was probably eventually remaindered or pulped. As late as 1956 the unearned balance remained unchanged.

Perhaps the observation of one philosopher applied in good measure to Bramah. 'He was a victim of that mania to which so many clever men are subject of liking that work best which they do worst.'[8]

Inevitably then it was back to Bramah's mythical China that had never failed to please critics, publishers and of course, his public. There was no great urgency to write another Kai Lung book. There was already a Kai Lung trilogy, *The Kai Lung Omnibus*[9] in preparation comprising the first three titles. Bramah could afford to rest on his laurels as indeed he did for a further six years.

Sources & Notes

1   Ernest Bramah. *The Bravo of London*. Cassell. London.1932 op. cit. p.8.

2   William White. *Twentieth-Century Literary Criticism.* op. cit. p8.

3   Jacques Barzun. *Twentieth-Century English Literature.* op. cit. p.9.

4   David Langford. 'Ernest Bramah: crime and Chinoiserie'. op. cit.

5   Ernest Bramah. *Best Max Carrados Detective Stories.* op. cit. Introduction by E. F. Bleiler. p.vii.

6   Quoted by Joan Seay in an essay on Ernest Bramah. *Dictionary of Literary Biography*. Vol. 70. op. cit. p.47.

7   ibid.

8   Julius Hare. *Guesses at Truth*. Taylor and Walton. London. 1898.

9   Ernest Bramah. *The Kai Lung Omnibus*. Quality Press. London. 1936.

CHAPTER EIGHTEEN

THE LAST KAI LUNG AND A POSTHUMOUS RETURN

Bramah had almost reached his allotted three score years and ten but his literary fecundity was undiminished. In the years following *The Bravo of London,* he continued to produce short stories, including those that were later to appear in *Punch.* In the same year he made the second of his only known broadcasts. It was a contribution to the series 'The BBC Presents the ABC' in which different speakers contributed short pieces themed according to the successive letters of the alphabet. Bramah's letter was 'W' and his subject 'Wizards', often to be found in Kai Lung plots. The late Alan Keith, still broadcasting sixty years later, presented the programme. Regrettably but understandably, he had no recollection of that particular broadcast.

Bramah's elder sister, a woman of independent means and character, (she travelled round the world alone when in her eighties) died in April 1939 at the age of eighty-five, her death being registered by Maisie. She left the house and its contents to Ernest as well as the income from other assets. There were no bequests to other siblings as her elder brother, Charles, had died in 1906 and youngest sister, Rose, in 1926. In Maisie's Will written in 1952, she refers to Ernest's and her own intention to leave this house to Ernest's two nieces the children of his brother Charles, instead of which she left them the proceeds of the sale of the house, a sum of £3,600.

Despite the rumours and imminence of war, after some thirty years, in early 1939, Ernest and his wife left Ravenscourt Mansions to move eastward. They leased a flat at 124 Holland Park Avenue, a prosperous area close to Notting Hill. A contributing factor for the move was probably the forty-six steps up to the Ravenscourt Mansions apartment that may have become too much for the ageing author.

Their new home was definitely an improvement on Ravenscourt Mansions in terms of size and location. It was a large, three-bedroomed flat in part of a terrace of elegant Victorian houses, a short distance from Holland Park itself, and looked out onto leafy Holland Park Avenue. The ground floor stretched out over the pavement to create shops. The flat is the largest one in the building as through some architectural quirk it extends into the building next door.

Unintentionally, evidence was found of the Bramahs' occupation of the flat. In 1975 a later owner removed a fire surround and found tucked into an unused chimney space a cache of antique coins wrapped in an old copy of *The Times*. It is unlikely they were hidden there to protect them from theft and forgotten perhaps in the chaos of their move to Weston-Super-Mare during the Blitz. Ernest was too addicted to his hobby to have deliberately left them behind when the risk of the building being bombed was not inconsiderable. (A bomb did in fact demolish a house opposite.) A more likely explanation is that Maisie took them back to London after leaving Weston-Super-Mare and hid them either for safety or, more likely, it was another act of eccentricity.

The Second World War broke out a few months after the move but what was to be called 'the phoney war' did not affect their way of life nor Ernest's work although he was now a sick man suffering with heart disease. While he was living in Holland Park Avenue he began work on the last Kai Lung book – *Kai Lung Beneath the Mulberry Tree*.[1] Its publication was enthusiastically greeted by the continually swelling number of appreciative readers and by the critics. Although four decades had passed since the first Kai Lung book there is no lessening of the humour, no deviation in the style and no diminishment in the strength of the writing. Characters still speak with amazing prolixity and circumlocution; the women archly hiding their emotions in thickets of words and double meanings. John Connell in his 1947 Third Programme talk,[2] 'The recluse who created Kai Lung' illustrated this with passages taken both *The Wallet* (1900) and Kai *Lung Beneath the Mulberry Tree* (1940).[3]

How unendurable is the position of a person who by the vicissitudes of fate is condemned to a detested lot! Why should the one who is speaking owing to an irrational father's unbecoming whim, be on the point of an alliance with a penurious and intellectually moth-eaten writer of third-rate verse when she had long in secret fixed her hopes on the congenial image of a profound philosopher, who in addition to being in every way a more trustworthy guide would have been able to satisfy her most fanciful ambitions?

This, Connell maintained, has precisely the same flawless texture, its sentences are modulated in precisely the same rippling rhythm as those passages Bramah wrote forty years earlier:[4]

'The unusual circumstances of the matter have already been put forth,' said an elderly Mandarin of engaging appearance, 'so that nothing remains to be known excepting the end of our despicable efforts to come to an agreeable conclusion. In this we have been successful, and now desire to notify the result. A very desirable and not unremunerative office, rarely bestowed in this manner, is lately vacant and taking into our minds the circumstances of the event, and the fact that Ling comes from a province very esteemed for the warlike instincts of its inhabitants, we have decided to appoint him commander of the valiant and bloodthirsty band of archers now stationed at Si Chose in the Province of Hu-Nan. We have spoken. Let three guns go off in honour of the noble and invincible Lin, now and henceforth a commander in the ever-victorious Army of the Sublime Emperor, Brother of the Sun and Moon, and Upholder of the Four Corners of the World.

What neither Connell nor indeed any other critic appear to have remarked upon is that never for one moment in this or the previous Kai Lung books does Bramah allow himself to be seen or felt behind the bland mask of his story teller. The impersonation is complete. *Kai Lung Beneath the Mulberry Tree* is a collection of tales that, unlike *The Moon of Much Gladness*, features Kai Lung both as a character and as the teller of tales as in *The Wallet*. The first part is a novella and concerns the adventures of Prince Ying who exchanges clothes with a peasant to go among his people in disguise. 'Prince Ying and the virtuous Mei' has both *The Prince and the Pauper* and *Cinderella* elements with a cast including two ugly sisters and the downtrodden relative who is a bullied lowly servant.

Among the treasures of the novella are tales of how Chess was invented and how Prince Ying saved his land from the dangers of printing and of gunpowder. There is however a strange contradiction between what Kai Lung tells his audience about the tales and at least two of the stories themselves. In 'The story of Yin Ho' Kai Lung challenges his audience:[5]

> ...can the index finger of denunciation be pointed to a single case where wrongdoing has flourished in the end or where the ultimate success and felicity of the one on whose behalf the circle's sympathy has been enticed has not been satisfactorily adjusted?

Yet in the preceding narrative 'Lin T'sing's ignoble alliance' it ends with the good Prince Ying and his beautiful and clever wife besieged by enemies retiring to their innermost sanctuary and then:[6]

> Unsheathing a light blade he habitually wore, Ying composed himself into a suitable position on the couch and after a reassuring glance towards the queen performed with a single stroke all that was necessary for a dignified self-ending. After a brief but sufficient interval spent in arranging his limbs and covering above Mei took from a concealed place in her robes a small crystal jar in which gold leaves floated among a delicately perfumed essence. When she had consumed the liquid and assured herself that nothing more remained to effect a becoming close she lay down by the prince's side and drew the coverlet over them.

And again in the 'The story of Yin Ho' the unfortunate hero having failed his examinations twelve times is, for topsy-turvy reasons, awarded a government post as Chief Detector of Hitherto Undetected Crimes.

Unfortunately his first assignment is to arrest his father-in-law. It concludes:

> ...he could not entirely free his mind of an element of suspense at the thought of what Hoa-mi's (his wife) attitude might be when she learned of what would by then have happened to her venerated father.

This is probably the most unsatisfactory end of any Kai Lung story since Yin Ho's dilemma is not resolved. Perhaps it was meant to continue after another appeal by Kai Lung for further contributions to be placed in his bowl as in 'The story of Sam-tso'.

> When Kai Lung had reached this point in the story of Sam-tso...it was his custom to rise and begin to roll up his weather-beaten mat but should there ensue any noticeable protest that the record was incomplete inasmuch as the minds of his hearers were still concerned with the various fortunes of those who had been involved he would willingly prolong the occasion. "The trend of your argument is pretty plain O verbose Kai Lung" one would happily then exclaim, "but we who remain are here to learn what happened to Sam-tso and those of the House of Wong and not to listen to your full throated persuasion. The more justice-loving among us have already generously contributed to your insatiable bowl and the less scrupulous are not likely to be enticed into doing so at this stage of your entertainment. However, here is an onion towards your evening rice and possibly others may be no less indulgent."

As indeed they were. The tale proceeded to its bitter-sweet end. Success and fortune crowning Sam-tso's enterprise while of his five siblings 'a spirit of frustration marked their passage' and they each sped on to disasters of different sorts.

Neither the tale of Prince Ying nor Yin Ho conforms to Kai Lung's claim of 'the ultimate success and felicity of the one on whose behalf the circle's sympathy has been enticed'.

A notable difference between this and the other Kai Lung books is the presence of a luxurious bedding of plump footnotes to explain incidents and references which, in previous books had been incorporated in the narrative. In 'The story of Ton Hi' the footnote spreads across almost the whole of two pages and is a subsidiary story in itself.

In one narrative, uniquely, the tale is written and not recited. 'It can no longer be concealed from the least intelligent of those who are so wasteful of their priceless time as to read these printed leaves.'

Kai Lung is also missing from two other stories. The effect of course, as in *The Moon of Much Gladness,* is to remove the delightful persuasive invitations to an audience to listen to his tales and their inter-action such as that which is illustrated earlier and which occurs at the beginning of many of the stories previously told. Fortunately for those readers who savour the compliments and barbs that precede the narrative Bramah returns to the old formula in the later chronicles.

Once again there is evidence that Bramah was not averse to re-cycling ideas as well as stories. There is some superficial resemblance between 'The story of Sho Chi' with his tame forest birds and a later one published in *Punch* 'Kewy Cho and the grateful song bird'.

The book is the equal of, and compares well with, the other four Kai Lung books. It was an immediate success and The Richard's Press reprinted it in 1944, 1946 and again in 1951. The book seems to have been undeservedly neglected in the U.S.A. According to the Mike Berro Bibliography[7] *Kai Lung Beneath the Mulberry Tree* did not find an American publisher until 1978.

There is little doubt Kai Lung paid a predominant part in changing the image of the evil, devious and Oriental typified in Sax Rohmer's books which featured the opium-smoking master criminal, Dr. Fu Manchu and who was perpetuated in hundreds of comics, boys' books, films and a regular feature on Radio Luxembourg. George Orwell's analysis of 'Boys' weeklies'[8] showed that in their stories foreigners conform to patterns with the Chinese characterised in these publications as menacing and treacherous. If a Chinese character appears, he is still the sinister pig-tailed opium smuggler and smoker. He is always Bret Harte's, Bramah's favourite author, 'The heathen Chineee'. The only thinkable role for an Asiatic in fiction up to that time was that of a felon. The gentle, wise and erudite Kai Lung may not have eliminated the stereotyping but he certainly modified it. Charlie Chan, at a later date, also contributed to improving the fictional image of the Chinese, although of course he was Hawaiian-Chinese, a fact overlooked by most of his devotees.

♦

In 1972 William White collected some of the aphorisms into one manuscript which was offered unsuccessfully to a number of publishers. A rejection letter from John Baker (now part of A. & C. Black) asks if White wanted them to send the typescript to another publisher or return it. Significantly the signatory stated 'Would that I could phrase this as Ernest Bramah would have done.'[9] A later communication from Black's states that they had arranged for a relatively new and conservative house to take the Kai Lung titles and suggesting this firm might publish a book to be called *The Aphorisms of Kai Lung*.

This company would appear to have been The Garnstone Press. A letter from them to William White[10] dated February 2nd 1973 stated that the 'other Kai Lung books were only selling at a rate of 190-200 books a year' which implies Garnstone Press had taken the titles. Bertram Rota a London Bookseller wrote in 1980[11] that 'the Garnstone reprints of Ernest Bramah's books are all out of print'. There is no evidence of a Garnstone Press imprimatur but it is of course possible they continued to print and sell the books using the Black plates.

Despite the slow sales Garnstone wanted to proceed with *The Aphorisms* but using the title *Kai Lung Says*. William White agreed to the change as he too felt their title was more commercial than the original.

In 1974 the correspondence was continuing but later that year White, obviously frustrated by Garnstone's indecision and financial frailty and being unable to get a decision from them, began offering the manuscript to American publishers. In 1975 he received a firm, but not particularly attractive, offer for it to be published as a chapbook from Capra Press. Financially it was less than rewarding; payment in copies and a royalty if sales exceeded 1,000. Whether White accepted the offer is not clear but in any event it was withdrawn in 1976. In 1979 he was trying to retrieve the manuscript from The American Baptist Historical Society – a strange choice for a publisher – without success. As late as 1980

The Aphorisms were still being offered. Regrettably all trace of the manuscript has been lost. The thought that it might still exist but dangles tantalisingly out of reach is intriguing.

Kai Lung Beneath the Mulberry Tree might have been the last in the series but the teller of tales was to make a posthumous return. In April 1973, at the suggestion of William White five other American enthusiasts, joined with him to underwrite a non-profit venture for another Kai Lung book to be called *The Kai Lung Six*.[12] It was to comprise six stories that had previously only appeared in *Punch* in 1940 and 1941 and had not been published in book form. They were therefore new stories to most Bramah aficionados who did not see *Punch* – not a widely distributed periodical in the U.S.A. The Introduction was by William White appropriately enough entitled 'Ernest Who?' It was also the basis for an article 'Is There an Ernest Bramah?' that subsequently appeared in a Korean magazine and doubtless was the result of White's visit to Korea as a Fulbright scholar.

A year later the proofs were ready and decisions had been taken on the jacket, binding, size, illustration and tentative cost which was estimated at about $7 per copy with a cover price of $10. There were to be special bindings for the original sponsors and for presentation copies that were to be given away. The book was published in 1974 under the title *The Kai Lung Six* with an edition of 250 copies, about a quarter of which were given to those who had provided capital for the venture, reviewers and others. The hope was to break-even at 200 copies. By August 1974 half of the original investment had been recovered from sales. In the end the price was $20 but despite being called 'over-priced' by William White the whole edition was sold within a few months and at least one London bookseller, Bertram Rota, wanted to buy copies for resale. The sponsors of the book, faced with a minimum of three months' delay to get a Library of Congress and an ISBN number decided to proceed without either.

Their enthusiasm for the posthumous publication led them to suggest both a Bramah party and exhibition but whether these events ever took place is not known.

One of the original sponsors wrote to William White that two further Kai Lung books were planned comprising unpublished stories with the second containing some of White's thirty-eight articles on Bramah, letters and a bibliography. It was hoped to get unpublished material from the Harry Ransom Humanities Center at the University of Texas where nearly all the Bramah material had been deposited. Clearly the idea did not come to fruition and *The Kai Lung Six* was indeed to be the last book featuring the eponymous storyteller.

◆

Some of the out-of-print Bramah writings may be re-issued. Changes in copyright law took the copyright protection from 1992 to 2012. Fortunately it may not be necessary to wait that long as William Charlton purchased the Copyrights from W. P. Watt. Charlton intends to publish or re-publish Bramah material for what is hoped will be a new generation of enthusiasts who have had no opportunity of engaging with the delights of his Chinese storyteller or the uncanny abilities of his blind detective. In addition there is a not inconsiderable volume of unpublished material still to see the light of day. Bramah himself listed thirty-five titles of unpublished manuscripts, but at what point in time that list was compiled it has not been established. The task is a considerable one given significant parts of the unpublished material are in Bramah's barely decipherable handwriting which William Charlton has been able to unravel.

The decline of interest in Kai Lung, partly because of lack of availability had, with much justification, been attributed by John Logan in a letter to William White in 1967[13] to 'The tempo of the times is not conducive to any widespread enjoyment of the stories. It takes a calm and contemplative person to enjoy the full flavour of the unique Kai Lung. He is out of step with the modern day world, but it is nice to get in step with him and slow the world down a bit.'

This last appearance of Kai Lung illustrates that it is not necessary to read all the Chinese tales to appreciate that Bramah was not writing about China nor was he satirising the Chinese. Far from it; it is Westerners, their ways and institutions, which are the targets and which he never fails to strike with precision and humour.

Writing in the *Northern Echo*[14] probably in the very early part of the twentieth century a prescient reviewer wrote that;

Literary prophecy is notoriously dangerous; but there seem to be grounds for believing that a hundred years hence Mr. Bramah's Kai Lung tales will still be read an admired.

He was right.

Sources & Notes

1   Ernest Bramah. *Kai Lung Beneath the Mulberry Tree*. The Richards Press. London. 1940.

2   John Connell. 'The recluse who created Kai Lung'. op. cit.

3   Ernest Bramah. *Kai Lung Beneath the Mulberry Tree*. op. cit. p.307.

4   Ernest Bramah. *The Wallet of Kai Lung*. Grant Richards. London. 1900. op. cit. pp.22-3.

5   Ernest Bramah. *Kai Lung Beneath there Mulberry Tree*. op. cit. p.140.

6   ibid. p.129.

7   www.mike@ernestbramah.com op. cit.

8   George Orwell. 'Boys' weeklies'. *Horizon*. London. March 1940.

9   H.R.H.R.C. op. cit. February 11th 1972.

10   H.R.H.R.C. op. cit. February 2nd 1973.

11   H.R.H.R.C. op. cit. April 9th 1980.

12   *The Kai Lung Six*. The Non-Profit Press. Tacoma. Washington. 1974.

13   H.R.H.R.C. op. cit. January 20th 1967.

14   H.R.H.R.C. op. cit. Extract of reviews compiled by Ernest Bramah. n.d.

Chapter Nineteen

THE THEATRE

Bramah wrote a number of plays and some stories were dramatised by other playwrights. The Jerwood Library of the Performing Arts has not been able to trace any professional productions in London or the Provinces other than the Old Vic Students' production of *Kai Lung's Golden Hours* already mentioned. Bramah definitely states, and there is no reason not believe him, that 'two of my one act plays adapted from Max Carrados stories are frequently performed at different London variety theatres and frequently broadcast'.[1] It is known that a play derived from an unsold story 'Cheerful tragedy' – *The Lesser Evil* – was performed at the Haymarket theatre in 1910 and *Blind Man's Bluff* at a theatre in Chelsea. Doubtless there were many others that have not been identified. Amateur theatre groups found Bramah plays most suitable for their limited means (and perhaps talents) and attractive to their audiences.

The Victorian & Albert Museum holds manuscripts of actors' parts for two plays adapted by Gilbert Heron for broadcasting and based on the stories *In the Dark* and *Blind Man's Buff*. While trying not to apply twenty-first century criticism to plays written nearly eighty years ago, it must be said that Heron does not appear to be a very good playwright. If Bramah could descend to melodrama Heron was pure barnstorming reminiscent of Tod Slaughter. After all 1930 was the year of Noel Coward's *Private Lives*, Somerset Maugham's *The Breadwinner* and Eugene O'Neill's *Mourning Becomes Elektra* not of *Maria Marten or Murder in the Red Barn*. The London theatre was vibrant and innovative.

The one script at the Theatre Museum that appears to be solely the work of Bramah is a dramatisation of 'The tragedy at Brookbend Cottage' that was originally in *Max Carrados*. A storm is a vital ingredient of the plot and, interestingly, the manuscript starts with guidance to the sound effects department. Bramah instructs; 'Thunder, though dramatically one of the most effective noises, is a two-edged weapon, and over-stressed it can become bathetic'. Perhaps not as bathetic as a character declaring "You fool! You sulky, wilful, sickly fool! ... At last I am rid of you for ever!" Possibly this outburst was the influence of Gilbert Heron. It is unquestionably his style and a very long way from the sure touch of Ernest Bramah. The play, which is thought to have been commissioned for broadcasting was never transmitted although in 1955 it was again under consideration and, as before, it was decided not to use it.

Among Bramah's papers with, alas, no indication if, when and where they were performed, are a number of short plays. There are manuscripts for plays called *The Last Groo-Groo*, *The Efficient Mrs. Higgs*, *Willow Plate*, (an adaptation of 'The embellishment of the willow plate pattern' and possibly the script used by the Old Vic Students production), *Lady Weedale's Diamond*, *Adventure* (taken from *The Bravo of London*), *Aggravette and Sadliso at Dinner* (a parody of Maeterlinck's *Alladine and Palomides)*, *The Game Played in the Dark*, *The Ingenious Mind of Mr. Rigby Lacksome.* (taken from *The Max Carrados Mysteries*), and the B.B.C. 1997 Radio broadcasts of *The Secret of Headlam Heights* and *The Ingenious Mind of Mr. Rigby Lacksome*. Adapted from 'Smothered in corpses' there is a burlesque for Cinema that appeared in print in 1919 in *The Living Age* (Boston) called *Smothered in Thrills* but it never reached the studio floor.

If Max Carrados offered excellent material for dramatisation the opposite is true of Kai Lung. It is perhaps understandable the stories, even when adapted for the stage, failed to find professional producers and were never performed (except the Old Vic students' production). The leisurely paces of the plots, the elaborate vocabulary and circumlocution and the subtlety of the humour and irony and above all the unending flow of maxims and euphemisms do not lend themselves easily to dramatisation. Grant Richards, who attended the Old Vic production, felt that the play did not capture the elusive quality of the stories of Kai Lung.[2]

There is little doubt the peculiar and unique essence of the Chinese stories is very difficult to transfer into a medium other than radio. One tale 'The invention of Yang Chung' was translated into Spanish with incidental music by Manual Lazerno. It was broadcast on September 19th 1951 in the Latin American Service of the B.B.C. The script, in Spanish, is still available in the archives of the B.B.C. but the score is lost. Alas, it does not seem any of the Chinese stories have ever featured in the B.B.C.'s many scheduled programmes of short story or serial readings and only very occasional broadcasts have been made by other organisations.

The South African Broadcasting Corporation paid Bramah the princely sum of £2.16.0.d. for a broadcast of 'The transmutation of Ling'. There is no record as to whether this was a reading or a dramatisation. There are references in correspondence to transmissions in Singapore/Malaysia in 1955. The topic(s) have not been identified.

There is a rare, if not unique, piece of dramatic criticism among the Bramah papers. The article called 'Two Camilles' probably intended for either *To-day* or *The Minster* could be described as a 'rave review'. His praise for Eleonora Duse as Marguerite Gautier in Dumas's *La Dame aux Camelias*, better known to opera Lovers as *La Traviata*, is unstinting.[3]

> Henceforth, beyond the stage, not a lip moved, hardly a finger stirred and through five acts the audience sat entranced; listening to the unfolding story of a courtesan, told to most in unknown tongue and relieved by singularly few dramatic incidents…in the auditorium people sat watching her and almost her alone.

It might be inferred from this and from his undoubted ability to satirise so perplexing a playwright as Maeterlinck in 'Aggravette and Sadliso at dinner' that Bramah's own taste in the theatre was for serious drama. He had however a familiarity with more plebeian performances in Music Hall and variety theatres. Chirgwin, The White-eyed Kaffir, who was top of the bill in Bramah's early days in London appears in one story, only in true Bramahian style he is playing Hamlet! Marie Lloyd, J. N. Maskelyn, the stage magician, Harry Lauder and Little Tich all make appearances. In later years he took his nephew and niece to the London Palladium and such variety performances as the Crazy Gang.

Kai Lung, Max Carrados and the other novels have not attracted the interest of the film industry. The Harry Ransom Humanities Research Center, Texas holds a film scenario *Safe Blind, Safe Find* but there is no evidence that this or any other of Bramah's writings were ever filmed. Even recognising that W. W. Jacobs's output was greater than Bramah's and his characters less esoteric, there is still a remarkable difference in their respective success rates in terms of the cinema. There have been almost fifty films (and one comic opera – Ethel Smyth's *The Boatswain's Mate*) based on W. W. Jacobs's stories including one of the most highly regarded Laurel and Hardy films *Our Relations*.

Perhaps Pinker, Jacobs's agent and who had once represented Bramah, had better connections in the film world than the Watt agency. There is a letter to Richards[4] in which Bramah writes 'The reason for this exception [him retaining all rights other than publishing] is that certain Max Carrados plays have been produced and I have given to the man who produced them a general undertaking for him to try and place the film rights. I hardly suppose he will.' Bramah was right, he didn't. A London would-be filmmaker in an undated letter to White, probably about 1980, expressed a determination to make a Kai Lung film and as late as 2004 an approach was made to William Charlton concerning filming *Kai Lung's Golden Hours*. Neither initiative developed beyond the inquiry stage. There is little doubt far worse plots found their way onto the screen mostly from the British film industry, particularly in the 1930s when it survived on what were called 'quota quickies'.[5]

If Bramah's activities and interests in the stage were catholic, there were nevertheless unexpected gaps in the theatrical interests of this clever, highly knowledgeable and cultured man.

Sources & Notes

1   H.R.H.R.C. Autobiographical note. op. cit.

2   Grant Richards. *Author Hunting.* op. cit. p.274.

3   H.R.H.R.C. op. cit. Manuscript.

4   H.R.H.R.C. op. cit. April 27th 1923.

5   'Quota quickies' were B features made to fulfil the requirement that every performance must contain a specified quota of British films. It was said of them by Alexander Korda that 'they didn't have to be good – they had to be ready by Tuesday'.

Chapter Twenty

AN 'EXCESSIVE ABSENCE OF INTEREST'

The Chief of Bowmen in 'The transmutation of Ling' is described as having an 'excessive absence of interest' a term that can be applied to three areas where Bramah also had 'an unendurable deficiency of resources' – art, music and sport.

As an Editor, and as an author of numerous books and articles, many of which were illustrated, it might be thought that Bramah would have given more than perfunctory attention to art and artists. But just as the great religious doctrinal controversies which so fascinated contemporary authors did not attract him as a topic neither did the various movements that inflamed and divided the world of art. Not even the tremors of the earthquake which Impressionism and Post-Impressionism caused reached him.

There is some confirmation of this lack of any real interest in painting and drawing in a brief comment in the article 'From Sydenham to St. Petersburg' when he wrote 'The museums and picture galleries – well, I confess that we had mutually agreed not to enter a single museum or picture gallery'.[1] This was a singularly shallow decision for a visitor to St. Petersburg with its wealth of artistic treasures and does betray a lack of aesthetic appreciation. The National Gallery rates one very brief mention in *The Optimist* where one character, like Ernest's sister, had had 'lessons in painting'.

Nevertheless despite apparently having little interest in illustration he commissioned artists and illustrators for the *London Year Book* and *The London Handbook*. Famous artists such as Aubrey Beardsley, Walter Sickert, Gordon Craig, Bernard Partridge, Byam Shaw and Lewis Baumer, (who had illustrated Bramah's second contribution to *To-day*) were either commissioned to provide drawings for articles and stories or their work was reproduced. Penrhyn Stanlaw, who was also a very regular *Punch* contributor, is credited with a caricature of Bramah in *The London Handbook*. Nathan Vanderlyn provided six illustrations for 'The rival rain-makers' also in *The London Handbook*.

Extant letters from one famous illustrator, Bernard Partridge, to Bramah are far from friendly and exhibit a degree of distrust in him or, more likely *The Minster* which he edited. In June 1895[2] he refused to work for them at their fee scale because he had received higher offers. Because of his suspicions he insisted on the fees being confirmed in writing. All his work was only to be used on the understanding that the original was to be returned and must be 'uninjured'. Most of the letters are highly critical of Bramah as editor and complaints and conditions abound, as well as refusals of commissions expressed in the most arrogant terms. '...but in the case of stories – this is a kind of work I almost invariably turn down.... . I prefer to do work that illustrates nothing but my own ideas'.[3] If this was typical of negotiating with artists it may well have affected Bramah's attitude towards illustration and illustrators. He, understandably, never asked Partridge to provide drawings for his articles or stories.

So far as his own books were concerned, he appears to have left the choice of illustrators largely to his publishers or editors. Bramah did suggest Penhrhyn Stanlaw but Grant Richards pointed out that he had given up illustration work. E. S. Hodson, a regular contributor to the *Strand Magazine* and Ernest Rhys both illustrated stories from *The Specimen Case* for *Cassell Magazine* (April 1907). J. Dewar Mills provided drawings for 'A bunch of violets' in the *Strand Magazine* (July 1924). George Wallace was an obvious choice as an illustrator since he had written and illustrated *The Big Game of Central and Western China*. The choice of the unidentified artists of some of the jacket illustrations, particularly *The Secret of the League*, one of the several editions of The *Wallet of Kai Lung* and *Kai Lung Unrolls His Mat* produced outstanding results.

It was Grant Richards who commissioned the American artist F. R. Kimborough to provide the cover design for *The Wallet*. It was claimed that the original American rights to *The Wallet* were purchased because the publisher, L. C. Page who bought 500 copies in sheets, found the jacket illustration particularly attractive. The design, to Grant Richards's great embarrassment, was in fact Japanese not Chinese.

Illberry Lynch, who was a follower of Aubrey Beardsley, undertook twelve Chinese designs for an American edition of the first tale from *The Wallet* 'The transmutation of Ling' which were much admired by Bramah. Grant Richards wrote 'The chief interest of the book consisted of the illustrations, there being a dozen plates in black-and-white by Mr Ilbery Lynch. These showed a wonderful skill in decorative line-work and one and all have been widely admired'.[4] Lynch also did the coloured plate for the 1923 edition of *The Wallet*.

One edition of *What Might Have Been* contains a single illustration signed 'Duncan'. The portrait of Max Carrados in *The Eyes of Max Carrados* is by the portraitist Ralph Peacock R.A. The cover drawing for the Hodder & Stoughton edition of *Max Carrados Mysteries* was by John Sewell. Ellen Edwards designed the jacket for *The Specimen Case*. The special luxury edition already mentioned of 'The story of Wan and the remarkable shrub' by the pre-apprentices at the School of Printing in the College of Arts & Crafts had six illustrations by W. J. Martindale an instructor at the College.

Wide as Bramah's interests were, it must be deduced that the illustrative arts were not a major concern to him. There are very few references to illustrators among the Bramah papers. This is very different to the attitude of other authors who were more often than not deeply involved in the choice of artist and subject. W. W. Jacobs, despite his somewhat relaxed approach to his own writings was intensely involved with illustrations. This could be of course because his artist, Will Owen, was also his life-long and closest friend.

◆

While art appeared to hold no great interest for Bramah, two other topics are particularly conspicuous by their absence in Bramah's work – music and sport. There must however have been some familiarity with Gilbert & Sullivan. W. S. Gilbert, whose humour almost certainly appealed to Bramah, is mentioned in several stories, and there is a comic policeman in the unpublished novel *The Optimist* who bears a considerable likeness to the police sergeant in *The Pirates of Penzance*.

In one plot, set in the twenty-ninth century, Bramah gently plays on a coincidence of names. Gilbert's Fairy Queen in *Iolanthe* sings of Captain Shaw[Chief of the London Fire Brigade], "Oh Captain Shaw/ type of true love kept under/Could thy Brigade/with cold cascade/ Quench my great love, I wonder". Bramah then proceeds to transmute George Bernard Shaw into Captain Shaw. The narrator's Guide explains "The last known reference to him [Bernard Shaw] is as Chief of the Metropolitan Fire Brigade".

Bramah quotes one of Gilbert's worst puns in 'The Oldest Known Poem in the World', in the *In Future* series.

> Bunthorne: "Do you yearn"
> Patience: "I earn my living"

Only one plot appears to have music as an important aspect of the tale. This is 'The dead march'[5] included in *The Specimen Case* and written in 1919. It is a tale that manages to include history, coins and a ghost. The relater finds 'a bit of silver, a denarius of Rome'. He rubs it, and Aladdin like, a Roman proconsul appears who is both a composer and critic of music and who was so offended by the playing of his Emperor that he left his court.

"You are a musician then?" I said.

"An amateur" he admitted carelessly. "Still, one who as a mere proconsul turned his back on a despot rather than endure his discords may be allowed to claim an ear."

My knowledge of music – or of despots – did not enable me to identify the particular ruler he alluded to. I sought enlightenment obliquely.

"Was he then so very poor a player?"

"He was not only that. After making due allowance for his exalted rank, he was, I would assert, the very worst player who has ever ventured to confront an audience."

There is a comic ghost story, 'A black business' published in *Land and Water* April 10th 1919 and in *The Specimen Case* (under the slightly different title 'A very black case', which is built around the ghost of a highly musical coal merchant although the music itself is not an integral part of the narrative.

Carrados was said to play the piano and to have loved chamber music and opera. Nevertheless there are no references in any of the plots to any actual operas or pieces of music. Although Maisie is thought to have played both the mandolin and piano, it can be deduced from Bramah's writings, that music was not important in his life, again a surprising deficiency in a cultured man of his time.

◆

Sport fares no better. Kong Ho makes satirical references to cricket, rugby and hockey. Max Carrados is said to be sport-loving and to have interests and was active as a boxer, golfer, a fisherman and a croquet player. Kai Lung was clearly not interested in sport and any references to outdoor games are difficult to find. There are passing references in some of the short articles and stories but nowhere does sport get more than the most casual mention, although judging from *The Mirror of Kong Ho* Bramah knew the rules of the sports Kong Ho writes about.

If Bramah lacked any real interest in music, art or sport there is some evidence that he understood and enjoyed gardening. (He seems to have had a particular liking for geraniums.) This is barely surprising given the large gardens at his childhood home, his farm, his homes at Marsden House, and Lothian Lodge both with gardens. However for most his life in London there was no opportunity to exercise his horticultural skills when for thirty years he lived in gardenless flats. Nevertheless there are stories and articles about gardening and gardens, which reveal both knowledge of and a love for them.

Sources & Notes

1   Ernest Bramah. 'Sydenham to St. Petersburg'. H.R.H.R.C. op. cit. n.d.

2   H.R.H.R.C. op. cit. 14th 1895.

3   ibid. n.d.

4   Grant Richards. *Author Hunting.* op. cit. p.272.

5   Ernest Bramah. 'The specimen case'. op. cit. pp.56-57.

CHAPTER TWENTY-ONE

THE MAN BEHIND THE MYSTERY

By 1940 almost all the successful writers of Bramah's generation were dead; Conan Doyle, Rudyard Kipling, John Buchan, Arnold Bennett and James Barrie. The gentle, humorous writers too; Jerome K. Jerome (who had been Bramah's role model), Israel Zangwill, Barry Pain, William Pett Ridge and W. J. Locke. In another three years the last of them were gone. W. W. Jacobs, Arthur Morrison and George Burgin and Ernest Bramah himself.

Some time in 1940 or 1941 Bramah and his wife left the London blitz for the safety of Weston-Super-Mare where they took up occupation at 40 The Boulevard. They probably chose Weston-Super-Mare to be close to Maisie's family, some of whom were living nearby in Clevedon. It was here at his wartime temporary home Bramah died, with Maisie at his side, on the 23rd June 1942 at the age of seventy-four from myocardial degeneration and arterio-sclerosis. He was cremated on June 26th at a private Bristol cemetery and his ashes were spread in the Garden of Rest.

Ernest's last months must have been a time of great personal depression, not only because of his deteriorating health but also because the country and the Empire which he loved so much were in a period of desperate crisis. He had lived through one world war and long enough into the second to see such decisive defeats as Dunkirk, the loss of Singapore, Malaysia and Burma. On the day of his death the Afrika Korps had recaptured Tobruk. Had he survived another year or two he might have died content with the long road to victory clearly in sight.

Obituaries appeared in many papers both in the Britain and the United States. The *Manchester Guardian*[1] surprisingly, since he was a Mancunian, gave him a mere two column inches, mostly factual whereas *The Times*[2] devoted three-quarters of a column which also included an assessment of his work. The *New York Times*[3] and the *New York Herald Tribune*[4] both carried full obituaries. The latter repeated the canard about him having lived in China and added to it by stating categorically that he wrote his Kai Lung books there.

Bramah's estate was £15,000 (over £400,000 in today's values) – a comfortable but not a huge sum for a successful author. His executors were his widow Maisie and the Public Trustee. There is some significance in the use of the Public Trustee. Possibly he felt that Maisie could not cope with the intricacies of proving the Will and distributing the bequests. There does not appear to have been any close friend or associate to whom he could delegate the task which, given his reclusive life style, is not surprising.

He left his widow a life interest in his estate including all the intellectual property. His sister, who had never married, had inherited a small income from her father's estate. Bramah's Will would have made this up to £300 per annum but his sister pre-deceased him in 1939. On Maisie's death three-quarters of the trust was to be divided equally between his four nephews and nieces. However for reasons which are completely inexplicable, other than perhaps Maisie's eccentricity, it appears that Ernest's nephew and niece received all the money from the sale of the property rather than an equal share of it with Maisie's nephew and niece.

The remaining quarter was to be divided between the Society of Authors' Fighting Fund and the Poor Box of the Metropolitan Police Courts. This last bequest reflects in a practical way Bramah's sympathy with miscreants, which can be found in some of his writing; for example Whitwash the convict in *A Little Flutter* and George Larch in *The Bravo of London*. 'George is the best copper-plate engraver in his line in England; he came out with a splendid character from the prison Governor – and not an earthly chance of getting a better job than rag picking'. The article 'Medallions made by gaol-birds' quoted in Chapter Fourteen also demonstrates this same sentiment.

A valuation of his literary estate at the time of his death made by his agent W. P. Watt for the executors shows that he was entitled to royalties on some thirteen titles, although some of the advances were still unearned. There is no explanation, other than it was an accidental omission for *The Specimen Case* not being included. The valuation also included receipts from anthologies, syndicated material and broadcasts. There was no attempt to place any values on the mass of unpublished material, presumably because whatever its intrinsic worth, until it was sold it had no value.

The valuation did not include the autobiographical manuscript because of Maisie's insistence that the parcel it was contained in was not to be opened. It was almost certainly destroyed unopened. Watt wrote to the Executors concerning the difficulty of valuing this manuscript unseen. He stated;[5]

> As to the manuscript of Mr Smith's autobiography, it is possible that it would have a value as an MS. It would certainly be impossible to value it without having it all read and it would be extremely difficult to value it even then. In fact, it seems to me at least arguable that, until it is published, it has no value at all except as a manuscript by Ernest Bramah.

Ernest's Will made provision for the cost of a memorial stone – a wish that was not fulfilled since he was cremated and he is now only an entry in the records of the Bristol General Cemetery Company. Ignoring this last request may reflect the alleged odd behaviour of his widow.

In 1944 Maisie presented to the Hammersmith Library copies of all the published works on the condition they were kept in the local collection for reference use only. In 1945 she also offered copies of anthologies which included Bramah stories, but the library did not take this up. They were however happy to have the three deluxe editions that had been produced for some of the titles. All the books continue to be held in the Hammersmith archives for reference purposes.

Handwriting analysis is not a science and neither is it acceptable to many people. It has however been used by biographers to augment other knowledge on such a disparate group of biographical subjects as P. G. Wodehouse, Margaret Thatcher, two of the Romanovs and Dennis Nilsen. Graphology, at the very least, can provide guidance to a greater understanding of the inner personalities and motivations of its subjects.

An analysis of Bramah's handwriting was carried out in 2000 by a leading graphologist Jane Patterson. It was made more exacting by having to use photocopies of letters rather than originals and largely confirmed much of what is known about him but adds some additional insights. In summary, the analysis shows him to have been an engaging, lively and interesting character, with no great materialistic ambitions but goal orientated. Other attributes were that he was logical and intuitive, unconventional and an originator of new aspects and ideas. Unsurprisingly the analysis identifies him as 'not socially confident or self-assured'. Other aspects of his personality were perceived as 'Dynamic, goes all out for his goal, but what he has achieved can cease to hold interest and there is a powerful need to progress further'. He is seen as having been exceptionally lucid but resisting mixing with people and needing his distance which today might be termed as needing his own space.

Among the small number of letters from, to and about Bramah, not one indicates anything other than formal relationships. It is, of course, possible that his personal correspondence was separated from his business letters and then destroyed by him or, more likely, Maisie. It is difficult to believe that, despite the fact he was non-gregarious, Ernest and Maisie were without a circle of friends – but probably not literary ones.

John Connell[6] had an ingenious theory about his attitude to publicity.

> Bramah was a secretive solitary because he had to be. His vision of China, which must have mattered to him far more than anything else, never tarnished, never dwindled in the light of common day, and never lost its strength. It was a young man's vision…which he maintained until well past seventy; but he did not risk its destruction by dissipating his energy on contacts with the literary world, however amiable and well-intentioned its approaches to him.

Bramah's efforts both for staying out of the public eye and keeping people at arms' length seems not have applied to quite the same extent where his hobby and passion – numismatics – was concerned. In a letter published in *Notes and Queries*[7] the writer stated that he found Bramah 'was far from difficult to approach by numismatists, and I had a pleasant letter from him in 1932 when I communicated to him a rather interesting discovery.'

◆

How does one assess the life of someone who so determinedly and successfully remained an enigma? He is surprisingly missing from most literary autobiographies and biographies of the period. The most unexpected omission is that of Jerome K. Jerome who had certainly been his role model, if not mentor, and who had taught him his editorial and writing skills. Others who knew him well and had worked with him are also silent – Alec Waugh, William Pett Ridge, St. John Adock, Charles Hind, Arthur Quiller-Couch and Edward Clodd by way of examples.

There is ample evidence in surviving correspondence of his desire not to meet people. Frequent excuses are given to avoid meetings. 'I am not very often in town', 'Out of town for a few weeks', 'moving about a great deal' and 'I am not often in town but hope to be able to call upon you within a week or two' 'I have been summoned away to the country' are among the excuses offered for either not meeting or cancelling previously arranged appointments. A letter to William White[8] from Patricia Butler, an employee of his agent, who knew Bramah stated, 'Ernest Bramah was, I think, not so much a solitary as one of the authors who wanted to keep his private and public life entirely separate.' An approach in 1936 by a journalist for an interview, which most authors would have been delighted to give, was met with a gentle refusal, a copy of the biographical notes he had prepared thirteen years earlier and a polite request not to write to him at home but care of A. P. Watt.

He frequently avoided giving his address in correspondence, using his father's and sister's or that of his publishers or agent instead or indeed giving none at all. As late as 1936 when he had been living at Ravenscourt Mansions for nearly thirty years for some correspondents he continued to use his sister's residence in Hendon. He gave no address at all in a 'thank you' letter to Hilaire Belloc and Peterborough writing in the *Daily Telegraph*[9] complained 'A year or so ago I had the rare distinction of receiving a letter from him commenting politely on some comment of my own. I should have replied – but there was no address on his letter.' Even his publishers did not always know where he was. Grant Richards in 1923 concludes a letter with 'I hope you are having a good holiday anyhow wherever you are'.

Writing to A. C. Bentley, Bramah refers to being incapacitated by acute bronchial trouble lasting many weeks. This might indicate that Bramah was an asthmatic. If he was an asthmatic it might in part account for his avoidance of publicity and social contacts and events. There was also the problem in later life with his throat that made eating slow and difficult and which perhaps would have been an embarrassment when dining in public or with people who were not close relatives.

Despite statements that he was a member of societies and clubs favoured by the literati, there is no evidence that supports this. While it might have been expected that he would have some link with the Numismatic societies, no trace of his association with them exists. P.E.N. and the Garrick did not attract him. He was not tempted by membership of, or being a guest at, the illustrious Omar Khayyam dining club which all the leading authors, publishers and agents either belonged to or attended their functions. With the exception of The Society of Authors, of which he was a member but played no part whatsoever in its affairs, there is not a shred of evidence to support the idea that he was in the slightest way a 'clubbable' man.

Ernest Bramah was never part of the usually well-rewarded lecture circuit. Indeed there is evidence he was a spectacularly poor speaker. His niece Rosemary persuaded him to address her sixth form Literary and Debating Society where, to her great embarrassment "he spoke in a dry fashion and was long winded and boring".

On being told by an American publisher 'I always had the feeling that you were a mythical person', Bramah responded;[10] 'There is something not unattractive in the idea of being a mythical person...though from the heroic point of view one might have wished that it could have been a 'mythological personage.'

Was Bramah revealing his own views when he has a character, Reginald Carfax, in *The Optimist,* declare "I think the phrase 'a keen sense of humour' is the most offensively banal in the English language? It's the quintessence of semi-detached suburban playfulness and is permeated with a spirit of amateur debating societies in their lighter moments."

As the manuscript contains much autobiographical material it could be that this reflected Bramah's feelings on the topic. Yet is undeniable Bramah had the most highly developed sense of humour. What else could it be called?

He was prepared to be the butt of other people's humour. In his B.B.C. talk he relates how in a library copy of Max Carrados he found a reader had written 'Max Carrados is not' and then discovered that the amateur critic's 'n' was an 'r'.

♦

That he was also a courteous man emerges clearly from his correspondence, all of which is well mannered, urbane and affable. It shows a meticulous adherence to good manners. As has been related, his concern and attempts to make amends for the inadvertent use of the title *What Might Have Been* when he found that it was also the title of a book by Cashel Hoey is typical of the man. He thanked Editors for reviews of his books. 'Will you please accept (and at a convenient opportunity convey to your book reviewer "D.L.M." also) my sincere thanks for the gratifying notice of *The Return of Kai Lung* appearing in a recent edition of the *Transcript*.'[11]

In a letter to George Orwell[12] he not only thanked him for his kind comments on *Max Carrados* but also accepted his reservations on Kai Lung. 'I could not conscientiously dispute that you have good grounds for your lack of interest,' There is in the Bramah papers a letter of appreciation to E. C. Bentley for mentioning Kai Lung in his memoirs. He writes to the editor of *The Sunday Referee*;[13] 'Notices of this generous scope and measure only comes one's way in the course of blue moons. If I thank a publication for giving me an ordinary good review (what seems to me to be a pleasant duty) what can I say about Mr. [Humbert] Wolfe's?'

Remarkably, there does not appear to have been a cross word between him and his many publishers other than the dispute with Grant Richards which was eventually resolved amicably. Bramah's dismissal of Pinker as his agent was undertaken without rancour and expressed in the most moderate of terms.

From scattered comments of those who had met him or

communicated with him (and indeed from his Will) a picture emerges of 'one of the kindest and the most amiable of men'. 'You have been the soul of generosity' Richards wrote. Another example of this generosity can be found in an extant book criticism. His admiration for G. K. Chesterton's Father Brown, a commercial rival of Carrados, is considerable declaring 'Father Brown is the one detective whom it is endurable to read twice in a lifetime…you never trouble about the flimsiness of the structure in wonder at the astonishing brilliance of the trappings…you can read or reread a Chesterton detective story over and over again with gratitude.'[14] His praise for Grant Richards's first novel *Caviare* was unstinting.[15] 'I found it literally impossible to tear myself away until the last page was reached. I certainly found it too easy to neglect other things once I had got into it.' He did take occasional good-natured digs at Conan Doyle (S. Holmes the detective in *A Little Flutter*) and, perhaps with a slight touch of asperity, George Bernard Shaw too, depicted as a Gilbertian character.

Grant Richards sketches him as '…small and – may I say – he does not look ferocious.' Hugh Greene who knew him says he was a small bald man with twinkly black eyes and reputation for immense kindness of heart. It is more than likely that the properties he owned and were occupied by his various relatives were either rent-free or for a purely nominal rent. When his nephew, John Barker, could not afford the College fees to study Horticulture, Ernest provided money to help him. In letters accompanying presents of toys for his nephews and nieces with characteristic thoughtfulness he writes: 'I thought I had better address the parcel to you [his sister in law] as it would be for you to say if they could have them just now…I thought for example if you want Jack to keep to his books particularly just now, you mightn't care about his having anything to take his mind off school work.'

◆

Whatever the qualities of the man, Mark Valentine in an article in *The Book Collector*[16] noted a 'sinister edge to his works and a detachment and even amorality in some Kai Lung tales'. He summed him up as 'a kindly misanthrope'. John Mortimer while unstinting in his praise of Bramah's literary skills and describing the Kai Lung stories as a 'literary tour de force' nonetheless found some stories 'slightly repellent' and could not see executions and torture as subjects for humour. In this he compares Bramah with W. S. Gilbert, presumably *The Mikado*[17] where both figure as an important part of the plot. E. F. Bleiler, despite his sympathetic comments on Bramah's personality that were quoted earlier, did recognise he had 'a secret liking for coarse melodrama'. Another unnamed American critic, on the occasion of a reprint in 1972, described him as 'a secretive man with a dash of sadistic prurience in his make up'. There is absolutely no evidence of prurience but there is undoubtedly sadism. In what is thought to be an unpublished piece 'The subtlety of Kang-Cheng', the principal character burns off a finger to bind himself to a vow to "seek out Kio-Feng…I will fall upon him…and taking him between my two hands I will crush him until his bones press out between my fingers." At the end of the story the spirit of Kang Chieng's father '…entered the body of Kio-Feng and squeezed his heart between its two hands until it became as dry and devoid of life as an uprooted sponge cast upon a burning sandbank…'

In the dramatisation of the Willow Plate story Fang has a gory end – decapitated and his head displayed to the audience.

Another example comes from 'The Emperor who meant well'.[18]

The street in which the false Khan lodged was purified of his presence by an all-consuming fire and a good many other people who were supposed to be implicated in one way or another were bowstrung, thrown into pits, buried in sand, knouted, bastinadoed, drawn over broken glass, compressed in cages lengthened on racks and inconvenienced in many other ingenious fashions with fire, water, cord, blade and blunt implements according to their degree of guilt.

In 'The vengeance of Tung Fel' there is a malign and sinister atmosphere of tragedy. Betrayal abounds; father betrays son, wife betrays husband, lover betrays lover and the Mandarin rules his people with a pitiless cruelty and unremitting terror. There is little of John Connell's 'gentle kindness' to be found in these tales.

◆

There are only three published photographs of the author; one in Grant Richards's book *Author Hunting* which shows the author about the age of fifty, serious but with a hint of a smile; one on the cover of the 1937 Penguin Books reprint of *Kai Lung Unrolls His Mat* and the third in *The Celestial Omnibus*, a trilogy of the first three Kai Lung books published some twenty year after Bramah's death. In these last two he appears to be in his middle or late sixties. He looked, to quote John Connell:[19]

> ...like an aged Mandarin of ancient lineage and ripe culture ...There was the high, dome forehead. There were the seams and the lines in the countenance drawn by irony, pity, laughing wisdom and a lifetime's rich and varied experience. There was the sage humility and the gentle kindness; and there, behind the owlish spectacles, was the sudden, sharp and violently illuminating gleam of wit.

It is a matter of speculation whether more published photographs in fact existed. A letter to William White from one of the sponsors of *The Kai Lung Six* refers to either publishing them as 'a collection, all at once or a few at a time'. Three photographs would hardly meet the criteria of either 'a collection' or 'a few at a time'. There are however family photographs showing Ernest as a very good looking young man, another in army uniform and one holding Maisie's hand. Hilary Fairfield, Bramah's great niece, uncovered some eight photographs in the National Portrait Gallery which must have been taken for publicity purposes but which it would seem were never used. It is doubtful to an extreme if the consortium which published *The Kai Lung Six* would have known about the collection at the National Portrait Gallery

There are apparently two caricatures of Bramah. The first in *The London Handbook* which shows him smoking but it is hard to reconcile this drawing with the later photographs probably because Bramah would have been only thirty at the time with a full head of hair. Richards stated that Bramah had been the subject of a caricature by Penrhyn Stanlaws who depicts him with large wings extending to his feet. Richards commented, 'The Ernest Bramah whom I know may very well carry such unusual appendages beneath his coat.'

◆

Like a great many authors he read omnivorously when young, not selectively, but Grant Richards[20] wrote:

> I never heard of any more interest in Chinese matters than in any other subject. One of the main difficulties now-a-days is to realise how much the educated man of Victorian days knew on a very large range of subjects. And he cannot have been at the Manchester Grammar School, nor with Jerome without having been "educated" in this particular way.

Again, according to Richards who probably knew him better than most other people, 'He eschewed the pleasures of the table – whether from compulsion or inclination I cannot say.' Richards may have gathered this impression from a letter Bramah wrote to him in 1912.[21] 'At first, I confess, the epicureanism of your amiable Charles put me off a little ("I shall have steak and kidney pudding" fits me).' In fact Ernest's interest in food was minimal and basic. His nephew, John Barker, recalled that on his visits to his uncle they would eat at the A.B.C. or J. Lyons's cheap cafés rather than the more luxurious Lyons Corner Houses. This choice of eating-places might have stemmed from the physical problem Ernest had developed which made swallowing difficult.

◆

Was he a misogynist or just a man of his time? He is certainly guilty of putting what now would be highly politically incorrect remarks into the mouths of his characters. Aphorisms about 'well meaning women' 'inferior half' and 'their place walking three paces behind men' can be found dotted throughout his work. 'It is less profitable to expect reason from a she-being of one's own house than it is to dig out a wasp's nest in pursuit of honey.' 'Authority becomes a woman as a saddle fits the back of a donkey.' 'It is possible to escape from an enemy carrying a two edged sword but not from the interference of a well-meaning woman' and 'a virtuous woman will cause more evil than ten river pirates.'

Another clue might be found in 'Chang Tao, Melodious Vision and the dragon'.

> ...Inspired by the uprisen sisterhood of the outer barbarian lands, we of the inner chambers of the Illimitable Kingdom demand the right to express ourselves freely on every occasion and on every subject, whether the matter involved is one that we understand or not.

These sorts of comments concerning those of the 'inner chamber' could of course represent either Bramah's interpretation of a Chinese view of women or his own attitude. This can only be a source of speculation because his heroines were perhaps a mix of brave self-sufficient, clever women (he had particular admiration for Nurse Edith Cavell who he regarded as a feminine role model) and weak submissives.

In *Max Carrados* both 'The clever Mrs. Straithwaite' and 'The comedy at Fountain Cottage' have skilfully portrayed and individualised female characters. Mrs. Straithwaite is intelligent and witty, if voluble, and hard-up Elsie Bellmark in 'The comedy at Fountain Cottage' is down-to-earth and practical. Other feisty heroines include; the ingenious and persistent Hwa Che in *The Moon of Much Gladness*; the assured, astute, impulsive New Woman but still essentially feminine, the adventurous and highly intelligent Irene Lisle in *The Secret of the League*; the sensible and business-like Irene in 'The geraniums'; and the wise, high-minded Hwa-Mei in *Kai Lung's Golden Hours*; the brave but not very sensible Norah Melhuish in *The Bravo of London*.

Nevertheless there are far more 'silly little me' characters. A weak, sickly Millicent Creake in 'The tragedy at Brookbend Cottage'; the flirtatious Hia Chou in 'The story of Sing Tsung and the exponent of dark magic'; the compliant, long suffering Hea-an in 'Lam-Hoo and the reward of merit'; the absurd Sybil in 'Smothered in corpses'; weak Aunt Mary in 'Uncle Henry and the investments'; the silly and hysterical mother and daughter, Lady Southwold and Nancy in 'The rival rain-makers'; the not very bright, or perhaps just teasing Irene, a very minor role in *The Optimist*. (Irene is a name that Bramah often gives to his female characters. Other Irenes appears in short stories – 'The super saleswoman', 'A domestic drama' and 'The geraniums'. Was there a special Irene in Bramah's life?)

Apart from passing references in two Max Carrados stories; one to the trouble which might be caused by Suffragettes when they are suspected, wrongly, of blowing up a Church and a second when they are accused of attacking post boxes, they are never the target for Bramah's anger or humour. He does however transfer them to his China when they appear as 'the uprisen sisterhood'. These references aside, the movement did not attract his comment except in a very casual way. At the time Bramah was writing *What Might Have Been* the Suffragettes were the source of much public attention and disapprobation and might well have fitted into the revolutionary policies of the government at the centre of the plot.

◆

There was nothing prurient in Bramah's work. All references to sex are always understated and as such conform largely to the general attitudes of the times. He refers very obliquely to sex problems both in *The Minster* and in the *Handbook for Writers and Artists*. In *The Moon of Much Gladness* the ambiguous affection of Chin-tung for Hwa-che who he thinks is a boy, is expressed innocently, as though Bramah had never considered the implication, as indeed he probably had not. In 'The disappearance of Marie Severe' he delicately tiptoes round the possibility of a paedophilic involvement.

> "Some man of good position, a friend and neighbour possibly, who sees this beautiful young creature – the school friend of his own daughters sitting before him in church it may be – and becomes the slave of his diseased imagination until he is prepared to risk everything for that one overpowering object. A primitive man for the time, one may say, or, even worse, a satyr or a gorilla."

Again in the same story he delicately refers to the villainess's posterior, she having sat on what she thought was a hypodermic needle. ' "But at the worst this is a very simple matter," protested Ellerslie [a Doctor],

"If you will let me dress the place." Miss Julp went as red as a swarthy-complexioned lady of forty-five could be expected to go. "How can I let you dress the place?" she snapped.'

An illicit affair in 'The tragedy at Brookbend Cottage', the villain's nefarious activities are described in terms that are positively decorous. "Yes, she is Austin's typist. His confidential clerk. His companion…there isn't a week-end that they do not go off together while you are left moping here." And again in 'The Kingsmouth spy case' Inspector Tapling explains, ' "She is not exactly Mrs. Muller, we believe, but she lives there, if you understand what I mean, Sir." "Perfectly," acquiesced Carrados in the same modest spirit.'

The Moon of Much Gladness has the servant, the beautiful Mei, warming the disguised, cold Prince Ying by joining him in his bed and sleeping next to him all night. The action is as innocent as a child climbing into her parents' bed for warmth and comfort. Even the most prurient mind would find it hard to find anything salacious in the whole episode.

D. J. Enright writing in *The Times Literary Supplement*[22] suggests that if Bramah knew that a 'shell-cow' was a Chinese term for a snail which is depicted by the characters for a shell and a cow then he might too have known that in *Kai Lung's Golden Hours* Hwa-mei, is described as the 'Golden Mouse' …'mouse' being an indecent slang term for female parts. He then goes on to write that it would be impugning Bramah's morals to suppose he was aware of this!

Unlike many of his contemporaries, women's appearances are rarely described except in more than a perfunctory way. This reflects, at least in part, his lack of interest in people and in social intercourse. The reader has no idea if Norah Melhuish, the main female character in *The Bravo of London* is short or tall, the colour of her hair, did she have an athletic figure? Was Mrs. Creake, the victim in 'The tragedy at Brookbend Cottage', wan, thin, greying? All Bramah tells his readers is that she was 'silent and aloof'. We only know that in 'Uncle Henry and the investments' Joan Ellicott is a schoolgirl and an orphan. We are not told if her aunt is middle-aged or old and all we can deduce about Irene in 'A domestic drama' is that she is 'still young and beautiful'.

Compare this with Gissing's[23] description of Miss Marcella Moxey in *Born in Exile*.

Her age was seventeen, but she had nothing of the sprightly grace proverbially connected with that time of life in girls; her pale freckled visage expressed a haughty reserve, intensified as soon as her eye fell upon the visitor. She had a slight well-proportioned figure and a mass of auburn hair carelessly arranged.

Trollope lingered long on his female descriptions.[24] Patience Woolsworthy in the 'The Parson's daughter of Oxney Colne' is:

...a pretty girl, tall and slender, with dark eyes and black hair. Her eyes were perhaps too round for regular beauty, and her hair was perhaps too crisp; her mouth was large and expressive; her nose finely formed, though a critic in female form might have declared it to be somewhat broad. But her countenance altogether was very attractive...

Clearly Bramah preferred to leave the question of appearances to the imagination of the reader because even Kai Lung's is never described.

◆

Ernest must have been a practising Christian in his youth as he was a Church Warden at Packwood Church near his farm. Whether he maintained his religious affiliations is not known. His writing career encompassed that period when there was a strong movement away from the Christian ethic as the arbiter of morals and behaviour to another moral code based on scientific scepticism and pragmatism which probably, given his interest in science, attracted him. Although his brother Charles, with whom he was on excellent terms, was an ordained priest, it cannot be deduced from either the autobiographical material available or from his literary output how strong his beliefs, if any, might have been. There is the occasional biblical quotation (and in one instance in 'Hautepierre's star' a very remote reference to St. Peter, that it might be thought, would only be familiar to biblical scholars) but nothing else that is indicative. There is no question but that, he held strong views on at least one religious group, Christian Science. He comments in 'The disappearance of Marie Severe' in *The Eyes of Max Carrados* are vituperative.

> "...my only daughter, was wantonly done to death by an ignorant and credulous woman who had charge of her, in the tenets of her faith. It is called Christian Science... . But Mrs. Severe deliberately said – her words – that Marie 'does not know what illness means'. That's their jargon. They hold that illness does not exist and so it has no meaning..."

The terms 'fanatics' 'trickery' are used to describe the movement. In contradistinction the Salvation Army receives his plaudits as in 'The last exploit of Harry the actor' in *Max Carrados*. A passage illustrating this has been quoted on page 110.

Indeed, the lack of almost any religious content or reference in his work seems to suggest that whatever his affiliations were in his youth, there was neither interest nor commitment. The dissent between the high, low and broad church, the boiling turmoil of doctrinal controversies and schisms that dominated church politics and provided such fertile material for Anthony Trollope, George Eliot and Mary [Mrs.Humphrey] Ward in the high Victorian period held no attraction for Bramah in the early twentieth century.

Racial prejudice, and anti-Semitism in particular, was as much a fact of life in Bramah's England as it is today even if in its most blatant form it is suppressed by political correctness. Anti-Semitism in Britain was largely mild antipathy, fuelled by financial disasters associated in Victorian and Edwardian minds with large-scale City manipulation by stereo-typical Jewish financiers. It is difficult to accept this attitude but it is anachronistic to criticise when viewed from twenty-first century perspectives. Up to the early part of the twentieth century at least, the public was largely insensitive to the unpleasantness of ethnic and religious intolerance, prejudice and antipathy. Perfectly decent people could hold views or advocate policies that now would appear shameful or evil. Moral and ethical attitudes change and change again. Anti-Semitism is again rife so that perhaps Bramah's comments would, alas, find more sympathetic readers.

Contemporary authors did not hide their anti-Semitism. Sidney

Horler could write 'The choicest collection of Hebraic types I have yet seen (even in New York) was to be observed. What it is about Bournemouth that attracts these pronouncedly Asiatic Jews I do not know.' Sapper was a rabid racialist as indeed were G. K. Chesterton, John Buchan, E. W. Hornung, Lytton Strachey and Henry James. Dorothy L. Sayers frequently wrote disparaging comments about Jews and put into the mouths of her characters anti-Semitic statements. 'The gentleman, rather curly in the nose and fleshy about the eyelids, nevertheless came under Mr. Chesterton's definition of a nice Jew, for his name was neither Montagu nor McDonald but Nathan Abrahams, and he greeted Lord Peter with a hospitality amounting to enthusiasm.'[25]

Bramah's attitudes were those of his time and it is not surprising if they seeped into his books. The stereo-typical Jew can be found in stories and articles. Bronsky in *The Bravo of London* is unquestionably a Marxist Jew. In 'An incident at Wethebey's' published in *The London Year Book* one of the bidders is described as 'a Jew who made all his bids by furtive winks, and who endeavoured, by amusing sallies, to distract his competitors' attention at critical moments'. And, ' "The gentleman is quite right" said the Jew, rubbing his hands delightedly, "I heard him myself..." He had never spoken a more obvious lie, or one which passed so unquestioned.'

Another character in *The Secret of the League* says "...and when it was a matter of fighting to grab someone else's hand to fatten up a gang of Stock Exchange Hebrews, I was with you through thick and thin..." In 'A topographical drama' he makes his villain '...A scheming Hebrew: one of the Newest Rich and an International Finance manipulator'. 'The great Hockington find' in *The Specimen Case* has two characters described as having Hebrew features 'but adopted good, solid, middle-class English cognomens'. In literature in general and for many years, along with the archetypal Chinese, Jews were of course always the villains of the plots.

Perhaps, like Trollope and the older Dickens, Bramah was ambivalent in his attitude, but he was unlike Trollope and Dickens in that their views softened in later works when Jews were written into the stories in a more sympathetic role. Dickens compensated for Fagin with the saintly Jew, Mr. Riah [*Our Mutual Friend*] and Trollope's Madame Max

Goesler [The Palliser Novels] and Anton Trendellsohn [Nina Balakta] were balanced against Augustus Melmotte [*The Way We Live Now*]. Bramah, unlike his eminent predecessors, seems not to have created any compensating characters. However, earlier in his career he had been prepared to write, or have written, an encomium on Lord Rothschild in an article 'Some well known Londoners' in *The London Hand Book* already quoted.

◆

Politically there is little doubt where Ernest Bramah stood. His book on his farming experiences reveals his youthful right-wing views. The episode, already related in Chapter Two when he gives his labourer a lesson in economics, does not show any difference from his later attitude.[26]

It will be recalled that at the end of the diatribe Scroggins, the labourer, is unimpressed and continues to maintain that 'fourteen shillings a week aren't much for a man to live on'. Was this the 'bloody-minded conservatism' Bramah blamed for the failure of his farm?

A decade after his farming career, as Editor of *The Minster,* he makes his views clear on the incompatibility of Socialism with patriotism.[27]

> And there is another thing: we have heard a great deal too much lately of that altruism and that socialism, which places a few minor questions of labour and heredity in front of man's natural feelings of patriotism and would endeavour to create an impossible bond of brotherhood between barbaric Eastern nations and civilised Englishmen.

What Might Have Been confirms his views, very firmly to the right – perhaps the far right. His private opinions are placed in the mouths of his characters. Orwell included this book in an essay 'Prophecies of fascism' which appeared in *Tribune* in July 1940 although fascism is not a word that Bramah would have been familiar with in 1907. The term was not current until used by Mussolini in 1919. Orwell wrote 'Ernest Bramah…was a sensitive, idealistic man whose private fears of the mob turned him into a passionate anti-democrat'.

Bramah's attitude to war is made clear in a number of articles but most particularly in *The Mirror of Kong Ho* where there is a particularly bitter attack on the government and the army concerning the Boer War which had ended five years before the book was published.

> These barbarians, less resourceful in device, have only just emerged from a conflict into which they do not hesitate to admit they were drawn despite protests. Such incompetence is characteristic of their methods throughout... . They at once sent out an army of those who could be readiest seized... . The result was that which the prudent must have foreseen. The more accomplished enemy, without exposing themselves to any unnecessary inconvenience gained many advantages by their intrepid power of dissimulation – arranging their garments and positions in such a way that they had the appearance of attacking when in reality they were effecting a prudent retreat...rapidly concealing themselves among the earth on the approach of an overwhelming force.[28]

The politicians fare no better under Bramah's lashing. Kong Ho continues

> In the meantime the adventure was not progressing pleasantly for those chiefly concerned at home...it was discovered that in the haste of embarkation the wrong persons had been sent, all those who were really the fittest to command remaining behind... . In the emergency, the most far-seeing recommended a more unbending policy of extermination... . The most effective measure...would be to capture all those least capable of resistance, concentrate them into a given camp, and then at an agreed signal reduce the entire assembly to...a smoking hecatomb of women and children.

Kong Ho's humorous reporting to his father does not conceal the strength of feeling Bramah expresses in this letter: '...with patriotic self-effacement [they] preferred to remain at home and encourage those who were fighting by pointing out their inadequacy to the task and their extreme unlikelihood of ever accomplishing it'.

There is no mention in any of his writings of the industrial and social disturbances in the post-war years, most particularly the general strike of 1926. His desire for seclusion must have clashed strongly with his antagonism to organised labour. In any event, it is difficult to envisage him driving a bus or tram.

There is perhaps even a nod towards eugenics – a much-discussed topic in the 1930s. Bramah has Kai Lung in *The Moon of Much Gladness* declare

> ...under a more judicious system the elderly, the infirm and the unremunerative were automatically weeded out by a process that was not unreasonable to themselves but convenient and economical to authority

and, as already quoted, he bemoans the use of 'magic powders' and 'scratching of cryptic emblems on the forearm' as a way of keeping river-pirates and hungry beggars alive. Of course it has to be asked, as with his Suicide article, was he joking?'

He also appears to believe that 'might is right'. In 'The war hawks' a member of the Cabinet declares "Mastery of the air overrides all strategies." In 'The war hawks' England is being attacked by apparently invincible German airships and is on the verge of surrender without offering resistance. The Prime Minister declares "There are only two classes of Powers today: Germany, and the rest of the world." 'Germany,' he wrote, 'had masked her strength, gained all the time she wanted and duped the suspicion and the activity of England by subterfuge.' Written in 1909, when good relations between Germany and Britain were deteriorating because of the rapid development of the German navy with the aim of reaching parity with the Royal Navy, it is barely surprising Bramah's intense patriotism should manifest itself in anti-German rhetoric.

Bramah may have been ultimately wrong in 'The war hawks' about dirigibles as the principal weapon of aerial warfare but he could never have seriously contemplated that his anticipation of kamikaze warriors and suicide bombers would become real and terrible weapons. "Every man will have to throw a missile from a distance of not more than thirty feet. Five pounds of thorite will grind up everything within a radius of fifty yards... . Every man who fails to blow himself into his constituent parts will have bungled", says Brampton Reed in the story.

♦

Bramah was certainly not unworldly. On the contrary. Even as a youth, taking on the lease of his farm, he insisted on knowing whether the freeholder had mortgaged it 'because it had a direct bearing on the relations between the landlord and tenant'.[29] His business skills were honed in the gentlemanly but nevertheless cut throat world of publishing. He used his knowledge of the economics of publishing and an understanding of the implications of the costs of authors' demands and changes. This made him a formidable negotiator with contributors and later with publishers and agents. It also enabled him to accommodate his own requirements to the realities of ensuring his works appeared before the public in a form and at prices that would engender sales.

An excellent example of this can be found in a letter to Pinker in 1907 when he offered a number of stories totalling 21,000 words. He writes[30]

> Do you care to have a complete set to offer as small books; 1/- or some similar price. I suppose it would be. I have four other articles in something of the same style which I would propose adding to make up to 30,000 words... . Other things being equal I should, of course, prefer them to be used serially and to get something from that source. Or would it be practicable to go on offering both serially and as a book and have a double chance?

Nothing unworldly about this.

He was more than capable of protecting his royalties and the subsidiary rights of his books. Frequent references can be found in correspondence to these issues. Bramah insisted that his agent, J. B. Pinker relinquished his representation for his books. The letter he wrote to Pinker in 1921[31] and quoted on page 127 clearly illustrates this.

In 1923 he was writing to Richards '...I will ask you to leave to me all subsidiary rights: that is to say everything except the exclusive right to publishing the book.'[32]

His editorial knowledge also stood him in good stead. He was able to challenge, usually successfully, excessive charges for proof corrections. Pinker writes on his behalf:[33]

The amount charged was £2.12.11. and he [Bramah] says he has looked up the proofs of both galley and page, and cannot imagine the cost of corrections should exceed 25% of the cost of composing. On the first few pages the corrections are fairly heavy but they would not average much spread over the entire book. Beyond these most of the corrections were literals and variations from copy, which the printers had introduced on their own responsibility.

There are many other examples of his probity. His correspondence with his agents frequently notifies them of commissions due to them about which they were probably unaware. He writes to Watt: 'I willingly agree to Mr. Stewart's correction of the system of assessing the royalty – the more so since, my own contribution being rather long, I was afraid that I might otherwise seem to be taking rather more than my proper share of the proceeds.'[34]

In 1928 J. C. Squire, then the Editor of *The London Mercury*, despite his enthusiasm for Bramah's work wrote on May 1929, '*The Mercury Story Book* is a venture to help the paper; do reduce your fees, or we will have to leave you out.'[35] They didn't. 'A topographical Drama' duly appeared in July 1929. In that year Bramah was complaining to Pinker that a fee of two and a half guineas for appearance in an American anthology 'strikes me as very little...they usually seem to give more than one gets from the English compilations and this one paid 5gns.'[36]

He was always insistent on retaining all play and film rights for all his books as well as, in some cases, anthology rights too. In 1939 he declined Allen Lane's, the founder of Penguin Books, terms for a reprint of *Kai Lung Unrolls His Mat* which led to a much-improved offer from Penguin Books. This included payment of royalties after one year on the entire edition even any unsold copies. On June 16th 1939[37] he writes to Allen Lane in slightly hurt tones, asking him to intervene to ensure prompter payment of his royalties before Watt put the debt out for collection.

It is not very agreeable for me to have to contemplate this with reference to one with whom I have so recently been in harmonious correspondence. At the same time Messrs. Watt are my agents, looking after my interests, and I cannot reasonably dissent from anything they consider necessary.... . You have recently taken the initiative of writing direct to me to bring about something that you wanted [signed copies of his books] and I have been able to facilitate the accomplishment of this. Isn't it worth while for you in return to give definite instructions for my accounts always to be put through promptly when they become due?

This type of correspondence has led to the suggestion that Bramah was always financially stressed. This is unlikely. The correspondence is much more indicative of his being a good businessman well able to look after his own interests both with publishers and his agents. The eleven Penguin Books impressions of his work on their own alone earned him over £8,000 between 1936 and 1940, the equivalent of an average annual sum of £55,000 – a very respectable income by any standards, particularly if royalties and fees from other books, anthologies and assignments are added.

Nevertheless the overall impression of the man is not of one to whom money was the overwhelming motivator as it was for his contemporary Arnold Bennett. Bramah's work is a denial of Bennett's cynical comment in his 1917 *Books and Persons*[38] that '...genuine artists ought to be indifferent to money. They are not. And what is still more curious, they will seldom produce their best work unless they really do want money.' This cannot be true of Bramah since his later works particularly the Kai Lung and Max Carrados stories were written when he was successful and prosperous.

He understood the need for marketing. He tried to persuade booksellers to place his books where they could easily be seen. A polite letter from W. H. Smith in July 1897 declined his request for 'special preference' on their bookstalls, presumably a prominent display. This was probably for *The London Handbook* since at this date his only book was *English Farming*. W. H. Smith's lack of enthusiasm can be understood, but this does not detract from Bramah's business-like attempts to get exposure for his publications.

While he had appointed effective and active agents to place his literary output, he was not prepared to leave the marketing wholly to them. He never hesitated to make direct approaches to editors but meticulously remitted commission to his agents even when they themselves had not placed his work.

He was well aware of the need for publicity for his edited journals as well as his books even if he eschewed it for himself. He ensured that *The London Handbook* was to be available for reference at 'principal institutions, clubs, stations, hotels, restaurants'. In contemporary marketing terms he was well aware of the need for 'exposure' and 'visibility'.

He was also a good advertising space salesman too. It is noticeable that several unsigned articles in *The London Handbook* in which the manufacturer or a product is mentioned also drew paid advertisements by the company mentioned. A dissertation on the merits of blacking seems to have attracted a half page advertisement at the front of the book by a manufacturer of that material. He persuaded the publishers to advertise *English Farming* in the *London Year Book* using quotations taken from favourable criticisms. (The author's name is not given.) All the evidence indicates his ability to generate advertising revenue.

He also sought endorsement for his publications from many prominent people, most particularly for the struggling *London Handbook*. On the 30th June 1897 he received a letter from Sir Brittany Brigge stating 'The Queen [Victoria] was pleased to accept the copy of his *London Hand Book.*' He was being wildly optimistic in sending a book to the Duke of York asking for an endorsement for it. A secretary wrote that 'his Royal Highness is unable to offer any opinion on the Handbook'. Later, when The Duke ascended to the throne as George V. Bramah tried again with similar results.

The Secretary to Lord Goschen, then Chancellor of the Exchequer, wrote to express thanks for the Handbook but 'it is contrary to his practice when books are forwarded to him to express any opinion on their merits'. With a good deal of astuteness and making the best of a bad job, Bramah appended the names of the rich and powerful to whom he had sent copies of the Hand Book and Year Book and who had not actually sent it back! 'Copies of this annual were graciously accepted by Her Majesty the Queen, Their Royal Highnesses the Prince and

Princess of Wales, Their Royal Highnesses the Duke and Duchess of York, Lord Salisbury and many others'.

Intriguingly in 1895 Bernard Shaw writes to thank him for a proposal and 'I should be of no use for the sort of thing you indicated'.[39] Alas it will never be known just what was 'the sort of thing' for which Bramah was trying to recruit Shaw. There are no Bramah letters in the Shaw archive. He was later to satirise Shaw in 'Feet and the Woman' that strongly suggested *Arms and the Man* was unintelligible. Shaw becomes a target again in 'Fame' a story in the *In Future* series. Looking back on the early twentieth century from the twenty-ninth century, the 'guide' who is the narrator explains that all literature, including Chaucer and Shakespeare, was in fact the work of Bernard Shaw. There is a statue of him but...

> I looked round. We had been standing by a plinth of a monument which I now recognised to be a colossal statue. Words graven on the pedestal met my eye but everything was fading and I had only time to read 'Be not afraid of greatness'. A trite motto; but then the statue itself was an excellent representation of Mr. G. K. Chesterton.

A greater mystery than Shaw's reply is an unfriendly postcard from Charles Dodgson [Lewis Carroll].[40]

Mr. Dodgson begs to inform Mr. Smith, who has evidently written under the impression that he claims, or at least acknowledges, the authorship of books not published under his name, that such an impression is wholly unauthorised, he does neither the one nor the other.

Nothing in the Carroll archive gives any clue as to the Bramah incorrect attribution or what it was Carrol refused to authorise.

◆

Few of his masters at the Manchester Grammar School would have foreseen that a pupil with such low-grade examination results would become the visionary, erudite, craftsman and subtle humorist who attracted the admiration of so many literary savants and authors. The boy who came out of school with such an unsatisfactory academic record and did not attend a university acquired an enviable vocabulary. Most people would need recourse to a dictionary to find the meaning of 'cicatrix' 'theurgal' 'paralogism' 'terebinthine' 'tabefaction' 'Eudaemonism'; all of which fit perfectly into the text with no suggestion of an author showing off or patronising his readers.

It is sometimes a problem to separate out Bramah's vivid imagination from the realities of science. His unremarkable performance in chemistry, twenty-second out of forty-five, did not stop him from inventing the fictional 24-pound thorite shell, 'which will grind everything up within 50 yards' and which David Langford[41] wrote; 'sounds nice and thunderous but it would not work since thorite exists but is merely an inert silicate of thorium'. Luck, not prescience, favours Bramah as although it was known in the early nineteenth Century that thorium was the mineral which is naturally radio-active, the use of the destructive power of radio-activity was still well in the future. The plans of a thorite torpedo are at the centre of the plot of 'The Kingsmouth spy case'. Moreover, in 'The war hawks' he also makes the gases generated by its explosive force 'arrest the action of an electrical discharge' thus cutting all wireless communication.

As was described in earlier chapters he successfully prognosticated fax and e-mail communication as well as the incredible anticipation of the Enigma code machine. He foresaw long before the experts, that air supremacy would be critical in war. Bramah's scientific and technical knowledge combined with his imaginative powers led to some predictions remarkable for their closeness to the eventual reality. In a story written about 1907 'The simple law' which looks back from the year 3007 he refers to interatomic action generated by the sun. Solar panels?

But he was not always so successful in his predictions. He was wrong, just as H. G. Wells was with his 1900 *War in the Air*, when they both saw airships as the main weapon of aerial warfare and of civilian travel. Using them for convoy protection in the First World War was successful but their role in bombing was limited. There is no recorded instance of two airships meeting in direct combat. The history of airships, particularly dirigibles, shows the predictions both for military and peaceful use were wildly out of line with the reality. The various disasters up to the Hindenburg in 1939 eliminated this form of travel as a serious competitor to fixed wing aircraft. Bramah's vision of flight by muscle power alone has not yet occurred and the likelihood of any future break-through seems very distant. His rainmaking machine may not have had any serious intent but it is no nearer realisation than the mostly unsuccessful cloud seeding.

In 'The disappearance of Marie Severe' he was medically correct. The diagnosis of an inflamed appendix, leading to acute peritonitis, by the use of a blood test was wholly accurate and in keeping with medical practice of the period. Clearly Bramah had taken the trouble to check his medical facts.

Bramah was a visionary with a fascination for unusual things and his erudition is undoubted. It shines through all his writing. To term him a polymath might be challenged, but the breadth of his knowledge and interests is irrefutable. He was deeply curious about the magical and supernatural but also all that was sanctified by age and custom. Aside from his keen interest in numismatics in which he was an expert, his knowledge extended over a wide range of subjects – law, philosophy, literature, history, Egyptology, astronomy, fossils, philately, the occult and many aspects of science. As the author of the manual on musketry training the list of his interests and knowledge must include at least some aspects of ordnance.

But if his interests and curiosity were catholic, they did not extend to other countries. In the article on the trip to St. Petersburg,[42] Bramah emphasises the point. 'I do not know what suddenly prompted Toby and myself to go to Russia for our ordinary, annual middle-class holiday this year'. After that foreign adventure no one could have accused him of being adventurous. He described himself as 'the most timorous of travellers'. He does not appear to have left the country again, taking his holidays in the types of resorts favoured by early twentieth century middle-class families. There is evidence of stays at Hastings at a Pelham Cottage that is listed as a 'lodging house' owned by a Mrs. Apps. There were also holidays at Bedford House in Sandygate in Kent, Rose Cottage near Lynmouth and Maiden Combe in Devon. Clearly no hotels for the Bramahs. There is also a mention of an unidentified 'Preston Beach' among the resorts where they stayed. Judging from the unpublished novel *The Optimist*, he was also familiar with Cornwall.

As for his own assessment of his extensive output, he contributed to an anthology of humorous stories based on each author's choice as their favourite. This perhaps gives an indication of Bramah's view of his own work. He selected 'The story of Ching-kwei and the destinies' from *Kai Lung Unrolls His Mat*. But a tongue in the cheek response to an inquiry as to his 'best' book does throw some doubt on even this statement. In a letter to an unknown recipient dated September 25th 1931 and found in a copy of *The Moon of Much Gladness*, Bramah writes:

> You say you would be interested to know which of my books I consider 'the best'. But surely it is an understood thing that really modest authors do not speak of their 'best' (except for trade purposes such as anthologies etc) but diffidently refer to 'my best bad book' or some pleasing evasion of that sort. However, even putting that aside there are difficulties to complicate the simple issue. Best? Well my 'Guide to the Varieties and Rarities of English Regal Copper Coins' is undoubtedly a better book on the subject of copper coins than my 'English Farming' is on the state of British agriculture. But as you have probably never heard of either book, that will not interest you. Let us say that if I happened to be sending someone a 'Kai Lung' book and wished to put the best face on the matter it would probably be 'Kai Lung's Golden Hours' and a Max Carrados book it would almost certainly not be 'The Eyes of Max Carrados'.

◆

But what of the widowed Maisie? She returned to the London flat, probably immediately after Ernest's death, where she remained until about 1956 after which her name no longer appears in the rating lists. She is in the electoral register, along with other names, as occupants of the flat but is missing from the Post Office Street Directory and the London Telephone Directory.

Her last traceable address was Fiddington House in Market Lavington in Somerset, a private lunatic asylum, to which she was admitted on March 15th 1957. Inevitably this leads to the supposition that at the age of eighty-three her mental condition was such as to require what is now called 'Sectioning'. Her eccentricity, or neurosis, expressed itself even at death. She was terrified of being buried alive and instructed that her wrists were to be cut to ensure she was indeed dead. This proved very difficult to achieve but her niece Rosemary was, in the end, able to ensure that her wishes were fulfilled.

Medical evidence in relation to those committed is not available until 100 years after their death so there is little to add to these bald facts. She died in St. Martin's Hospital Bath of broncho-pneumonia and an acute intestinal obstruction on July 23rd 1957. Fiddington House itself was demolished in 1962 but its records are held at the Wiltshire and Swindon Record Office.

Among the many strange acts by Maisie was an attempt, reported by *The New York Times*, to suppress information on the place of Ernest's death, ignoring Ernest's instructions for a burial rather than cremation and the destruction of the manuscript of the autobiography.

Whether the suggestion of her great niece Hilary Fairfield that Maisie was 'eccentric' applied throughout her life and whether she deteriorated to the extent she was committed to an asylum is not knowable. The only extant letters written to the Hammersmith Librarian in 1944 and 1945 are both sensible and sensitive.

On May 30th 1944 she wrote[43] '...I do not feel as though I should care for you to have these just because we [sic] have offered them – unless they are to be of value'. She took the nineteen books along personally and discussed them with the Chief Librarian. It is also notable that she signed all her letters 'M. Bramah', not Smith, although as the death certificate shows the name 'Bramah' was never changed by Deed Poll.

Her estate was valued at £25,600 (equivalent to over £420,000 today). It is obvious she had not squandered Ernest's bequest. Her brother Alan who was to be the beneficiary of the residual estate had died before Maisie. A codicil of that date refers to him as her 'late brother'. There are two aspects of her Will that are of note. First, she replicated Ernest's bequests to his brother's children, the Society of Authors and the Metropolitan Courts Poor Box. Second, she left all the intellectual rights to Bramah's agent W. P. Watt, son of the founder of the Agency and now running it, and eleven volumes of literary letters of famous people. Were these letters Bramah received from the many prominent authors with whom he was in contact, both as a commissioning Editor and as an author in his own right? There has been no trace of the eleven volumes that would be of enormous literary value as well as contributing to a deeper understanding of Bramah and his relationships with his peers.

The gift of the copyrights of her husband's work is almost inexplicable and again it might have been an act of eccentricity. The literary estate in terms of royalties owed at the time of his death was not particularly great so as a gift its monetary value was small. Perhaps it was a gesture of gratitude both for A. P. Watt's work on Bramah's behalf and for his friendship although there is nothing supports the view that Ernest's relationship with Watt was anything but a business arrangement. There is no evidence from correspondence of them being friends.

In 1959 Ernest's manuscripts were sold at an auction at Sotheby's. There were thirty-five lots but two of them, which were autobiographical accounts of Bramah's early life, were withdrawn. The Harry Ransom Humanities Center purchased twenty-four items and two New York dealers purchased the remainder. What is of interest was the high prices, even by the standards of the day, which were obtained; £3,015 or at 2007 values, nearly £50,000.

In 1960 Maisie's heirs sold the coin collection to a numismatic dealer. The largest part of the collection was re-sold in 1996 to an American collector. Those found in Ernest's London home long after his death are still in the hands of the family who occupied the flat.

◆

Enthusiasm for Bramah's books is at present greatest in the U.S.A. According to Mike Berro's research there were at least eleven editions of his books in the 1970s. More recently there has been revived interest among publishers with printings of *The Mirror of Kong Ho, What Might Have Been, The Wallet of Kai Lung, Kai Lung's Golden Hours* and a new edition of four previously unpublished stories. This last book is to be published in the U.S.A. in 2006. Project Gutenberg offer copies of *Kong Ho* and *Kai Lung's Golden Hours*, on-line and without charge. Other titles are available commercially over the Internet. It is even possible to purchase facsimile copies of the original jackets of some of the books.

Ernest Bramah wrote fourteen fiction books, three of which he, if not his public, regarded as critical failures. All of them were reprinted, some very many times. It is, at the very least, a respectable record for any writer. The American publications *Twentieth-Century Literary Criticism* Volume 72[44] devotes ten pages to Ernest Bramah and the *Dictionary of Literary Biography*[45] six pages. In 1959 William White[46] felt that Bramah had never received the critical attention and public support that the quality of his work justified. Had Bramah lived he would have been delighted to see that, over sixty years after his death, many reprints are appearing in various formats. The reasons behind this resurgence of popularity in America are far from clear. It has yet to occur to the same extent in the United Kingdom although there are signs that it will happen.

Over the years his works have been translated into German, Spanish, Portuguese, Finnish, Dutch and Swedish. There was a French translation of *Max Carrados* as recently as 2004.

The Public Lending Rights statistics do not enable a judgement to be made on the popularity of Bramah's books in the United Kingdom. Only books with an I.S.B.N. number are reported. Moreover few, if any, libraries have been willing or able to replace old books under the strict financial constraints they have been subject to for many years. It is significant that some Bramah books command very high prices in the second hand and antique book market and not just as collector's items.

Ernest Bramah's career began inauspiciously with an incomplete education and a failed attempt in agriculture, yet through self-education, a love of science, and a remarkable imaginative creativity he died a successful and honoured writer of delicate, artificial and ingenious stories. There is nothing quite like them in English literature.

Sources & Notes

1   *Manchester Guardian*. June 29th 1941.

2   *The Times*. June 28th 1942.

3   *New York Times*. June 28th 1942.

4   *New York Herald Tribune*. June 28th 1942.

5   Documents relating to the literary estate were provided by Mike Berro.

6   John Connell. 'The recluse who created Kai Lung'. op. cit.

7   T. O. Mabbett. *Notes and Queries*. Oxford University Press. November 6th 1943.

8   H.R.H.R.C. September 28th 1965.

9   *Daily Telegraph*. June 30th 1942.

10 *The Specimen Case*. op. cit. p.20.

11 *Transcript*. Boston. (Bramah does not give a date when the review appeared.)

12 George Orwell Archive. University of London.

13 Berg Collection of English and American Literature. New York Public Library. op. cit.

14 H.R.H.R.C. Typescript. op. cit. p.3.

15 Grant Richards. *Author Hunting*. op. cit. p.48.

16 Mark Valentine. *The Book Collector*. London. July 1997. op. cit. p.48.

17 B.B.C. 'A good read'. op. cit.

18 H.R.H.R.C. op. cit.

19 John Connell. 'The recluse who created Kai Lung'. op. cit.

20 Society of Authors. Grant Richards Archive. op. cit.

21 Grant Richards. *Author Hunting*. op. cit. p.274.

22 D. J. Enright. 'A Chinese never-never land'. op. cit.

23 George Gissing. *Born in Exile*. Nelson. London. 1892 p.76.

24 Anthony Trollope. *Courtship and Marriage*. Trollope Society. London. n.d.

25 Dorothy L. Sayers. *Lord Peter Finds the Body*. Gollancz. London. 1928. The very Jewish Victor Gollancz, an indefatigable defender of minorities, did not try, or if he did, failed to restrain her.

26 Ernest Bramah. *English Farming and Why I Turned it Up*. op. cit. p.26.

27 *The Minster.* December 1895. op. cit. p.673.

28 Ernest Bramah. *The Mirror of Kong Ho.* op. cit. pp.64-65.

29 Ernest Bramah. *English Farming and Why I Turned it Up.* op. cit. p.26.

30 Rare Books and Special Collections Library University of Illinois. Urbana. op. cit. August 1st 1907.

31 The Berg Collection of English and American Literature. op. cit. October 22nd 1921.

32 H.R.H.R.C. op. cit. April 27th 1923.

33 John Murray Archive. March 11th 1909.

34 The Berg Collection of English and American Literature. op. cit. January 18th 1933.

35 H.R.H.R.C. op. cit. September 11th 1928.

36 H.R.H.R.C. op. cit. November 9th 1929.

37 University of Bristol Library. Special Collections. January 28th 1938.

38 Arnold Bennett. *Books and Persons.* Chatto and Windus. London 1917.

39 Society of Authors. Bernard Shaw Estate.

40 Alderman Library. University of Virginia. September 4th 1895.

41 David Langford. 'Ernest Bramah: crime and Chinoiserie'. op. cit.

42 Ernest Bramah. 'Sydenham to St. Petersburg'. op. cit.

43 Ernest Bramah. Collection. Hammersmith and Fulham Archives Centre. May 30th 1944.

44 *Twentieth-Century Literary Biography.* op. cit. pp.1-10.

45 *Dictionary of Literary Biography.* op. cit. pp.45-50.

46 William White. 'Kai Lung in America'. Paper read at The American Studies Association of Michigan. March 21st 1958.

The last words should be those that Ernest Bramah Smith put into the mouth of Ton Hi the proprietor of the many-sided shop under the gilt sign of The Inconspicuous Elephant, in the least frequented byways of Shenking. His wish was "to remain unostentatiously in the discreet background and gain the esteem of the more reputable deities ..."

BIBLIOGRAPHY

Books

English Farming and Why I Turned It Up	1894
A Handbook for Writers and Artists: A Practical Guide to the Press and to Literary and Artistic Publications	1898
The Wallet of Kai Lung	1900
The Mirror of Kong Ho	1905
What Might Have Been: the Story of a Social War (also called The Secret of the League)	1907
Max Carrados	1914
Kai Lung's Golden Hours	1922
The Eyes of Max Carrados	1923
The Specimen Case	1924
Max Carrados Mysteries	1927
Kai Lung Unrolls His Mat	1928
Short Stories of Today and Yesterday	1929
A Guide to the Varieties and Rarity of English Regal Copper Coins. Charles II-Victoria. 1671-1860	1929
A Little Flutter	1930
The Moon of Much Gladness (entitled The Return of Kai Lung in the USA)	1932
The Bravo of London	1934
The Kai Lung Omnibus	1938
Kai Lung Beneath the Mulberry Tree	1940
The Celestial Omnibus	1963
Best Max Carrados Stories	1977
The Kai Lung Six (previously uncollected short stories)	1974

◆

For the most recent and complete bibliography (September 2000) giving details of different editions, including special editions of single stories, anthologies, articles and short stories published in different periodicals see the Mike Berro website. www.mike@ernestbramah.com

The Bulletin of Bibliography Vol. 32 No.12 contains an admittedly incomplete list of Bramah writings in various journals compiled by William White. To that list can be added the following but it is emphasised the listing is still far from complete.

Some well known Londoners	*The London Handbook* 1897
The rival rain-makers	*The London Handbook* 1897
The world a-wheel	*The London Handbook* 1897
A modest defence of constitutional Suicide	*The London Year Book* 1898
The art of perjury	*The London Year Book* 1898
Brevets of London characters	*The London Year Book* 1898
An incident at Wethebey's	*The London Year Book* 1898
Hautepierre's star	*The Ladies Realm* 1908
Deakin and the ghost	*Land and Sea.* 1919
The geraniums	*Windsor Magazine* June 1924
Our illustrative interview	*Quarterly Journal of the Book Club of Detroit* 1972
Ledwulf and the modest maid	*Odyssey* n.d. but probably 1977
William revisits the old home	*Odyssey* n.d. but probably 1977
Authors' corrections	*Bluegrass Literary Review* 1980
In the dark	University of Mississippi Studies in English 1980

◆

William White also traced Bramah inclusions in anthologies. This list was published by *The Bulletin of Bibliography* January-March issue 1973. To White's list can be added the following but again emphasising it is far from complete.

Great Short Stories of Detection, Mystery and Horror	Gollancz 1928
Great English Short Stories	Liverwright 1928
Short Stories Today and Yesterday	Harrap 1929
Second Century of Detective Stories	Hutchinson 1930
Short Stories of Detection, Mystery and Horror Second Series	Gollancz 1931
My Best Story (Second Edition)	Faber 1933
Best Detective Stories of the Year	Dutton 1933
World's Great Detective Stories	Daily Express 1934
A Century of Detective Stories	Hutchinson 1935
The Great Book of Humour	Odhams Press 1935
Murder by Experts	Collins 1936
Tales of Detection	Dent 1936
Fifty Enthralling Stories of the East	Odhams Press 1937
Twentieth Century Detective Stories	Odhams Press 1938
Ellery Queen's Challenge to Readers	Sampson Low 1938
Fifty Famous Detectives of Fiction	Odhams Press 1938
Twentieth Century Detective Stories	Sampson Low 1948
The Rivals of Sherlock Holmes	Penguin Books 1971
The Best Max Carrados Detective Stories	Dover 1972
Novels of Adult Fantasy Volume II	Ballantine 1973
The Max Carrados Portfolio	Silicone Despatch 2000
Sleuths: 23 Great Detectives of Fiction	Publisher not known
Century of Spy Stories	Hutchinson n.d.

Additionally, *The Short Story Index* published by H. W. Wilson Company. New York 1955 also contains titles not to be found in the other lists.

◆

Apart from books, articles and plays not mentioned in the text there are further titles that have been identified and are given below. The list is based substantially on William Charlton's research at the Harry Ransom Humanities Research Center. Few of them are dated and no publication information is available nor has any been located. This does not necessarily mean that they were not published. Some of the material is hand-written and others are typescripts.

Stories

The vanished book
The discipline of young Eggleston
The red splinter
The cake mad gentleman
Abracadabra
A disgraceful story
Rosemary for remembrance
Sidelights of tragedy
A victim of circumstance
The guinea stamp
Max and the water maiden
Lady N
The leash of fate
Science from an uneasy chair
Sweet simplicity
More and more (an extract from a novel)
The last Plantagenet
The result of an accident
En passant
The complete art
The hard man
Sukie and the horse doctor
Tomorrow
Cumulative
Revolution
A celestial laureate
Miss Hem and the microbe
The marquise ring

Articles and Sketches

All about them
Authors' corrections
The awakening of Henry
Book trade gossip
Bullet holes in the wall
Business friendship
The collectors' room
The complete art
Cultural hints for April
Curious engraved tokens
Excavating
Fascination of the tragic
Felix Henderson
Gathos the cow doctor
Instructing the natives
Liz
New advertising
Our illustrative interview
Our pet white elephant
Penny of Edward 1
A pocket portrait of English sovereigns
Pearce and plenty
Phases of a year of war
Popular fallacies
A remarkable blunder
Smoki cigretto
Specialist's eye
Suburban gardening for pleasure and profit
The specialisation of coins
Trailing moss
Was Julius Caesar ever in London?

Plays

A Cheerful Tragedy
Darkness and Composure
The Efficient Mrs. Higgs
In the Dark
Kai Lung's Golden Hours
Safe Bind, Safe Find
The Tragedy at Brookbend Cottage
Two Birds

Index